THE SOLDIERY OF WEST VIRGINIA

IN THE

FRENCH AND INDIAN WAR; LORD DUNMORE'S WAR; THE REVOLUTION; THE LATER INDIAN WARS; THE WHISKEY INSURRECTION; THE SECOND WAR WITH ENGLAND; THE WAR WITH MEXICO.

AND

Addenda relating to West Virginians in the Civil War.
The Whole Compiled from Authentic Sources.

BY

VIRGIL A. LEWIS, M. A.,
State Historian and Archivist.

Reprinted From

Third Biennial Report of the
Department of Archives and History
State of West Virginia

CLEARFIELD

Reprinted for
Clearfield Company, Inc. by
Genealogical Publishing Co., Inc.
Baltimore, Maryland
1991, 1996, 1998, 2002

Originally published as Third Biennial Report
of the Department of Archives and History, State
of West Virginia, Charleston, 1911
Excerpted and reprinted: Genealogical Publishing Co., Inc.
Baltimore, 1967, 1972, 1978
Library of Congress Catalogue Card Number 67-28603
International Standard Book Number 0-8063-0210-0
Made in the United States of America

CONTENTS.

CHAPTER I. DISCOVERY, EXPLORATION AND EARLY SETTLEMENTS IN WEST VIRGINIA.

CHAPTER II. WEST VIRGINIA PIONEERS IN THE FRENCH AND INDIAN WAR—GENERAL BRADDOCK'S ARMY IN WEST VIRGINIA.

CHAPTER III. WEST VIRGINIA FRONTIERSMEN IN LORD DUNMORE'S WAR—ROLLS OF THE ARMY—THE BATTLE OF POINT PLEASANT.

CHAPTER IV. WEST VIRGINIANS WHO WERE SOLDIERS AND PENSIONERS IN THE REVOLUTIONARY WAR—THE WAR FOR INDEPENDENCE.

CHAPTER V. WEST VIRGINIANS IN THE INDIAN WARS AFTER THE REVOLUTION—THE LATER INDIAN WARS.

CHAPTER VI. WESTERN VIRGINIA SOLDIERS IN THE ARMY ORGANIZED FOR THE SUPPRESSION OF THE WHISKEY INSURRECTION IN WESTERN PENNSYLVANIA IN 1794.

CHAPTER VII. WEST VIRGINIANS IN THE SECOND WAR WITH ENGLAND—THE WAR OF 1812—CORRESPONDENCE CONNECTED THEREWITH.

CHAPTER VIII. WEST VIRGINIANS IN THE WAR WITH MEXICO, 1847-1848.

CHAPTER IX. ADDENDA RELATING TO WEST VIRGINIA SOLDIERS IN THE WAR BETWEEN THE STATES—DATA RELATING TO THOSE KILLED IN BATTLE; ACCIDENTALLY KILLED; DIED OF DISEASE AND WOUNDS, ETC.

PREFACE.

The men who reared the first cabin homes in the Eastern Pan-Handle, together with those who pioneered the way for civilization throughout all the trans-Allegheny Region extending from the Alleghenies to the Ohio, were as brave as any who ever dared the perils of a wilderness—one inhabited by wild beasts and savage men. In their veins flowed the blood of half the civilized nations of the world—English, German, Welsh, Scots, Scotch-Irish, Irish, and Dutch—men representing the old Teutonic and Celtic peoples—men whose ancestors had helped to make history on the battlefields of Europe—some of them on that of Hastings. Transplanted from the Old World to the wilds of the New, their descendents—those who became frontiersmen in Western Virginia—now West Virginia—lost naught of the heroism, valor and bravery of their forefathers.

THE FRENCH AND INDIAN WAR—In this struggle between the French and Englishmen for territorial supremacy in the Valley of the Ohio, these frontiersmen marched with Braddock's army to the fatal field of Monongahela; and later waged battle with the French and Indians in the Valley of the South Branch of the Potomac; on the banks of the Opequon, in sight of the Blue Ridge; and erected and defended frontier forts in the Greenbrier Valley.

LORD DUNMORE'S WAR—In Lord Dunmore's War, large numbers of them from the Valley of Greenbrier river were in the battle of Point Pleasant at the mouth of the Great Kanawha, October 10, 1774; while hundreds of them marched with Lord Dunmore from the Eastern Pan-Handle and the South Branch Valley, to the very heart of the Ohio wilderness where the treaty of Camp Charlotte, then agreed upon, made possible the treaty of Pittsburg the next year, by the terms of which the Indians were kept quiet until 1778, thus enabling General Gates—then a resident of West Virginia—to collect the frontier soldiery from New York to Georgia, and overthrow Burgoyne at Saratoga; and at the same time, make possible the settlement of Kentucky whereby a base of operations was formed for General George Rogers Clarke's conquest of the Illinois Country, by which the Jurisdiction of Virginia, and, later, the. sovereignty of the United States, were extended to the Mississippi river.

THE AMERICAN REVOLUTION—When the Revolution came, nowhere else could be found more patriotic or determined spirits than were the inhabitants of Berkeley and Hampshire counties, the frontiersmen of the "District of West Augusta," and the dwellers in the Greenbrier Valley, then in the county of Botetourt, but so soon to be included in that of Greenbrier. All were ready at the first drum-tap of that struggle, and no sooner did they learn of the stirring scenes in Massachusetts, than hundreds of them hastened away to Pittsburg—then believed to be within the confines of Virginia—and there in convention assembled, pledged their lives to the cause of American liberty. How well these Western Virginia men made good these pledges is in part, at least, shown in the following pages.

THE LATER INDIAN WARS—These border men throughout the years of the Revolution, were forced to wage war alike against the Britton from the sea, and the savage from the wilderness beyond the Ohio. The Indians there residing—Shawnees, Miamis, Delawares, Wyandotts, Mingoes, and Ottawas—had been allies of the British in the Revolution. They sometimes warred among themselves, but all were united in one purpose—that of carrying on a war of extermination against the frontier inhabitants—the pioneers of Western Virginia. This they continued from the close of the Revolution in 1783, until General Wayne broke the savage power at the battle of Fallen Timbers, August 20, 1794—a period of twelve years—in all of which time parties of Western Virginians were under arms defending the infant settlements, against a savage foe.

THE WHISKEY INSURRECTION.—The year 1794 is an important one in American history. It was characterized by what is known as the Whiskey Insurrection in Western Pennsylvania. A United States Army numbering fifteen thousand men from New. Jersey, Pennsylvania, Maryland and Virginia, was organized and marched westward to suppress the insurrection. Of these nearly five thousand were from the last named State, and of these hundreds were Western Virginians who rendezvoused at Moorefield, in Hardy county, preparatory to joining the main army at Cumberland in Western Maryland.

THE WAR OF 1812—When the Second War with England—that

of 1812—came, Virginia called upon her sons to defend her soil from the foot of the invader, and no where else did that call meet with a readier response than among the hills and valleys of Western Virginia. From the summits of the Alleghenies to the Ohio, many hundred men hastened away to Norfolk, to defend the shorelands of Virginia, while other hundreds—a brigade of fifteen hundred men collected at Point Pleasant, at the mouth of the Great Kanawha river—marched away across the State of Ohio to render faithful service under General Harrison in the Valley of the Maumee river.

THE WAR WITH MEXICO—Again these Western Virginians responded nobly to the call of the Governor of Virginia for volunteers for service in the war with Mexico. Three Companies—one from Berkeley county, one from Jefferson county, one from the counties bordering on the Ohio, and a detachment from Monongalia —saw service on the table-lands of Mexico. Hundreds of others who could not be received, tendered their service, and the highest ranking Virginian—Colonel John F. Hamtramck—who saw service in that war, was from Jefferson county, now in West Virginia.

ROLLS OR ROSTERS.

The rolls or rosters of the Military organizations of Western Virginians in these wars, are such as have been collected—originals or copies—and deposited in the State Department of Archives and History. Others may yet be found, for there is abundant evidence to show that there were a number of organizations in these wars of which no lists of the men serving therein, are now known to exist. Some additional ones may appear when the records of these wars now deposited in the archives of the War Department have been printed, which, it is hoped, may be done within the next few years. Meanwhile, research on the part of this Department will be continued, that, if possible, other documents may be found containing or revealing the names of early West Virginians in these early Wars.

INTRODUCTORY AND EXPLANATORY

THE FOUNDING OF VIRGINIA.

The 10th of April, 1606, was a great day in the history of North America. On that day King James I. granted to the "Virginia Company of London," a corporation composed of men of his kingdom, "Letters Patent or License" to make habitation, plantation, and to deduce a colony of sundry of our people into that part of America, commonly called Virginia, * * * and do therefore, for us, our heirs, and successors, grant and agree, that Sir Thomas Gates, Sir George Somers, Richard Hackluyt, and Edward-Maria Wingfield, adventurers of and for our city of London, and all such others, as are, or shall be joined unto them of that Colony, shall be. called the First Colony; and they may begin their said first plantation and habitation at any place upon said coast of Virginia, or America, where they shall think fit and convenient, between the four and thirty and one and forty degrees of latitude; and they shall have all lands * * * from the said first seat of their plantation and habitation by the space of fifty miles of English statute measure, all along the said coast of Virginia, or America, towards the west and southwest as the coast lyeth, with all the islands within one hundred miles, directly over against the sea coast * * * from the said place of the first plantation and habitation for the space of fifty like English miles, all alongst the said coast of Virginia and America, towards the east and northeast, or towards the north as the coast lyeth, together with all the islands within one hundred miles directly over against the said sea coast. * * * from the same, fifty miles every way, on the sea coast, directly into the main land by the space of one hundred like English miles; and shall and may inhabit and remain there; and shall and may also build and fortify within any the same, for the better safeguard and defense according to their better discretion.''[1]

It will be seen from the foregoing description of the boundaries of the Colony of Virginia, that what is now West Virginia, was

---
1. Hening's "Statutes at Large" of Virginia, Vol. I., pp. 57, 58, 59.

not included therein; but this was done by the sixth section of the second Charter granted to the Virginia Company of London, bearing date May 23, 1609, when the boundary of the Virginia Colony was so enlarged as to include "all those lands, countries, and territories situate, lying, and being, in that part of America called Virginia, from the point of land, called Cape or Point Comfort, all along the sea coast to the northward two hundred miles; and from the said point of Cape Comfort, all along the sea coast to the southward two hundred miles, and all that space and circuit of land, lying from the sea coast of the precinct aforesaid, up into the land throughout from sea to sea west and northwest"—that was, from the Atlantic to the Pacific Oceans. The zone within this grant being four hundred miles wide, of course, included the present State of West Virginia.[2]

The Virginia Company of London had, as the object of its creation, the founding of an English Colony on the Atlantic coast of Virginia. Three small vessels, no one of which would now be thought worthy to attempt the passage of the Atlantic, were secured by the Company, and lay at anchor on the Thames, at Blackwell, in Middlesex county, three miles above London. They were the "Susan Constant," of one hundred and twenty tons burden, commanded by Captain Christopher Newport; the "Godspeed " of forty tons, Captain Bartholomew Gosnold; and the "Discovery," a pinnace of twenty tons. The little fleet left Blackwall, December 6, 1606, having on board colonists to the number of one hundred and seven, who bade adieu to the shores of the Old World, to find a home in the wilds of the New. January 1, 1607, when, buffeted by contrary winds, the vessels cast anchor in the "Downs," on the south coast of England, where they were detained for six weeks. Then the storms abated, and again the sails were spread and the little fleet stood out to sea. On April 26th, the entrance to Chesapeake Bay was reached, and to the points on either side, the colonists gave the names of Charles and Henry, in honor of the sons of King James. Further within the bay, upon another projection, they bestowed the name of Point Comfort, because of the comfortable anchorage they found there. Then Captain Newport, the acting admiral of the little fleet, steered the vessels up a majestic river, which they called the James, in honor of their beloved sovereign. The voyage was continued for fifty miles, when a landing was made on the north bank, where, on the 13th day of May, 1607, these Middlesex

---

2. Hening's "Statutes at Large" of Virginia, Vol. I., p. 88.

county men laid the foundation of Jamestown, *the oldest permanent English settlement in North America.* Here, on the banks of the James, had landed the men who were destined to light a lamp of liberty which all the tyranny of after ages could not extinguish. It was here that representatives elected by the people of eleven boroughs, assembled, and on the 30th day of June, 1619, organized the House of Burgesses—the first representative legislative body in the New World.

From Jamestown, as the population was increased by the arrival of colonists from over-sea, settlements were made at other points along the great river; whence they spread, as the years sped away, over the Tide-Water Region, and thence into the Piedmont Region, even to the eastern base of the Blue Ridge. So rapidly did the population increase, that in 1671—but sixty-four years after the settlement at Jamestown—there were forty thousand English-speaking people in Virginia.

CHAPTER I.

DISCOVERY, EXPLORATION, AND EARLY SETTLEMENTS IN WEST VIRGINIA.

As stated, hardy pioneers had, previously to 1664, extended the domain of civilization even to the eastern base of the Blue Ridge; but of the region beyond that "Rocky Barrier," nothing whatever was known, for the most daring adventurer had not, as yet, penetrated its vast solitudes. But the exploration and conquest of the wilderness was the mission of determined spirits, and the time was near at hand when white men should traverse this hitherto unknown region, and return to tell the story of its wonderful resources.

The first West Virginia river discovered by white men was called New River, its upper course having been discovered in 1641, by Walter Austin, Rice Hoe, Joseph Johnson, and Walter Chiles. [1] It was a *new river*, one flowing northwest, in an opposite direction from those east of the mountains—hence the name New River.

The Ohio river, which forms the western boundary of West Virginia, was discovered by Robert Cavalier La Salle—the most eminent French explorer of the New World. It was in the year 1663, that Europeans first heard of the Ohio river, and this information came from the Indians to Dallier, a French missionary in Canada. It was reported to be almost as large as the St. Lawrence. This information inspired the adventurous spirit of La Salle with a desire to behold the great river. Accordingly, with Indian guides, he began his journey via Lake Onondagua, now in New York. In October, 1669, he reached the Allegheny river, which he descended to its confluence with the Monongahela, and thence continued down the Ohio as far as the Falls—now Louisville, Kentucky. He was the first European on the Ohio river, and the first that saw the western part of West Virginia.[2]

It is probable that the first white men who saw any part of the eastern portion of the State of West Virginia, were those composing the party under John Lederer, a German explorer in the service of Sir William Berkeley, Colonial Governor of Virginia. In

---
1. Hening's "Statutes at Large" of Virginia, Vol. I., p. 262.
2. Parkman's "La Salle and The Discovery of the Great West," pp. 29, 30.

company with Captain Collett, nine Englishmen and five Indians, he, on August 30, 1670, set out from York river and proceeded by way of the Falls of the Rappahannock, near the present city of Fredericksburg; thence to the mouth of the Rapidan river; thence along the north side of the Rappahannock, to the base of the Blue Ridge; and thence to the summit of that mountain barrier, from which, at a point south of the present Harper's Ferry, the explorers looked down upon and across the Lower Shenandoah Valley— now included in the counties of Jefferson and Berkeley—a first view of the old part of West Virginia.[3]

The first English-speaking men within the present limits of West Virginia, were those composing the exploring expedition under Captain Thomas Batts. These, in addition to himself, were Robert Fallam, Thomas Wood, Jack Neasam, and Per-e-cu-te, the latter a great man of the Appomattox Indians. This party, acting under authority of a commission granted fourteen years before, by the House of·Burgesses—the Colonial legislative body of Virginia —to Major Abraham Wood. "For ye finding out the ebbing and flowing. of ye waters on ye other side the Mountains, in order to ye Discovery of ye South Sea;" left the Appomattox town near the site of the present city of Petersburg, Virginia, on Friday, September 1, 1671, and toiling onward to the westward, crossed the Blue Ridge, thence over what is now known as Peters' Mountain; and thence, through the present West Virginia counties of Monroe, Summers and Fayette, until the 16th of September, when they "had a sight of a curious River like the Appomattox river in Virginia, and the Thames at Chelsea, in England, and broad as that river at Wapping, but it had a fall that made a great noise." The party had reached the Great Falls of the Great Kanawha river, distant ninety-six miles from the Ohio. Here, on the 17th, they took formal possession of the region and proclaimed the King in these words: "Long live King Charles ye 2d, King of England, Scotland, France, Ireland and Virginia, and all the territory thereunto belonging; Defender of ye Faith, etc." Guns were fired, and with a pair of marking-irons, they marked trees; "1st C. R." (Charles Rex I.) for his Sacred Majesty, "2d W. B." for the Governor (Sir William Berkeley): "3d A. W." for Major Abraham Wood, (promoter of the expedition); another for Per-e-cu-te (who said he would turn Englishman); and also, another tree for

---

3. Discoveries of John Lederer on three Several Journeys from Virginia, over the Mountains. March, 1669, to September, 1670." London, 1682.

each of the company. Then the homeward journey began, and all arrived at the Falls of the Appomattox river on the first day of October, except Thomas Wood who died on the expedition.[4]

In 1716, Governor Alexander Spottswood resolved to learn more of the Mountain Region of Virginia. He accordingly equipped a party of thirty horsemen, and heading it in person, left Williamsburg, the Colonial Capital, June 20th, that year. Day after day the journey continued until the Blue Ridge was reached and crossed by way of Swift Run Gap. Descending to the river, now the Shenandoah, the party bestowed upon it the name of "Euphrates." It was crossed and recrossed; then a night was spent upon its banks; then the return journey began, and from the Blue Ridge, the adventurers, looking westward, beheld in the distance, the lofty peaks of the Great North Mountain, in what is now Pendleton county, West Virginia. On arriving at Williamsburg, the Governor established the "Trans-Montane Order or Knights of the Golden Horse-shoe," giving to each of those who accompanied him, a miniature horse-shoe, some of which were set with valuable stones, and all bearing the inscription, "*Sic juvat transcendere montes,*—Thus he swears to cross the mountains.

About the year 1725, John Van Meter, a representative of an old Knickerbocker family early seated on the Hudson, traversed the valley of the South Branch of the Potomac—the *Wap-pa-tom-i-ca* of the Indians. He was an Indian trader, making his headquarters with the Delawares, on the Susquehanna. Thence he made journeys far to the southward, to trade with the Cherokees and Catawbas.[5] It was he who first told the story of the wonderful fertility of the land in the Lower Shenandoah and South Branch Valleys.

FIRST WHITE SETTLEMENTS IN WEST VIRGINIA—THE FRONTIER IN 1756.

The first white man to find a home in West Virginia, was Morgan *ap* Morgan, who in 1726, reared a cabin on the site of the present village of Bunker Hill in Mill creek District, Berkeley county. The next year, a number of Germans from the Valley of the Susquehanna in Pennsylvania, crossed the Potomac at what has been known for more than a hundred years, as the old "Pack-Horse

---
4. Captain Batts' Journal is printed in Fernow's "Ohio Valley in Colonial Times," pp. 220-229; and in the "Introductory Memoir" to Darlington's edition of Christopher Gist's Journals," pp. 18-21.
5. See Kercheval's "History of the Valley of Virginia," p. 46.

Ford," and about a mile above on the southern bank of that river, founded a village which they named New Mecklenberg, in memory of their early home in the Fatherland, and such it continued to be called, until changed to that of Shepherdstown, by an Act of the House of Burgesses in 1762. In 1734 Richard Morgan obtained a grant for a tract of land in the vicinity of New Mecklenberg, and there made his home. Among those who came at the same time and settled along the Upper Potomac in what is now the northern part of the West Virginia counties, of Berkeley and Jefferson, were Robert Harper (at Harper's Ferry) William Stroop, Thomas and William Forester, Israel Friend, Thomas Shepherd, Thomas Swearingen, Van Swearingen, James Formanfi Edward Lucas, Jacob Hite, James Lemon, Richard Mercer, Edward Mercer, Jacob Van Meter, Robert Stockton, Robert Buckles, John Taylor, Samuel Taylor and John Wright. In 1735, the first settlement was made on the South Branch of the Potomac by four families of the name of Coburn, Howard, Walker, and Rutledge. The next year Isaac Van Meter, Peter Casey and numbers of others found homes in the valley of that river in what is now Hampshire and Hardy counties; and within the next few years, cabin homes dotted the valleys of the Opequon, the Great and Little Cacapon rivers, and that of Lost river and Back and Patterson Creeks.

Thus far the early West Virginia settlements had been confined to the region drained by the upper tributaries of the Potomac river. Now, we turn to notice the first pioneer of West Virginia in the valley of Greenbrier river. In 1749, the Greenbrier Land Company was organized. It consisted of twelve Members or Stock-holders, among whom were its President, Hon. John Robinson, the Treasurer of the Colony of Virginia, and long the Speaker of the House of Burgesses; Thomas Nelson, for thirty years the Secretary of the Council of State; and John Lewis the founder of Staunton and two of his sons, William and Charles, This Company was granted the right, by the Governor and Council to survey and take up a tract of land containing one hundred thousand acres of land, lying and being on Greenbrier river, and now in the West Virginia counties of Pocahontas, Greenbrier and Monroe. Four years were allowed to make surveys and pay rights for the same. Andrew Lewis, (afterward General Andrew Lewis of the Revolution) was appointed surveyor and agent for the Company and, in execution of his commission, he in 1754 and prior thereto, surveyed and sold small parcels of this land to sundry persons, who hastened to settle thereon.[5] Col. John Stuart the historian of the Greenbrier Valley, says, that "previously to the year 1755, Andrew Lewis had completed surveys for the quantities aggregating more than fifty thousand acres.[6] When Andrew Lewis came to the Greenbrier river in 1749, he found Stephen Sewell and Jacob Marlin, both of whom had fixed their abode at the mouth of Knopp's creek on the site of the present town of Marlinton, in Pocahontas county."[7]

In 1750, Dr. Thomas Walker with five companions two of whom were Ambrose Powell and Colby Chew, when returning from a tour of exploration in the Kentucky wilderness, crossed the New river at the mouth of the Greenbrier, June 28, 1750, and then journeyed up the latter stream, July 6th ensuing they were at the mouth of Anthony's Creek now in Greenbrier county, where Dr. Walker wrote in his Journal: "There are some inhabitants on the branches of Green Bryer, but we missed their Plantations."[8] Evidently there was a very considerable population in the Greenbrier Valley prior to the year 1755.

On February 23, 1756, Captain Teaque sent to the Lords of Trade, London, a "List of Tithables" in Virginia which he had prepared under the direction of the Government. Upon this as a basis, he estimated the population of Virginia to be 173,316 whites, and 120,000 negroes. Taking his estimate for Hampshire county, and estimating for that part of West Virginia then included in Frederick and Augusta counties, we may conclude that in West Virginia at that date there were about 11,000 whites and 400 blacks.[9] If an irregular or broken line be drawn from the Blue Ridge through Harper's Ferry and Charles Town in Jefferson County; Martinsburg, in Berkeley County; Berkeley Springs, in Hardy County; Petersburg, in Grant County; Upper Tract and Franklin, in Pendleton County; Clover Lick, in Pocahontas County; and thence through Monroe County to Peter's Mountain, it will pass centrally through the region in which resided at that time the pioneer settlers of West Virginia, as shown by contemporary documents.

5. See Call's "Reports of Cases Argued and Decided in the Court of Appeals of Virginia," Vol. IV, p. 28.
6. Stuart's "Memoirs of the Indian Wars and other Occurrences," p. 38.
7. Stuart'- "Memorandum," written in 1798, in Deed Book No. 1 in the County Clerk's Office, Greenbrier County, West Virginia.
8. Rive's "Annotated edition of the Journal of Dr. Thomas Walker," p. 67.
9. "Dinwiddie Papers," Vol. II, pp. 345, 352, 374.

CHAPTER II.

THE FRENCH AND INDIAN WAR.

GENERAL BRADDOCK'S ARMY IN WEST VIRGINIA IN 1755—THE SOLDIERY OF THE WEST VIRGINIA FRONTIER DURING THE WAR.

(From 1754 to 1763.)

From the coming of the first white settlers to West Virginia, to the year 1754—a period of nearly thirty years—the white men and Indians dwelt together in peace and harmony. The Shawnees had their wigwams at "Old Town," Maryland, opposite the mouth of the South Branch of the Potomac; at the "Indian Old Fields," now in Hardy county, in the valley of that river; and at the "Shawnee Springs," now Winchester, in Frederick county, Virginia; while a band of Tuscaroras were on Tuscarora Creek, in the vicinity of Martinsburg, now in Berkeley county, West Virginia. "But," says Kercheval, "in the year 1753, emissaries from the Western Indians came among the [Shenandoah] Valley Indians, inviting them to cross the Allegheny Mountains; and in the Spring of 1754, they suddenly and unexpectedly moved off, and immediately left the Valley."[1] This movement was evidently made under the influence of the French. Both France and England had been engaged but recently in the War of the Austrian Succession, and the truce secured by the terms of the treaty of Aix-la-Chapelle afforded to both an opportunity to push their schemes of colonization into the Ohio Valley—a region which both claimed but neither possessed. But the final struggle for territorial supremacy in America was at hand. "The country west of the Great Mountains is the center of the British Dominions," wrote Lord Hillsborough. The English occupied the point at the "Forks of the Ohio"—now Pittsburg—and began the erection of a fort; The French came down the Allegheny river, dispossessed them and completed the fort, calling it Fort Du Quesne. In 1755, the English General, Edward Braddock, with the 44th and 48th Royal Infantry Regiments, came to Virginia, and having been joined by a large force of provincial troops, marched against Fort Duquesne; but when within ten miles thereof, his army was shot down by the French and Indians on the fatal field of Monongahela. Then began a war of ex-

---
1. Kercheval's "History of the Valley," p. 58.

termination—a border war carried on against the West Virginia settlements. This continued for seven long years, in all of which the French and Indians or the latter alone, carried death and desolation all along the frontier of civilization. The West Virginia pioneers nevertheless stood their ground and, aided by companies of rangers from the older Virginia settlements, warred successfully against their barbarian enemies until the close of the war in 1763.

The following are partial lists of the Companies of Rangers employed on the upper tributaries of the Potomac, and in the Greenbrier river—the West Virginia frontier—during the French and Indian War; that is from 1754 to 1763:—

CAPTAIN ANDREW LEWIS' COMPANY OF RANGERS, IN SERVICE IN 1754.

(*Source*—Crozier's "Virginia Colonial Militia," pp. 9-57.)

OFFICERS.

Andrew Lewis	Captain	Robert Graham	Sergeant
John Savage	Lieutenant	Thomas Stedman	Corporal
William Wright	Ensign	Joshua Baker	Corporal
John McKully	Sergeant	David Wilkinson	Drummer

PRIVATES.

Abaham Mushaw	James Milton	Andrew Fowler
John Biddlecomb	Jacob Gowen	John Allan
Robert Murphy	Henry Bailey	Thomas King
Bartholomew Burns	John Brown	William Chaplain
James Fulham	Henry Neale	John Davis
John Thurstan	Benjamin Gauze	Patrick McPike
Thomas Burney	John Hart	Michael McCannon
John Maston	George Gibbons	Matthew Jones
Terrence Swiney	William Holland	Thomas Pierce
John Smith	John Gallihon	Thomas Burras
Patrick Smith	Casper Moreau	Samuel Arsdale
John Mulholland	John Chapman	George Malcom
James Cammack	Samuel Hyden	Philemon Waters
Charles Waddey	William Dean	John Campbell
James Smith	Nicholas Morgan	Francis Rogers
William Stallions	Barnaby Ryley	Pledge Ward
Henry Bowman	Nathaniel Deadman	James Ford

CAPTAIN WILLIAM PRESTON'S COMPANY OF RANGERS, AUTHORIZED BY AN ACT OF THE HOUSE OF BURGESSES JUNE 8, 1757, IN SERVICE UNTIL MAY 4, 1759, WHEN IT WAS ABANDONED.

(*Source*—Crozier's "Virginia Colonial Militia," pp. 9-57.)

OFFICERS.

William Preston ....Captain
Charles Lewis .... Lieutenant
Archibald Buchanan .....Sergeant
Charles Smith .... Sergeant
William Davis...........Sergeant
Joshua Cummings ...... Corporal
Thomas Saunders........Drummer
Dr. Thomas Lloyd ....Surgeon

PRIVATES.

John Davis
James Hulman
Nicholas Smith
John Johnston
Frederick Fitzgerald
David Graham
William Anderson
William Hutcheson
William Jackson
John Carlisle
John Vachob

Moses Fisher
Bond Estle
John Miller
Thomas Kinkead
William Stewart
Francis Riley
John Codare
Lofftus Pullin
William Black
Robert Graham

Solly Mulliear
Gardner Adkins
Samuel Campbell
John Estle
Thomas McGregor
Robert Hall
John Pryor
John Kinkead
George Gwinn
Thomas Hicklin

CAPTAIN WILLIAM PHILLIP'S COMPANY OF RANGERS, IN SERVICE IN 1763.

(*Source*—Crozier's "Virginia Colonial Militia," pp. 9-57.)

OFFICERS.

William Phillips...........Captain
Joseph Bickley..........Lieutenant
James Bullock.............Ensign
William Hughes...........Ensign
Joseph Terry.............Sergeant
Charles Barrett..........Sergeant
John Hall ....Sergeant
William Hughes..........Surgeon

PRIVATES.

William McGehee
Nathaniel Branham
Robert Hall
James Twopence
Clabourne Routhwell
Phillip Cosby
John Freeman

John Gilbert
William Bibbs
James Ratcliff
John McCoy
John Lemay
Zacheus Cosby
Charles Hester

Chapman White
James McGehee
James Smith
John Sanders
Robert Goodwin
Dabney Carr
William Brock

Captain John Dickinson's Company of Rangers, in Service in 1757-59.

(*Source*—Crozier's "Virginia Colonial Militia," pp. 9-57.)

OFFICERS.

John Dickinson...........Captain   Robert Gillispie, Sr.......Sergeant
John Baller .... Sergeant   Humphrey Madison ....Ensign
Thomas Kelly ....Corporal

PRIVATES.

John Fulton	William Shields	David Galloway
James Johnston	Edward McMullin	John McMullin
Thomas Carpenter	Jacob Parsinger	Abraham Parsinger
Philip Parsinger	Patrick Carrigan	Andrew Jameson
Solomon Carpenter	Ezekiel Johnson	Peter Wiley
Joseph Willis	John Taylor	William Davis
Peter Wiley	John Wiley	William Hamilton

Captain Peter Hogg's Company of Rangers, in Service from 1754-58.

(*Source*—Crozier's "Virginia Colonial Militia," pp. 9-57.)

OFFICERS.

Peter Hogg...............Captain   Samuel Powell ....Sergeant
James Dunlap ....Lieutenant   William Vaughan ....Sergeant
James Taylor.............Ensign   William Armstrong......Corporal
John Clark ....Sergeant   David Laird ....Corporal

PRIVATES.

Thomas Scott	Thomas Galbreath	Francis Gibbs
William Smith	James McMahon	Daniel Grubb
John Johnson	George Ehrmantrout	James Riddle
John Furnace	James Shaw	John Pence
James Milligan	Henry Shackleford	

Captain Samuel Overton's Company of Rangers, in Service in 1755-56.

(*Source*—Crozier's "Virginia Colonial Militia," pp. 9-57.)

OFFICERS.

Samuel Overton..........Captain   Ansolem Clarkson........Sergeant

PRIVATES.

John Penix	William Watson	Richard Foster
Charles Jenkins	James Ratliff	George Sims
Thomas Jones	Charles Jenkins	Edmond Foster
William Foster	James Melton	William Ahorn
John Shepperson	Peter Clarkson	

CAPTAIN ROBERT RUTHERFORD'S COMPANY OF RANGERS, IN SERVICE IN 1758-59.

(*Source*—Crozier's "Virginia Colonial Militia," pp. 9-57.)

OFFICERS.

Robert Rutherford........Captain   William Darke...........Corporal
Edward Luce.............Sergeant   Jonathan Seaman ....Corporal
John Rouse..............Sergeant

PRIVATES.

John Dastforan	James Shirley	Jacob Rush
Joseph Hedges	Richard Bowen	Alexander Lemon
Walter Shirley	Jervice Sherly	Robert Buckles, Jr.
Thomas Bright		

CAPTAIN WILLIAM CHRISTIAN'S COMPANY OF RANGERS, IN SERVICE IN 1760-64.

(*Source*—Crozier's "Virginia Colonial Militia," pp. 9-57.)

OFFICERS.

William Christian........Captain   William Carvin..........Sergeant
James Barnett ....Sergeant

PRIVATES.

Thomas Miller	John Collins	John Turnley
William Melton	Dumas Lane	Nathan Gibson
James Ritchey	James Twopence	John Lea

Of other Companies of Rangers in service on the West Virginia frontier during the French and Indian War were those of Captains Christopher Gist, John Smith, Joseph Fox, John McNeal, Charles Lewis, Samuel Meredith, Archibald Alexander, Christopher Hudson, Obediah Woodson, Thomas Fleming, Thomas Bullet, James

McGavok, John Anthony, Robert Breckenridge, William Cox, Alexander Sayer, John Blagg, George Berkeley, ———— Temple, and ———— Hubbard. The work of erecting and garrisoning forts on the frontier during this struggle was performed by the companies of Washington's First Virginia Regiment, the headquarters of which was at Fort Loudoun, now Winchester, the seat of justice of Frederick county, in the Shenandoah Valley. These companies were composed of men from this valley and from Virginia east of the Blue Ridge.

The depredations of the French and Indians upon the white settlements during the years of this War, were particularly fatal on the frontier settlements of West Virginia. They destroyed the settlement of Foyle and Tygart on Tygart's Valley river; that of the Eckarleys at Dunkard's Bottom on Cheat river; and that at the mouth of Decker's Creek on the Monongahela. Then scalping parties overran all the region drained by the upper tributaries of the Potomac and the Greenbrier rivers; and then carried death and desolation eastward to Jackson's river and to the Lower Shenandoah Valley. Everywhere dark mysterious clouds of malignant spirits hung upon the horizon, threatening every moment to overwhelm and exterminate the half-protected pioneers in their wilderness homes, and there was scarcely a settlement in all the region from the Potomac to the New River that did not experience some of the fatal effects of the terrible storm of savage warfare which raged so fiercely around them. Then there were battlefields on the soil of West Virginia. The battle of Great Cacapon River was fought in what is now Bloomery Magisterial District, in Hampshire county, April 18, 1756, between a detachment of one hundred men, of Col. Washington's regiment, under Capt. John Mercer, on one side, and a body of French and Indians on the other. The battle of Lost River was fought in the Spring of 1756, in what is now Lost River Magisterial District, Hardy county, between West Virginia frontiersmen under Capt. Jeremiah Smith, and a body of fifty Indians commanded by a French officer. The battle of the Trough was fought in 1756, in what is now Moorefield Magisterial District, Hardy county; between a body of seventy Indians, allies of the French, and a Virginia garrison from Fort Pleasant near by. The massacre at Fort Seybert occurred in May, 1758, in what is now Bethel Magisterial District, Pendleton county, on the south fork of the South Branch of the Potomac, twelve miles east of the present town of Franklin; the Fort was attacked by Shawnee Indians, under their celebrated chief, Killbuck; the garrison surrendered and all were massacred, save one.

EXPEDITION OF GENERAL EDWARD BRADDOCK—MARCH OF THE BRITISH ARMY THROUGH THE EASTERN PART OF WEST VIRGINIA.

The year 1754 closed with the French in complete possession of the Ohio Valley. But a war was in progress which, in its results, was to change the geography of a continent and exert a powerful influence in moulding the destiny of nations. Both nations —France and England—speedily mustered veteran regiments fresh from the battle-fields of the Old World and transferred them to the wilds of the New. In mid-winter 1755, General Edward Braddock, a British General, sailed from the harbor of Cork, Ireland, with two regiments destined for Virginia. February 20th, the ships which bore them across the Atlantic, arrived in Chesapeake Bay, and proceeded up the Potomac river to Alexandria, where all were disembarked preparatory to the march through the wilderness, the object being the recovery of Fort Du Quesne at the forks of the Ohio—now Pittsburg. The troops which came with Braddock were the 44th and 48th Royal Infantry Regiments, commanded respectively by Sir Peter Halket and Colonel Thomas Dunbar. Sir John St. Clair was the Quarter-Master-General, and Lieutenant Robert Orme was the chief aid to the General. From Alexandria, the army moved up the Potomac, passing the site of the present city of Washington, and proceeded to Fredericktown, in Maryland. Its progress from there to Wills' Creek, now Cumberland, the metropolis of western Maryland, is a subject of intense interest to every student of West Virginia history. This is because a large part of the distance marched between these points was through what is now the eastern part of the State. In this connection the following from the Journal of Lieutenant Orme is of special interest:—

"As no road had been made to Wills' Creek on the Maryland side of the Potomack the 48th Regiment was obliged to cross that river at Congogee. (now Conococheague Creek, Washington county, Maryland,) and to fall into the Virginia Road near Winchester. The General ordered a bridge to be built over the Antietam (Creek), which being finished, and provision laid on the road. Colonel Dunbar marched with his Regiment the 48th, from Fredericktown, Maryland, on the 28th of April, and about this time the bridge over the Opeccon in Virginia, now in Berkeley County, West

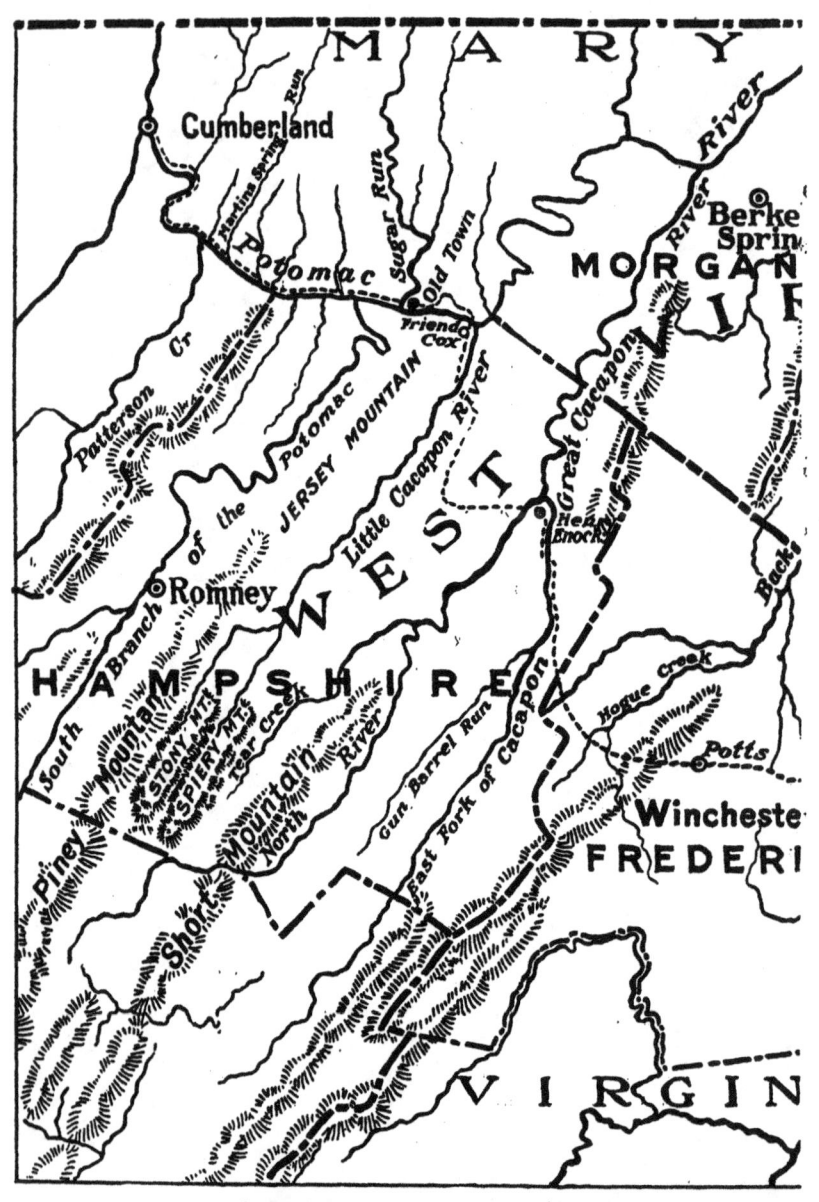

SKETCH SHOWING BY DOTTED LINE THE ROUTE PURSUED BY BRADDOCK'S

The Army crossed the Potomac from Maryland into Virginia, at Evan ginia House of Burgesses, October 9, 1744—eleven years before—at the mo side of the Opequon river by the pioneer home of John Evans; thence to t Henry Enocks, in the "Forks of Capon;" and thence to that of Friend Cox, it recrossed the Potomac into Maryland, and pressed on to Fort Cumberla

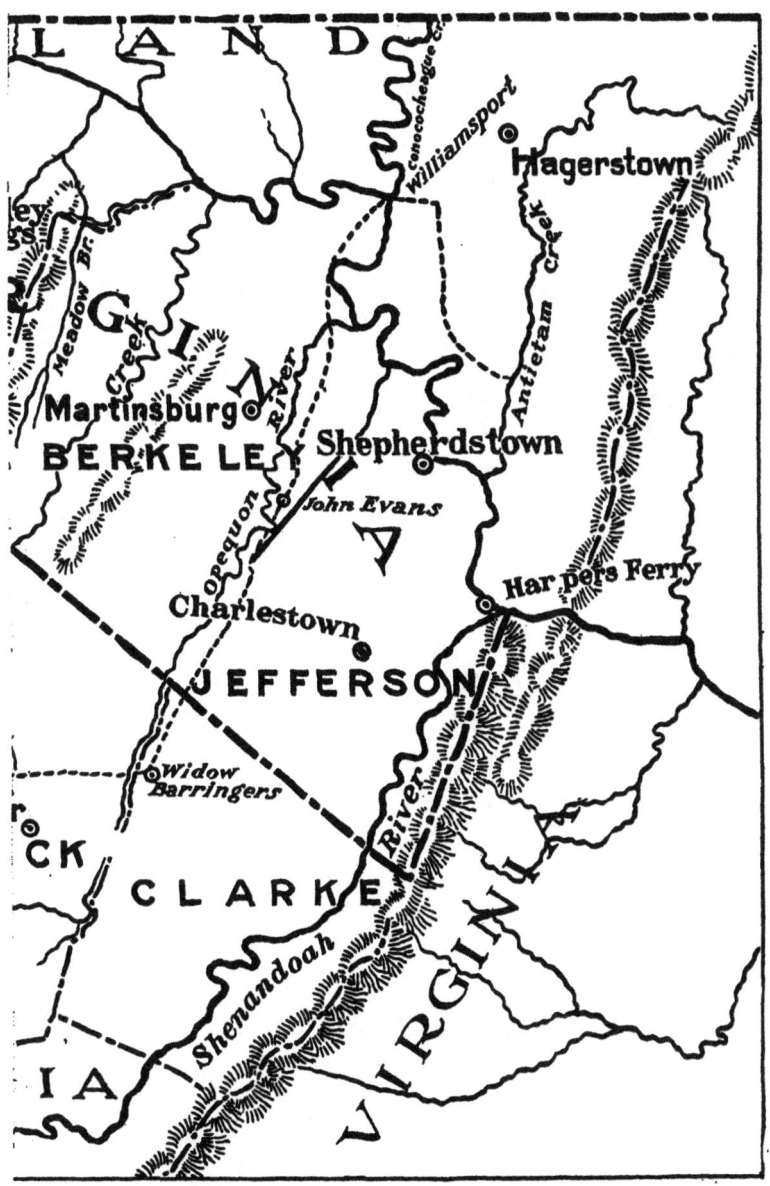

ARMY THROUGH THE EASTERN PAN-HANDLE OF WEST VIRGINIA.

Watkin's Ferry, which had been established by an Act of the Vir-
ith of Conococheague Creek. Thence it proceeded up the eastern
1at of the widow Barringer; thence to that of one Potts; thence to
at the mouth of Little Cacapon river; where, at the "Ferry Fields"
ad—now Cumberland City, in Western Maryland.—V. A. L.

Virginia, was finished for the passage of the artillery, and floats were built on all the rivers and creeks."—"Journal of Lieutenant Robert Orme, printed in Sargent's "History of Braddock's Expedition," pp. 308, 309.

On the 29th of April the 48th Regiment, under Colonel Dunbar, took up its line of march from Frederick, Maryland, to the mouth of Conococheague Creek, now in Washington county, that State; thence across the Potomac river into Virginia; and thence across and up the Qpequon river to the vicinity of Winchester, in Frederick county; thence westward and north westward over the mountains, to the "Forks of Cacapon", in Hampshire county, now West Virginia; and thence to the mouth of Little Cacapon, where the army crossed the Potomac and was in Maryland again. The following description of the progress of the army through eastern West Virginia is quoted from what is known as the "Seaman's Journal."[2] which was doubtless written by Lieutenant Spendelowe, of the detachment of Marines sent by Commodore Keppel of the British fleet, with Braddock on his expedition to the Ohio:—

"April 29th, 1755. We began our march [from Fredericktown] at 6, but found much difficulty in loading our baggage, so that we left several things behind us, particularly the men's hammocks. We arrived at 3 o'clock at one Walker's, 18 miles from Frederick, and encamped there on good ground; this day we passed the South Ridge [South Mountain] or Shannandah [Shenandoah] Mountains, very easy in the ascent. We saw plenty of Hares, Deer, and Partridges: This place is wanting of all refreshments.

On the 30th:—at 6, we marched in our way to Connechieg, where we arrived at 2 o'clock, 16 miles from Walker's: this is a fine situation, close to the Potomack. We found the Artillery Stores going by water to Wills' Creek, and left two of our men here.

May 1st:—At 5, we went with our people, and began ferrying the Army &c. into Virginia, which we completed by 10 o'clock, and marched in our way to one John Evans,[3] where we arrived at 3 o'clock—17 miles from Connecochieg, and 20 from Winchester. We got some provisions and forage here The roads now begin to be very indifferent.

On the 2nd:—As it is customary in the Army to halt a day after 3 days march we halted today to rest the Army.

On the 3rd:—Marched at 5 in our way to one Widow Barringer's, 18

---
2. Printed in Sargent's "History of Braddock's Expedition," pp. 366-389.
3. The John Evans here mentioned was the builder and defender of Fort Evans, a stockade, which was situated about two miles east of south from the site of the present town of Martinsburg, in Berkeley county. It was partially erected in 1755, and completed the following year. Scarcely was it ready for occupancy, when the French and Indians made an incursion into the vicinity, and the people, among them the founders of Martinsburg, found refuge in this fort. Then it was besieged, but the heroism of those within saved the fort from distruction, and themselves from Massacre.—Kercheval's "History of the Shenandoah Valley," (first edition), pp. 94, 95; also Aler's "History of Martinsburg and Berkeley County," p. 39.

miles from Evans: this day was so excessively hot that several officers and many men could not get on till the evening, but the body got to their ground at 3 o'clock. This is 5 miles from Winchester, a fine station if properly cleared.

On the 4th:—Marched at 5 in our way to one Potts—9 miles from the Widow's—where we arrived at 10 o'clock. The road this day was bad: we got some wild turkeys here: in the night it came to blow hard at N. W.

On the 5th:—Marched at 5 in our way to one Henry Enock's,4 being 16 miles from Potts, where we arrived at 2 o'clock. The road this day over prodigious mountains, and between the same we crossed over a run of water 20 times in 3 miles distance. After going 15 miles we came to a river called Kahapetin, (Cacapon) where our men ferried the Army over and got to our ground, where we found a company of Peter Halket's encamped.5

On the 6th:—We halted this day to refresh the Army.

On the 7th:—We marched at 5 in our way to one Cox's,6 12 miles from Enock's This morning was very cold but by 10 o'clock it was prodigiously hot. We crossed another run of water 19 times in 2 miles, and got to our ground at 2 o'clock, and encamped close to the Potomack.7

On the 8th:—We began to ferry the Army over the river into Maryland, which was completed at 10, and then we marched on our way to one Jackson's, 8 miles from Cox's. At noon it rained very hard and continued so till 2 o'clock, when we got to our ground, and encamped on the banks of the Potomack. A fine situation, with a good deal of clear ground about it."

4. Henry Enock was residing in the "Forks of Cacapon" as early as 1750, five years before General Braddock's Army passed that place. April 23, 1750, George Washington, Surveyor for Lord Fairfax, surveyed for John Newlon a tract of land containing 315 acres, beginning at a hickory. "Henry Enock's Corner, and thence with his line N. 12, E. 260 Poles to another of Henry Enock's Corners." Henry Enock was one of Washington's chain-carriers, when surveying land for John Parker in Little Cacapon river, April 26, 1750—See "A Book of Surveys begun July 22, 1749," printed in Toner's edition of Washington's "Journal while surveying for Lord Fairfax in the Northern Neck of Virginia beyond the Blue Ridge." p. 111.

5. The Company belonged to the 44th Regiment which marched over the same route in advance of the 48th. This is evident from the statement of Lieutenant Orme, who says that "no road had been made to Wills' Creek on the Maryland side of the Potomac," by which any part of the Army could proceed. When General Braddock arrived at Wills' Creek, on May 10th, he preceeded the 48th Regiment, and found six companies of the 44th encamped at that place. The Company overtaken at the "Forks of Cacapon," May 5th, by the 48th Regiment, was evidently the rear guard, or company, of the 44th. The entire army must therefore have marched through eastern West Virginia. —V. A. L.

6. Young George Washington, in the employ of Lord Fairfax, was on the upper Potomac in 1750, and April 25th of that year, "Surveyed for Friend Cox, a certain tract of wast Ld Situate in Frederick Coty and on Potomac & Little Cacaphon & bounded as followeth:" a tract containing 240 acres.—See "A Book of Surveys begun July 22, 1749," printed in Toner's edition of Washington's "Journal while surveying for Lord Fairfax in the Northern Neck of Virginia beyond the Blue Ridge." p.. 111.

7. "The army struck the Little Cacapehon (though pronounced Cacapon. I have used for the occasion the spelling of Washington, and various old documents,) about six miles above its mouth, and following the stream, encamped on the Virginia side of the potomac, preparatory to crossing into Maryland. The water is supposed to have been high at this time, as the spot is known as "Ferry Fields," from the army havng been ferried over."—See Loudermilk's "History of Cumberland, Washington's First Campaign, and Braddock's Expedition," p. 141.

April 30th Braddock left Fredericktown with his staff and a body-guard of light horse. Before leaving Alexandria, he had purchased from Governor Horatio Sharpe, of Maryland, a chariot, one of the cumbersome carriages of that day, and made his journey through eastern West Virginia with a degree of style, far better suited to the streets of London, than the roadway through the forests of Berkeley county and over the Hampshire hills at that time. He arrived at Wills' Creek—Fort Cumberland—where he found in camp, six companies of the 44th Regiment; nine companies of Virginia Rangers, and Independent companies from North Carolina, South Carolina, New York and Maryland.

From Cumberland the army began the march to Fort Du Quesne, and it was the evening of the 8th of July, when the columns, for the second time, reached the Monongahela river at a point ten miles distant from that fortress. On the next day a crossing was affected and once more the ranks were formed on the level plain before them. The order to march was given but scarcely were the columns in motion when a deadly fire was poured in upon them. It came from a body of eight hundred French and Indians concealed in the dense forest and this was continued until of the twelve hundred men who crossed the Monongahela that morning, sixty-seven officers and seven hundred and fourteen privates were either killed or wounded. Braddock was among the latter, and four days later he died, his name evermore to be associated with defeat. The remainder of the army returned to Fort Cumberland and thence the West Virginians and Virginians proceeded to their homes and to Philadelphia.

CHAPTER III.

WEST VIRGINIA SOLDIERS IN LORD DUNMORE'S WAR.

In the year 1774, John Murray, Earl of Dunmore, was the governor of the Colony of Virginia; hence Dunmore's War was a designation applied to a series of bloody deeds engaged in by the Virginia frontiersmen and the warriors of the Indian Confederacy of the Ohio Wilderness, that year.

At this time, Berkeley county, formed in 1772, included its present area with that of the whole of Jefferson, and a part of that of Morgan. Hampshire county, not only had its present extent but a portion of Morgan, and all of the counties of Hardy, Grant and Mineral. Augusta county then stretched away from the Blue Ridge to the Ohio, and to the Upper Valley of that river, even, as was asserted, beyond Fort Pitt. That part of this county lying west of Hampshire, was known as the "District of West Augusta" its boundaries being then undefined. Botetourt county, created in 1769, from the southern portion of Augusta county, likewise extended from the Blue Ridge across West Virginia, to the Ohio river; the line separating it from Augusta county, extending north fifty-five degrees west, and crossing Greenbrier river at the southern end of the Marlin Mountains, terminated on the Ohio river, near the present village of Belleville, now in Wood county, West Virginia. Thus all that part of West Virginia lying between the said line and the Great Kanawha river, was included in Botetourt county. Fincastle county, organized in 1772, from the southern part of Botetourt, also extended westward from the Blue Ridge to the Ohio, and included within its limits all of West Virginia lying between the Great Kanawha and Big Sandy rivers. At this time there were probably twenty thousand white people living in what is now West Virginia.

In the ten years intervening between the close of the French and Indian War in 1763, and the year 1774—that of Lord Dunmore's War—there was comparative peace and quiet along the Western Frontier; and for this reason, this period has been called the "Halcyon Decade of the Eighteenth Century." But hostilities began in the spring of 1774, and a savage warfare with all its horrors, was waged upon the defenseless settlements of the Western

Border. Messengers bore tidings of this to Williamsburg, the old Colonial Capital of Virginia, and the House of Burgesses—the legislative body of the Colony—directed Lord Dunmore to prosecute a war against the Indian nations of the Ohio Wilderness. As a preliminary movement to this, he ordered Major Angus McDonald to proceed with four hundred men, from the Lower Shenandoah Valley, by way of Wheeling, against the Wakatomika and other Indian towns in the Muskingum Valley, northwest of the Ohio. This was done but little accomplished, beyond exciting the Indians to increased acts of barbarity. Meantime, Governor Dunmore crossed the Blue Ridge, and, in the Lower Shenandoah Valley, fixed his headquarters at "Greenway Court" the home of Lord, Thomas Fairfax. Here a thousand men were collected—five hundred from Frederick county, under Colonel Crawford, and five hundred from Berkeley county commanded by Colonel Adam Stephen. Governor Dunmore assumed command of this force, and heading it in person, proceeded to the Ohio. At Fort Pitt, he was joined by the "West Augusta Battalion" commanded by Major John Connolly. At Wheeling another hundred men were added to the ranks, and with his force thus augmented to thirteen hundred men, Lord Dunmore descended the Ohio to the mouth of Hockhocking river, where, at its mouth he reared a stockade fort to which he gave the name of Fort Gower, in honor of Lord Gower, his personal friend in the British House of Lords.

Here Dunmore awaited the arrival of intelligence from the Southern Division of the army which he had ordered General Andrew Lewis to collect at "Camp Union" on the Big Levels of Greenbrier,—now Lewisburg, West Virginia. This Division was composed of a Regiment from Augusta county, commanded by Colonel Charles Lewis; a Regiment from Botetourt county under Colonel William Fleming; a Battalion from Fincastle county, at whose head was Colonel William Christian. A company of Minute Men under Colonel John Field, from Culpeper county; a Volunteer Company under Captain Francis Slaughter, from Dunmore (now Shenandoah) county; a company of Bedford County Riflemen under Captain Thomas Buford; and a company of Kentucky Pioneers under Captain James Harrod. This Division left Camp Union, in September, and proceeded to the Ohio river on which, at the mouth of the Great Kanawha, on Monday, October 10th, 1774, the greater part of it was engaged in the battle of

Point Pleasant, the most desperate struggle ever waged between white men and Indians in America.[1]

Singularly enough no rolls or rosters of any of the companies with Major Angus McDonald, or with Lord Dunmore are known to be in existence. In the Southern Division under General Lewis there were thirty company organizations; and of these the rolls of eleven have been preserved. They are as follows:—

IN THE AUGUSTA COUNTY REGIMENT.

A LIST OF CAPTAIN WILLIAM NALLE'S COMPANY OF VOLUNTEERS IN THE AUGUSTA COUNTY REGIMENT.

(*Source*—Thwaites and Kellogg's "Documentary History of Lord Dunmore's War," p. 405. Original in the Library of the State Historical Society of Wisconsin)

OFFICERS.

William Nalle, ... Captain.
Martin Nalle, ... Lieutenant.
Jacob Pence, ... Ensign.
John Bush, ... Sergeant.
William Bush, ... Sergeant.
Bernard Crawford, ... Sergeant.

PRIVATES.

Shadrick Butler,	William Feavill,	Robert Hains,
Moses Smith,	Stephen Washburn,	Israel Meaders,
Henry Owler,	John Griggsby,	Richard Welch,
Zacarias Lee,	John Goodall,	Benjamin Petty,
Michael Jordan,	Bruten Smith,	James Todd,
William Spicer,	James Washburn,	Charles Brown,
James Alexander,	George Rucker,	Joseph Ray (or Roay),
William Scales,	John Bright,	Jenty Jackson,
John Owler,	George Fuls (or Fultz)	James Miller,
George Harmon,	John Chisholm,	Adam Hansbarger,
Henry Cook,	John Breden,	Thomas Brooke,
Henry Miner,	Chesley Rogers,	Zapaniah Lee
Zachiaus Plunkenpiel,	Micajah Smith,	William Smith,
John Deck,	John Fry,	John Williams,
Joseph Butler,	James Selby,	James Reary,
Abraham Rue,	Jacob Null,	John Null.

Total 54.

---

1. For full details relating to Lord Dunmore's War, see Thwaites and Kellogg's "Documentary History of Dunmore's War;" the "Revolution on the Upper Ohio," by the same authors; "American Archives," Fourth series Vols. I. & II.; "Journals of the Virginia House of Burgesses," and Ford's "Reprint of the Journals of the Continental Congress."

IN THE BOTETOURT COUNTY REGIMENT.

A LIST OF CAPTAIN JOHN MURRAY'S COMPANY OF VOLUNTEERS IN THE BOTETOURT COUNTY REGIMENT.

(*Source*—Thwaites and Kellogg's "Documentary History of Lord Dunmore's War," p. 40C. Original in the Library of the State Historical Society of Wisconsin.)

OFFICERS.

John Murray,[2] ....Captain.
William McKee,[3].......................Lieutenant.
Samuel Wallace, ...Lieutenant.
Adam Wallace..........................Ensign.
William Taylor,........................Sergeant.
Moses Coiler, ...Sergeant.
John Larken, ...Sergeant.
John Simpson, ...Sergeant.
Barney Boyls, ...Sergeant.

PRIVATES.

John Nelson,
John Gilmore,
James Arnold,
George Milwood,
Thomas Nail,
Ezekiel Kennedy,
William Simpson,
Robert Wallace,
George Cummings,
Daniel Blair,
Nicholas Mooney,
Stephen Harris,
Moses Whitby,
John Kelsey,
William Cochran,
Thomas Hedden,
Jonathan Watson,
James Neely,
William Conner,
William Brown,
Andrew Wallace,
William Johns,
William Lyons,
Hugh Logan,

Stephen Arnold,
John Sedbury,
Andrew Evans,
John Lapsly,
John Jones,
Thomas McClure,
Thomas Pearry,
John Eager
 (or Edgar),
Thomas Burney,
Solomon Brundige,
Daniel Fullin
 (or Pullin),
James Gilmore,
Hugh Moore,
James Logan,
Presley Gill,
Hugh Logan,
John Miligan,
William Bradley,
James McCalister,
Isaac Trimble,
Andrew Alden,
John McMurray.

James Hall,
William Moore,
William MacCorkle,
Joseph McBride,
James Walker,
John Moore,
Peter Cassady,
John Griggs,
James Crawley,
Daniel Simpkins,
John McClure,
David Wallace,
James Cunningham,
Joseph Gibson,
John Logan,
John Coiler,
William Neely,
Peter Higgings,
John McGee,
John Barkley,
Peter McNeal,
James Brambridge,
James Simpkins.
          Total   78.

---

2. Killed at Point Pleasant.
3. Assumed command of the company when Captain Murray was killed.

A List of Captain Philip Love's Company of Volunteers, in the Botetourt County Regiment.

(*Source*—Thwaites and Kellogg's "Documentary History of Lord Dunmore's War," p. 407. Original in the Library of the State Historical Society of Wisconsin.)

OFFICERS.

Philip Love, ...Captain.
Daniel McNeill, ...Lieutenant.
John Mills,...............................Ensign.
William Ewing, ...Sergeant Major.
Francis McElhaney,....................Quarter M. S.
Shelton Taylor, ...Sergeant.
James Alexander,4.....................Sergeant.
John Crawford,.........................Sergeant.

PRIVATES.

Robert Owen,
Samuel MtGumery
  or (Montgomery)
Thomas Pierce,
Charles Byrne,
William Hooper,
Thomas Welch, Jr.,
William Armstrong,
Thomas Brown,
George Craig,
John Buchanan,
James Franklin,
Richard Collins,
Griffin Harriss,
John Robinson,

Samuel Andrews,
William Teasy,
Thomas Armstrong,
Thomas Gilbert,
Samuel Savage,
Patrick Conner,
Daniel McDonald,
James Neeley,
Richard Wilson,
Charles Davis,
William Hanson,
James M. Guillin,
John Jones,
John Todd,
William Scott,

John Todd,
John Dunn,
Abraham DeMonts,
Thomas Welch, Sr.,
Joseph Pain,
James Simpson,
Abraham Moon,
Robert Smith,
William Franklin,
James McDonald,
John McGinnis,
John Marks,
Daniel Ormsbey.

—Total 50.

A List of Captain John Lewis'[5] Company of Volunteers in the Botetourt County Regiment.

(*Source*—Thwaites and Kellogg's "Documentary History of Lord Dunmore's War," p. 409. Original in the Library of the State Historical Society of Wisconsin.)

OFFICERS.

John Lewis,..............................Captain.
John Henderson,........................Lieutenant.
Robert Alliet, or (Elliott)..............Ensign

---

4. Wounded at Point Pleasant.
5. This Captain John Lewis was a son of General Andrew Lewis, and a cousin of Captain John Lewis, (son of Thomas) of the Augusta Regiment, his father being a brother of the General.—V. A. L.

Samuel Glass, ...Sergeant,
William Bryans, ...Sergeant.
Peter Huff, ...Sergeant.
William Wilson, ...Sergeant.
Samuel Estill, ...Sergeant.
John Donnally, ...Fifer.
Thomas Alisbury, ...Drummer.

PRIVATES.

John Swope,	Alexander Kelley,	Edward Eagin,
James Ellison,	John Deniston,	James Stuart.
John Savage,	Christopher Welch,	James Crawley,
James Dulin,	Isaac Fisher,	Peter Ellenburg.
Andrew Kissinger,	Samuel Barton,	William Clifton,
Joseph Love,	Leonard Huff,	Thomas Huff,[6]
Samuel Croley,	William Isum,	Isaac Taylor,
Martin Carney,	Peter Hendricks,	John Hundley,
Henry Howard,	Molastine Peregrine,	Walter Holwell,
James McNutt,	Samuel Burcks,	Nathan Farmer.
Gabriel Smithers,	Thomas Edgar,	James Carlton.
Mathew Polug,	Thomas Canady	William Jones,
(or Pogue)	(or Kanady)	William Robinson,
Richard Packwood,	John Arthur,	Robert Boyd,
Samuel Huff,	Edward Wilson,	Philip Hammond.
John Reyburn,	Isaac Nichol,	Thomas Carpenter,[6]
James Burtchfield,	Solomon White,	David Cook,
Jeremiah Carpenter.	Solomon Carpenter,	Robert Bowles,
John Bowman,	Jacob Bowman,	Hugh Caperton,
James Burnsides,	Dennis Nail,	Adam Cornwell,
Mathew Creed,	Mathew Jewitt,	John Carpenter,
William Boniface,	Robert Davis,	Matthias Kissinger,
Henry Bowyer,	Thomas Burnes,	
Adam Caperton,	William Mann,	—Total 78.

A List of Captain John Stuart's Company of Greenbrier Valley Volunteers in the Botetourt County Regiment.

(*Source*—Thwaites and Kellogg's "Documentary History of Lord Dunmore's War." p. 410. Original in the Library of the State Historical Society of Wisconsin.)

OFFICERS.

John Stuart............................Captain.
(Manuscript torn),..................... ———.
James Donnally,........................Sergeant.
Charles O'Hara.........................Sergeant.
Skidmore Harriman,.....................Sergeant.

---

6. Wounded at Point Pleasant.

PRIVATES.

Daniel Workman,
Robert O'Hara,
John Pauley,
Andrew Gardiner,
Thomas Ferguson,7
Henry Lawrence,
Edward Smith,
William Clendenin,
Joseph Day,
John Burke,
John Doherty,
Samuel Williams,

James Pauley,
Archibald McDowell,
Quavy Lockhart,
John McCandless,
John Crain,
John Harris,
Spencer Cooper,
Jacob Lockhart,
Charles Kennison,7
John McNeal,
William O'Hara,

James Clarke,
William Hogan,
Samuel Sullivan,
Thomas Gillispie,
William Dyer,
Joseph Currence,
Daniel Taylor,
George Clendenin,
William Ewing,
Joseph Campbell.

—Total 37.

A LIST OF CAPTAIN ROBERT McCLENNAHAN'S COMPANY OF GREENBRIER VALLEY VOLUNTEERS IN THE BOUTETOURT COUNTY REGIMENT.

(*Source*—Thwaites and Kellogg's "Documentary History of Lord Dunmore's War," pp. 410-411. Original in the Library of the State Historical Society of Wisconsin.)

OFFICERS.

Robert McClennahan,8 ....Captain.
William McCoy, ...Lieutenant.
Mathew Bracken,8.....................Ensign.
Thomas Williams 8 . ...Sergeant.
William Craig,.......................Sergeant.
Samuel Clarke,.......................Sergeant.
William Jones,.......................Drummer.

PRIVATES.

John Harmon,
David Cutlip,
James Gilkeson,
Edward Thomas,
Lewis Holmes,
John Williams,
John Patton,
James Guffy,
John Cunningham,
James Kinkead,

James Morrow, Sr.,
Evan Evans,
Patrick Constantine,
William Hutchinson,
Richard Williams,
Thomas Ellias,
Thomas Cooper,
Francis Boggs,
George Kinkead.

James Morrow, Jr.,
William Stewart,
William Custer,
Edward Barrett,
James Burrens,
Charles Howard,
William McCaslin,
John Vaughn.

—Total 34.

7. Wounded at Point Pleasant.
8. Killed at Point Pleasant.

A List of Captain Henry Pauling's Company of Volunteers in the Botetourt County Regiment.

(*Source*—Thwaites and Kellogg's "Documentary History of Lord Dunmore's War," p. 411. Original in the Library of the State Historical Society of Wisconsin.)

OFFICERS.

Henry Pauling............................Captain.
Edward Goldman,9 ....Lieutenant.
Samuel Baker,..........................Ensign.
Obediah H. Trent,......................Sergeant.
Robert Findley,........................Sergeant.
James Woods,..........................Sergeant.

PRIVATES.

Robert Watkins,	William Holley,	Joel Doss,
William Thompson,	Dangerfield Harmon,	Stephen Holston,
William Ray,	Dudley Callaway,	William Canaday,
James Wilson,	John Frazer,	George Davis,
John Clerk,	Richard Rollins,	Michael Looney,
Thomas McCreary,	Charles Ellison,	John Agnew,
John Gibson,	David Belew,	Andrew Rogers,
James Donahoo,	Andrew Harrison,	George Zimmerman,
Robert Ferrell,	Alexander Caldwell,	William Gilliss,
Thomas Wilson,	Mathew Ratcliff,	William Glass,
Edward Ross,	Thomas Reid,	Joseph Whittaker,
John Fitzhugh,	David Condon,	Richard LeMaster,
Isham Fienquay,	John Hutson,	William McCallister,
James King,	Edward Carther,	Martin Baker.
Jeremiah Jenkins,	James Lynn.	
Philip Hanes,	James DeHority,	—Total 52.

THE FINCASTLE COUNTY BATTALION.

A List of Captain Evan Shelby's Company of Volunteers from the Watagua Valley, in the Fincastle County Battalion.

(*Source*—Thwaites and Kellogg's "Documentary History of Lord Dunmore's War,"p. 412. Original in the Library of the State Historical Society of Wisconsin.)

OFFICERS.

Evan Shelby,10 ....Captain.
Isaac Shelby,11 ....Lieutenant.
James Robertson,.......................Sergeant.
Valentine Sevier,......................Sergeant.

---

9. Wounded at Point Pleasant.
10. Assumed chief command on the field of battle after Colonels Lewis, Fleming, and Field had fallen.
11. Took command of his father's company, who had assumed command of the field.

PRIVATES.

James Shelby,
Henry Shaw (or Span),
John Williams,
George Brooks,
George Ruddle
  (or Riddle),
Arthur Blackburn,
William Casey,
Conrad Nave,
Elijah Robison,
  (Robertson)
Jarrett Williams,
Peter Torney (Forney),
Samuel Vance,
Samuel Samples,
Hugh O'Gullion,
Joseph Hughey,
  (or James Hughey),

John Sawyer,
Daniel Mungle,
  (or Mongle),
John Carnack,[12]
Isaac Newland,
Emanuel Shoatt,
Robert Herrill,
  (Handley,)
Mark Williams,
Richard Burck,
Reece Price,[12]
Julius Robison,
William Tucker,
Samuel Fain,
Benjamin Grayum,
  (or Graham),
Barnett O'Guillion,
John Bradley,

John Findley,
Frederick Mungle,
Andrew Terrance
  (or Torrance),
Abram Newland,
Abram Bogard,
George Armstrong,
John Stewart,[12]
John Riley,
Richard Holliway,
Charles Fielder,
John Fain,
Samuel Hensley
  (or Handley),
Andrew Goff,
Patrick St. Lawrence,
Bazaleel Maxwell.
  —Total 49.

A Partial List of Captain William Campbell's Company[13] of the Fincastle County Battalion.

(*Source*—Thwaites and Kellogg's "Documentary History of Lord Dunmore's War," p. 400. Original in the Library of the State Historical Society of Wisconsin.)

OFFICERS.

William Campbell,........................Captain.

PRIVATES.

Philemon Higgins,
John Johnston,
John Lewis,
Coonrad Sterns,
Richard Lyhnam,

Benjamin Richardson,
Stephen Hopton,
Auldin Williamson,
John Neil,
William Champ,

Joseph Newberry,
Richard Woolsey,
William Hopton,
William Richardson,
John Boles.
  —Total 16.

---

12. Wounded at Point Pleasant.
13. There were 39 men in Captain Campbell's Company, but the names of only 15 of them have been preserved.

A LIST OF CAPTAIN JAMES HARROD'S COMPANY OF KENTUCKY PIONEERS IN THE FINCASTLE COUNTY BATTALION.

(*Source*—Thwaites and Kellogg's "Documentary History of Lord Dunmore's War," p. 420; Original in the Library of the State Historical Society of Wisconsin; also Collin's "History of Kentucky," Vol. II, p. 517.)

OFFICERS.

James Harrod,14..........................Captain.

PRIVATES.

James Blair,	James Harrod,	Thomas Harrod,
James Harlan,	John Crawford,	Jared Cowan,
John Clarke,	John Crow,	Azariah Davis,
John Cowan,	Robert Gilbert,	David Glenn,
William Fields,	Silas Harlan,	Evan Hinton,
James Hamilton,	James Knox,	James McCulloch,
Isaac Hite,	Azariah Reece,	Jacob Sandusky,
Alexander Petrey,	James Sodousky,	Benjamin Tutt,
John Shelp,	David Williams,	John Wilson.
James Wiley,	Thomas Glenn.	
James Brown,	Abraham Chapline,	—Total 32.

THE INDEPENDENT COMPANIES.

Of the Independent Companies,—the Dunmore County Volunteers, the Culpeper Minute Men, and the Bedford County Riflemen,—but one roster, that of the latter, has been preserved. This follows:—

A LIST OF CAPTAIN THOMAS BUFORD'S BEDFORD COUNTY RIFLE COMPANY OF VOLUNTEERS.

(*Source*—Thwaites and Kellogg's "Documentary History of Lord Dunmore's War," p. 409. Original in the Library of the State Historical Society of Wisconsin.)

---

14. In the spring of 1774, Captain James Harrod, a Pennsylvanian by birth, collected at the mouth of Grave Creek, now Moundsville, Marshall county, West Virginia, a party of thirty-one young men, for the purpose of making a settlement in Kentucky. Descending the Ohio to the mouth of the Kentucky river, they thence journeyed through the wilderness to the Big Spring, now in Mercer county. Here they were engaged in founding Harrodsburg, the oldest town in Kentucky, when they were discovered by Daniel Boone and Michael Stoner who had been sent by Lord Dunmore to warn John Floyd, Deputy Surveyor of Fincastle county, Virginia, which then included all of Kentucky, together with his assistants, then at the Falls of the Ohio, that an Indian War was begun. Harrod and party abandoned their settlement, and proceeded to the Holston Valley, where he and twenty-seven of his men joined the Fincastle Battalion, and with Christian, arrived at Point Pleasant the evening after the battle.—V. A. L.

OFFICERS.

Thomas Buford,15......................Captain.
Thomas Dooley,......................Lieutenant.
Jonathan Cundiff,....................Ensign.
Nicholas Meade,......................Sergeant.
William Kenedy,......................Sergeant.
John Fields,.........................Sergeant.
Thomas Fliping,......................Sergeant.

PRIVATES.

Abraham Sharp,	Absalom McClennaham,	William Bryant,
William McCollister,	James Scarbara,	John McClennahan,
James McBride,	John Carter,	Adam Lynn,
Thomas Stephens,	Thomas Hall,	William Hamrick,
Nathaniel Cooper,	John Cook,	Mr. Waugh,
John McGlahlen,	John Campbell,	Wi'liam Campbell,
Robert Boyd,	Thomas Hamrick,	William Kerr,
Garrott Kelley,	James Ard,	William Deal,
John Bozel,	John Welch,	William Overstreet,
Robert Hill,	Samuel Davis,	Zachariah Kennot,
Augustine Hackworth,	William Cook,	Uriah Squires,
James Boyd,	James Dale,	Robert Ewing,
Francis Seed,	William Hackworth,	John Roberts,
Joseph White,	Joseph Bunch,	Jacob Dooley,
Thomas Owen,	John Read,	John Wood.

—Total 52.

From the foregoing official rosters it will be seen that they contain five hundred and thirty-one names. If to these we add those of the captains, of the nineteen companies, whose names are known, but of which we have no rosters, we shall have a total of five hundred and fifty names of the men who were with the Southern Division, or left wing of Dunmore's Army, commanded by General Lewis.

---
15. Died of wounds the night after the battle.

CHAPTER IV.

WEST VIRGINIANS WHO WERE SOLDIERS AND PENSIONERS IN THE REVOLUTIONARY WAR—THE WAR FOR INDEPENDENCE.

West Virginia did her full part in the War for Independence, and may be regarded as the "fourteenth link in the American Chain." West Virginians were on nearly all the battlefields of that war, from Bunker Hill to Yorktown, and it may be safely said that there are more graves of Revolutionary soldiers in West Virginia than in any other American State, outside of the thirteen original Commonwealths.

COUNTY ORGANIZATION IN WEST VIRGINIA DURING THE REVOLUTION.

At its beginning—1775—there were about thirty thousand white people—men, women and children—residing in West Virginia. Then Augusta and Botecourt counties both extended across West Virginia, from the Blue Ridge to the Ohio, while the other units of government were Berkeley and Hampshire counties and the "District of West Augusta," the latter of which was, by an Act of the Virginia Assembly, in 1776, divided, and the counties of Monongalia, Ohio and Yohogania formed therefrom. By a westward extension of Mason and Dixon's Line, the greater part of Yohogania fell into Pennsylvania, and the residue was added to Ohio county. In 1776, the historic old Fincastle county was extinguished and the counties of Kentucky, Washington and Montgomery created therefrom. The last named of these counties extended to the Ohio, and included within its limits all of that part of West Virginia lying between the Great Kanawha and Big Sandy rivers. By legislative enactment, Greenbrier county was formed in 1777, from the western part of Botetourt, and extended to the Ohio river. Such was the county organization of West Virginia during the Revolution.

FIRST CALL FOR WEST VIRGINIA SOLDIERS IN THE REVOLUTION.

These counties, as is shown by contemporary documents still extant, responded freely to every call for men, and for supplies as well, made upon them throughout the long years of that struggle. By an ordinance of the Virginia Convention, of July, 1775, provision was made for raising two Regiments, of four hundred men each, for the defense of the Colony. Of these, one hundred men were to be enlisted in the "District of West Augusta" and stationed at Pittsburg; twenty-five more, also from "West Augusta," were to serve at Fort Fincastle (afterward Fort Henry) at Wheeling; and still one hundred more, to be raised in Botetourt county—then extending westward to the Ohio river—to serve in Fort Randolph, at the mouth of the Great Kanawha, now Point Pleasant, West Virginia.[1]

SECOND CALL FOR WEST VIRGINIA SOLDIERS FOR THE CONTINENTAL ARMY.

In October, 1776, the Virginia Assembly passed an Act preparatory to raising six battalions of Infantry on Continental Establishment; and under this, Ohio county was required to send to the army two captains, two first lieutenants, two second lieutenants, and two ensigns; Monongalia county, three captains, three first lieutenants, three second lieutenants and three ensigns; Berkeley county, one captain, one first lieutenant, one second lieutenant, and two ensigns; Hampshire county, one captain, one first lieutenant, one second lieutenant, and one ensign. It was further required that each captain should bring into the field twenty-eight men, each first lieutenant, twenty men, each second lieutenant, sixteen men, and each ensign, ten men. This meant one hundred and forty-eight men from Ohio county; two hundred and twenty-two from Monongalia; eighty-four from Berkeley; and seventy-four from Hampshire. In addition to this, Augusta county, which then extended westward to the Ohio river, was required to send two captains, two first lieutenants, two second lieutenants, and two ensigns, with one hundred and forty-eight men, one-half of whom ought to be credited to West Virginia. Botetourt county, which likewise extended to the Ohio, was required to send two captains, one first lieutenant, one second lieutenant and one ensign, with one hundred and two men, one-half of whom ought likewise be credited to West Virginia. And further: Fincastle county, which also extended to the Ohio river, was required to send one captain, one first lieutenant, one second lieutenant, and one ensign, with sev-

---

1. Hening's "Statutes at Large," of Virginia, Vol. IX, p. 13.

enty-four men, one-half of whom should be credited to West Virginia. Thus it was that the quota of officers and men of West Virginia, under the call of 1776, numbered seven hundred and thirty-five men.[2]

THIRD CALL FOR WEST VIRGINIA SOLDIERS.

In October, 1777, an Act of Assembly provided for speedily recruiting the Virginia Regiments on Continental Establishment. Under this call, the quota of Berkeley county was fifty-two men; that of Hampshire, thirty-three men; that of Monongalia, forty men; that of Augusta (one-half credited to West Virginia), ninety-seven men; that of Botetourt (one-half credited to West Virginia), sixty men; that of Montgomery (just formed from Fincastle, and one-half credited to West Virginia), thirty men; and that of Ohio county, such number as was equal to one twenty-fifth part of its able-bodied men.[3]

FOURTH CALL FOR WEST VIRGINIA SOLDIERS.

At the October Session of the Virginia Assembly, in 1778, another act was passed providing for further recruiting the Virginia Regiments on Continental Establishment; and under its provisions, the counties of Berkeley, Greenbrier (just formed from Botetourt), Hampshire, Monongalia and Ohio were each required to send to the field, before the first day of May ensuing, every twenty-fifth man of their entire enrolled militia. Each of these who would enlist for eighteen months, was to receive a bounty of three hundred dollars; and to all who enlisted for three years, or during the war, the sum of four hundred dollars.[4]

FIFTH CALL FOR WEST VIRGINIA SOLDIERS.

In May, 1779, an act was passed by the Assembly providing for raising a body of "Volunteers for the Defense of the Commonwealth." Therein it was provided that for the protection of the western pioneers against the Indians (who had become the active allies of the British), and other enemies, two battalions, of five hundred men each, should be raised in the counties on the western side

---

2. Hening's "Statutes at Large," of Virginia, Vol. IX, pp. 179, 180, 181, 182.
3. Hening's "Statutes at Large," of Virginia, Vol. IX, pp. 339, 340.
4. Hening's "Statutes at Large," of Virginia, Vol. IX, pp. 588, 589.

of the State—Ohio, Monongalia and Greenbrier, and in Western Augusta and Western Montgomery, the two last named extending from the Shenandoah Valley to the Ohio river. Here was a requisition on West Virginia for one thousand men, their terms of service being nine months from the ensuing tenth of June.[5]

SIXTH CALL FOR WEST VIRGINIA SOLDIERS.

Again, later in this May Session of 1779, another act was passed providing for the organization of four Regiments—two for the defense of the eastern coast, and two for that of the Western frontiers. This force was to be raised by a requisition upon every county of the State—Berkeley, Greenbrier, Hampshire, Monongalia and Ohio included—for one twenty-fifth part of their enrolled militia.[6]

SEVENTH CALL FOR WEST VIRGINIA SOLDIERS.

The urgency for men in the ranks of the Revolutionary army increased, and in May, 1780, the Virginia Assembly passed an act. providing for recruiting the quota of that State for the Continental army. By its provisions Berkeley, Greenbrier, Hampshire, Monongalia and Ohio, with other counties were required to send to the army every fifteenth man of their enrolled Militia between the ages of eighteen and fifty years. If these were not supplied within thirty days by volunteers, then any deficit was to be made up by draft.[7]

EIGHTH CALL FOR WEST VIRGINIA SOLDIERS.

General Washington and the Continental Congress continued to call upon Virginia for more men, and, in October, 1780, her Assembly passed another act making provision for recruiting the State's quota of troops to serve in the Continental army. By its provisions, Berkeley county was required to furnish sixty-eight men; Greenbrier, thirty-four men; Hampshire, sixty-three men; and Monongalia, South of Mason and Dixon's Line, thirty men. These levies were to be supplied by volunteers from each county.[8]

5. Hening's "Statutes at Large," of Virginia, Vol. X, pp. 18, 19, 20.
6. Hening's "Statutes at Large" of Virginia, Vol. X, pp. 32, 33.
7. Hening's "Statutes at Large" of Virginia, Vol. X, pp. 257, 258.
8. Hening's "Statutes at Large" of Virginia, Vol. X, pp. 327, 328, 329.

NINTH CALL FOR WEST VIRGINIA VOLUNTEERS, IN THE REVOLUTION.

In 1781, at the May Session of the Virginia Assembly, it was enacted that the Governor should immediately appoint a district officer in each county—Berkeley, Greenbrier, Hampshire, Monongalia and Ohio included—to recruit, by voluntary enlistments, soldiers for the term of two years or during the war, each soldier to be not less than five feet and four inches, not a deserter nor subject to fits, but of able body and sound mind, and fit for immediate service. For all such men enlisted, the recruiting officer was to receive twenty shillings each.[9]

LAST CALL FOR TROOPS FOR THE CONTINENTAL ARMY.

The last call by Virginia for troops for the Continental Army, was made by the General Assembly in May, 1782. It was then enacted that for the purpose of recruiting three thousand men to complete the State's qouta on the Continental Line in the Army of the United States; each of the counties—Berkeley, Greenbrier, Hampshire, Monongalia and Ohio among them— should furnish every fifteenth militia-man, who should be not less than five feet four inches in height, of able body, sound mind, and between the ages of eighteen and fifty years, whose term of service should be three years or during the war.[10]

GREENBRIER COUNTY MEN IN THE CONTINENTAL ARMY AND WITH GENERAL CLARK IN THE ILLINOIS COUNTRY.

In 1779, it was provided by the Assembly that every able-bodied freeman who should enlist for the protection and defense of Illinois County, should receive a bounty of seven hundred and fifty dollars, at once, and one hundred acres of land at the end of the war.[11]

Greenbrier men entered this service, as is shown by the letter of Colonel Andrew Donnally, of that county, dated March 27, 1781, to Governor Thomas Jefferson; in which he says: "That part of our militia, which in obedience to your Excellency's order, were to be sent to join General George Rogers Clark, have gone with much alacrity."[12] At this time Greenbrier with a militia enrollment of

---
9. Hening's "Statutes at Large" of Virginia, Vol. X, pp. 433, 434.
10. Hening's "Statutes at Large" of Virginia, Vol. XI, p. 14.
11. Hening's "Statutes at Large" of Virginia, Vol. X, pp. 26, 27.
12. "Calendar of Virginia State Papers," Vol. 1, p. 601.

550 effective men, had 174 of them in the Continental Army or with Clark in the Illinois Country. Similar conditions existed in other West Virginia counties at that time.

CLOTHING, BEEF AND WAGONS SUPPLIED BY WEST VIRGINIA COUNTIES FOR THE CONTINENTIAL ARMY.

Not only did West Virginia do her part in supplying men for the Revolution, but in furnishing supplies as well. The Assembly passed, at the October Session of 1780, an Act for supplying the Continental Army with clothing. Therein it was provided that every suit should consist of "two shirts of linen or cotton, one pair of overalls, two pairs of stockings, one pair of shoes, and one wool, fur, or felt hat, or leather cap." Requisitions were made on the several counties for so many suits—on Berkeley county for seventy-one suits; on Greenbrier, for eight suits; and on Hampshire, for twenty-six suits. Each county was divided into as many militia districts as there were suits to be furnished. It was further provided that each one of these "districts should furnish one good beef, weighing at least three hundred weight nett." Thus did Berkeley county furnish seventy-one suits and seventy-one head of cattle; Greenbrier, eight suits and eight head of cattle; and Hampshire, twenty-six suits and twenty-six head of cattle. It was still further provided by this Act that each county supplying suits of clothing and beef cattle should also, on or before the first day of March ensuing, "furnish and provide one good and servicable waggon with a good cover and a team of four good horses and complete harness with a driver who shall serve as a driver one month at the expense of each county respectively." Official accounts still extant show that Berkeley, Greenbrier, and Hampshire counties did this.[13]

WEST VIRGINIA BECOMES THE BACK DOOR OF THE AMERICAN REVOLUTION:

In the year 1777, West Virginia became what may be called the "Back Door of the Revolution." It was then that Henry Hamilton, the British Lieutenant-Governor at Detroit, succeeded in inducing the Indians of the Ohio Wilderness to become the allies of the British and as such they began hostilities against the West Virginia frontier in the autumn of that year. From Detroit they obtained arms, ammunition, and all other supplies for their barbarian warfare.

---

13. Hening's "Statutes at Large" of Virginia, Vol. X, pp. 338, 339, 340, 341, 342, 343.

Lord Chatham denounced the alliance between Great Britian and the American savages as a "disgrace.—a deep and deadly sin;" but his protest availed nothing, and barbarian alliance began and continued until the close of the Revolution. On the 1st day of September, 1777, an Indian army three hundred strong, consisting of Mingoes, Shawnees, Delawares, and Wyandots, under the leadership of Simon Girty, and carrying the British colors, massacred twenty men under the walls of Fort Henry, and then laid siege to the fort. This continued for a night and two days when the besiegers withdrew, having lost between forty and fifty killed and wounded. In April, 1778, a body of Indians appeared before Fort Randolph at the mouth of the Great Kanawha; Lieutenant Moore, with some men from the garrison sallied forth to drive them off. They fell into an ambuscade, and he and three of his men were killed and the others saved themselves by a precipitate flight to the fort. In May of the same year, a large body of Indians laid siege to this fort, attacked it furiously, and for a week kept the garrison closely besieged. Finding that they made no impression upon the fort they killed the cattle about it, and withdrew. A few days later, the army which had besieged Fort Randolph, attacked Fort Donnally about ten miles northwest of Lewisburg, in Greenbrier county, and it was furiously assailed throughout the day, until the arrival of reenforcements under Captain John Stuart, from Lewisburg, late in the evening when the attack was abandoned. On the eleventh day of September, 1782, Fort Henry at Wheeling, was a second time besieged. This time the attacking force consisted of about three hundred Indians—Shawnees and Delawares—under the command of George Girty, and a company known as the "Queen's Rangers" commanded by Captain Pratt, from Detroit. They marched to the attack in regular file, headed by drum and fife, with the British flag flying over them. A surrender in the name of the British Governor was made, and "the best protection King George could afford," was promised. To this, contemptuous answers were made by the dauntless inmates of the fort. The attack began and continued for three days, when the assailants withdrew because of the approach of a strong re-enforcement under Captain Williamson. This was the most important event of the Revolution, in West Virginia. Thus from the autumn of 1777, to that of 1782, did the savage allies of Great Britain wage a relentless warfare against the West Virginia frontier, and in addition to the events mentioned, there was scarcely a month, in the whole period of four years, in which, depredations and atrocities were not committed on the defenseless settlements. The Indians were as much the allies of the British, as were the Hessians, and the military movements in West Virginia from 1777 to 1782, are as much those of the Revolution as were those of Trenton or Germantown.

In the autumn of 1777, when it became known that the Indian Nations northwest of the Ohio would become the allies of Great Britain, an invasion of their country was planned, this to be commanded by General Edward Hand. A call for troops for this purpose was made on the West Virginia frontiersmen, and Major George Skillern raised two companies in Botetourt county, which, with forty Greenbrier county men under Captain William Renick, repaired to Point Pleasant, at the mouth of the Great Kanawha river. At the same time and for the same purpose, Captain William Foreman, of Hampshire county, collected a company of men in the South Branch Valley, and marched to the Ohio, arriving at Fort Henry, now Wheeling, on the 15th of September, fifteen days after the first siege at that place. On Sunday, the 26th ensuing, a great column of smoke was seen down the river and David Shepherd, a County-Lieutenant of Ohio county, believing that the Indians had set fire to the deserted Fort Tomlinson, on the Grave Creek Flats— now Moundsville—dispatched Captain Foreman with forty-five men to that place. No Indians were seen, the fort was intact and the troops spent the night at that place. The next day when returning to Wheeling, the party fell into an ambuscade at "McMechen Narrows," on the Ohio river, now in Marshall county, and twenty-one of the Virginians were killed at the first fire and several badly wounded. The sad event is known in pioneer annals as "Foreman's Defeat," and long was heard the sorrowful story in the homes of the South Branch Valley and among the Hampshire Hills.

A PARTIAL LIST OF THE HAMPSHIRE COUNTY MEN AT THE DEFEAT OF CAPTAIN WILLIAM FOREMAN AT "McMECHEN NARROWS" BETWEEN THE SITES OF WHEELING AND MOUNDSVILLE, WEST VIRGINIA, SEPTEMBER 27, 1777,

(*Sources*—"The American Pioneer." Vol. II. pp. 347, 348, 349, 350; DeHass' "History of the Early Settlement and Indian Wars of Western Virginia," pp. 230, 231, 232, 233, 234, 279; "Journal of the Virginia House of Delegates." Session beginning October 5, 1778. p. 47.)

OFFICERS.

William Foreman,........ Captain   David Wilson, ...Ensign
Anthony Miller,........Lieutenant

PRIVATES.

Edward Peterson,	Benjamin Powell,	Hambleton Foreman,
James Greene,	John Wilson,	Jacob Pugh,
Isaac Harris,	Robert McGrew,	Elisha Shriver,
Henry Riser,	Bartholomew Viney,	Anthony Miller,
John Vincent,	Solomon Jones,	William Ingle,
Nathan Foreman,	Abraham Powell,	Samuel Lowry,
Samuel Johnson,	Jacob Ogle,	Abraham Powell,
John Collins,	Robin Harkness,	William Linn.

PROPERTY LOST BY SOLDIERS AT FOREMAN'S DEFEAT.

(*Source*—DeHass' "History of the Early Settlements and Indian Wars of Western Virginia," p. 279.)

The following document, bearing date six days after the bloody tragedy, and which has been preserved, is connected with it:—

"A list of the effects lost, of sundry soldiers of Captain William Foreman's company of Hampshire county volunteers, appraised by Lieutenant Anthony Miller, and Ensign David Wilson, officers of said company, being duly qualified for that purpose.

		£	s.	d.
1	Captain William Foreman—A rifle-gun, £11 5s. shot pouch and horn, 10s. pocket compass, 5s. blanket, 30s.	13	17	6
2.	Edward Peterson—A rifle-gun, £11 5s. shot pouch and horn, 10s. blanket. 30s....................	13	5	0
3.	Benjamin Powell—A rifle-gun, £12 10s. a blanket, £1 17s. 6d., shot pouch and horn, 12s. 6d.,............	15	10	0
4.	Hambleton Foreman—a rifle-gun, £11 5s., a blanket, 30s., shot pouch and horn, 10s...............	13	5	0
5.	James Greene—A rifle-gun, £10, a blanket, 37s. 6d.,....	11	17	6
6.	John Wilson—A rifle-gun, £10, shot pouch and horn, 7s. 6d., blanket. 22s. 6d.,.......................	11	10	0
7.	Jacob Pew—A rifle-gun, £8 15s., shot pouch and horn 10s. blanket 18s. 9d.,........................	10	3	9
8.	Isaac Harris—A rifle-gun, £12 10s., shot pouch and horn, 10s. blanket, 37s. 6d.,......................	14	17	6
9.	Robert M'Grew—A blanket, 22s. 6d.,.................	1	2	6
10.	Elisha Shivers—A blanket, 22s. 6d.,.................	1	2	6
11.	Henry Riser—A blanket, 37s. 6d.,...................	1	7	6
12.	Bartholomew Viney—A blanket, 22s 6d.,.............	1	2	6
13.	Anthony Miller—A blanket, 22s. 6d.,................	1	2	6
14.	John Vincent—A blanket, 30s.,.....................	1	10	0
15.	Solomon Jones—A blanket, 30s.,....................	1	10	0

16. William Ingle—A blanket, 22s. 6d.,	1	2	6
17. Nathan Foreman—A blanket, 22s. 6d.,	1	2	6
18. Abraham Powell—A blanket, 37s. 6d.,	1	17	6
19. Samuel Lowry—A blanket, 30s.,	1	10	0
20. Samuel Johnston—A rifle-gun, £7 10s. shot pouch and horn, 10s blanket, 22s. 6d.,	9	2	6

JUDGEMENTS:—We, the subscribers, do hereby certify that the within specified appraisements are just and true to the best of our judgments and that the several articles were lost in the late unhappy defeat near M'Mechen's narrows, on the 27th of September, 1777—as witness our hands, this 3d of October, 1777.

                      (Signed)   Anthony Miller, *Lieutenant.*
                                        David Wilson, *Ensign.*
Sworn before me,   David Shepherd."

NOTES ON CAPTAIN WILLIAM FOREMAN'S DEFEAT.
(From the Journals of the General Assembly of Virginia.)

"Monday, November 2, 1778, the General Assembly received a petition of" John Wilson and others; setting forth, that some of the petitioners, and those whom the others represent, being engaged in the defence of the western frontiers in September, 1777, were fired on by a number of Indians, when half of the party were killed on the spot, and many of their guns and blankets thereby lost, and praying some compensation for the same.

"Friday, November 6, 1778. Mr. Lee, from the committee of Public Claims reported, that the committee had, according to order, had under their consideration, several petitions to them referred, and had come to several resolutions thereupon, which he read in his place, and afterwards delivered in at the clerk's table, where the same were again read and agreed to, as followeth:"

"1. Resolved, that it is the opinion of this committee, That the petition of John Wilson and others, who were part of the militia ordered out by Gen. Hand, from the county of Hampshire, under the command of Captain William Forman, in defence of the western frontiers, praying to be allowed for the loss of their guns, blankets, powder horns and pouches, in an engagement with the Indians in the month of September, 1777, is reasonable; and that there ought to be allowed to the petitioners, the several sums following, to wit, John Wilson, £91.10s.: Solomon Jones, £1.10s.; Abraham Powell, £2; Samuel Lowery, £1.10s.; Anthony Miller, £1.10s.; the representatives of William Forman, £11; of Edward Peterson, £11; of Benjamin Powell, £14.15s; of Samuel Johnson, £10; of Isaac Harness, £13; of Jacob Pugh, £10; of Elisha Shivers, £7; of Robert M'Grew, £1.10s; of Henry Riser, £1.10s; and of Bartholomew Viney, £1 10; and that the same ought to be charged in the accounting of this Commonwealth, against the United States of America."

"SHEPHERDSTOWN MEN IN THE REVOLUTIONARY WAR."

Under date of February 5, 1850, the *Register* then published by Hardy & McAuly at Shepherdstown, Jefferson county, West Virginia, printed, under the above caption, a lengthy article giving the names of officers and privates who served in the Revolutionary Army from Shepherdstown and its vicinity, then in Berkeley county, but after 1801, in Jefferson county. Their names with rank and memoranda in the said article, appearing as it did, sixty years ago, were as follows:

NAMES.	RANK	MEMORANDA.
William Darke	Brigadier-General	Colonel, afterward General, served throughout the Revolution, both North and South; commanded the Virginia Regiment at St. Clair's defeat in the Northwest Territory, November 4, 1791. Died at Duffield's Station in 1801.
Joseph Swearingen	Colonel	Entered the Army as a Lieutenant in the fall of 1775, and was in active service throughout the Revolution. Promoted to a Captainoy for gallantry at the battle of Brandywine, and at the close of the war had risen to the rank of Colonel.
John Morrow	do	Entered the army at an early age to fight in the cause of liberty; a noble specimen of a soldier; no other man left his country's service more honored than he.
Henry Bedinger	Major	Joined the army when quite a youth, and distinguished himself in several brilliant engagements. He died near Shepherdstown at an advanced age.
Dr. Nicholas Shell	Surgeon	A native of Germany; emigrated to America before the Revolution; served as a surgeon for six years. Died at Shepherdstown in 1803, beloved by all who knew him.
Charles Morrow	Captain	Was an officer of high standing; served three years in the southern campaigns with credit to himself and honor to his country.
Thomas Morrow	do	Served two years in the army of the North; taken prisoner at battle of Long Island, and though exchanged, died soon after because of ill-treatment on board a British prisonship. He was the youngest of the "Three Morrows."
Abraham Shepherd	do	A brother of the founder of Shepherdstown, and an officer of high repute in the Revolution. When difficulties were apprehended with France in 1799, he raised a company of Jefferson county men in which James Glenn and Raleigh Morgan were lieutenants. He died in 1825, and was buried with military honors.
Michael Bedinger	do	A brother of Major Henry Bedinger; was an accomplished and gallant officer. Removed to Kentucky at the close of the war.
Christian Orndorff	do	Distinguished himself in the battles of Bennington and Skeensborough. Died on his farm near Shepherdstown.

"Shepherdstown Men in the Revolutionary War."—Continued.

NAMES.	RANK.	MEMORANDA.
James Glenn	Captain	Volunteered as a private in the war of the Revolution, and rose to the rank of Captain; was at St. Clair's defeat, where he carried from the field his friend Lieutenant Raleigh Morgan, of Jefferson county, who was fatally wounded.
William Morgan	do	Distinguished for his bravery among distinguished comrades.
John Boyer, (Byers?)	do	Served in the Pennsylvania Line, and died in York County, that State; he was physically powerful and a brave soldier.
Thomas Turner	do	A brave soldier, distinguished among the heroes of Jefferson county.
Jacob Haynes	do	A brave soldier of the Revolution. It was he who afterward did the iron work for James Rumsey, in his experiments in steam navigation.
Ludwig Myers	do	Served in the Revolution as a Captain of Infantry; he was a brave soldier.
Burkett Riger (Reger?)	do	Served during the Revolution under Colonel, afterwards General William Darke.
Cato Moore	Lieutenant	Born on the eastern shore of Maryland; came to Shepherdstown at an early age. Enlisted in the Continental Army, and was so severely wounded at Brandywine, that he was forced to resign his commission.
Lemuel Riger (Reger?)	do	Was a brother of Captain Burkett Reger, and like him, served under Colonel William Darke.
Jacob Eaty	Drummer	No memoranda.
Jacob Wysong	do	No memoranda.
Medlar	do	No memoranda.
Fayette Wysong	Fifer	No memoranda.
William Lucas	Private	Known to his companions in arms as one of the bravest of the brave. He was the father of Hon. Robert Lucas, who was the Governor of Ohio from 1812 to 1836.
John Kearsley	do	A brave soldier, one possessed of a spirit and determination that rendered him "fit for any emergency."
Michael Cookus	do	Served throughout almost all of the Revolutionary period.
James Peacock	do	No memoranda.
Philip Robb	do	In service throughout almost all the years of the Revolutionary period.
Peter Staley	do	In service in nearly all the years of the war.
Martin Ernst	do	Was a Hessian who deserted the British army at the battle of Princeton, and jo'ned the American army. Settled at Shepherdstown, and was a Revolutionary pensioner to the end of his life.
Henry E Beller	do	Upward of fifty years of age when he entered the army, but served to the end of the war. Died about 1784, near Bedington, in Berkeley county.
John Eckhart	do	No memoranda.
Jacob Likens	do	No memoranda.
John Randall	do	Spent nearly all the years of the war in the army.
Henry Unseld	do	No memoranda.

"Shepherdstown Men in the Revolutionary War."—Continued.

NAMES.	RANK.	MEMORANDA.
George Shaver	do	Was in the army almost constantly during the war.
William Wilson	do	No memoranda.
Thomas Crockett	do	No memoranda.
Peter Fisher	do	A veteran of the Revolution. Died in 1844, while serving as toll collector on the Smithfield and Shepherdstown Turnpike, and was buried with military honors.
John Darnheffer	do	A good soldier in the Revolution, and a soldier in Captain Glenn's Berkeley County company at St. Clair's defeat.
George Reynolds	do	Served throughout the Revolutionary period.
John Neal	do	Was a brave Revolutionary soldier, and was a member of Captain Glenn's Berkeley County company at St. Clair's defeat.
Michael Delrock	do	A Hessian; deserted to Americans at battle of Princeton, and proved himself to be a true and brave soldier in the American army.
Daniel Folk	do	Was with Arnold at Ticonderoga, and with General Montgomery, at St. Johns, Montreal and Quebec. He died near Shepherdstown in 1838.
Robert Hoffman	do	A native of Shepherdstown; was in the front rank of the American Army at the battle of Germantown.
James Kretzer	do	No memoranda.
Thomas Thornburg	do	No memoranda.
Joseph Turner	do	A man of great strength, often carried the musket and knapsack of a wearied soldier in addition to his own.
Christy Young	do	Served with Gates and Greene in the Carolina campaigns.
Burruck Butt	do	Served with Gates and Greene in their Southern campaigns.
George Ox	do	A Hessian; deserted from the force under Kniphausen and enlisted under the banner of Pulaski. Followed the business of butcher in Shepherdstown after the war.
John Haynes	do	No memoranda.
Thomas Johnson	do	No memoranda.
John Loar	do	No memoranda.
Philip Loar	do	No memoranda.
Anthony Kearney	do	No memoranda.
Adam Antler, Sr.	do	No memoranda.
Phillip Antler	do	No memoranda.
Jacob Fachler	do	Was a member of Captain David Morgan's company, was with Arnold at Quebec, and was taken prisoner while fighting within the ramparts of that city. He taught school in Shepherdstown for more than thirty years after the Revolution.
John Pearce	do	

"Shepherdstown Men in the Revolutionary War."—Continued.

NAMES.	RANK.	MEMORANDA.
John Angell	do	Served in the campaigns of Generals Gates and Greene in the Carolinas, and was a member of Captain Glenn's company at St. Clair's defeat.
John Miller	do	No memoranda.
Adam Mohler	do	No memoranda.
George Powell	do	Was with "Mad Anthony" Wayne at the Storming of Stoney Point.
Lewis Ronemous	do	Served as a member of the body-guard of General Horatio Gates.
Conrad Ronemous	do	A member of the body-guard of General Gates.
Andrew Ronemous	do	Member of the body-guard of General Gates.
Daniel Bedinger	do	Joined the army when sixteen years of age; taken prisoner at White Plains, and suffered great privations.
Conrad Byers	do	No memoranda.

It has been frequently asserted that Shepherdstown furnished more officers and soldiers to the Revolutionary army, than any other town in Virginia, and from an examination of records, it would appear that this assertion has foundation in truth.

A Nearly Complete Muster Roll of Captain Hugh Stephenson's Company of Riflemen of 1775-6.

(*Source*—Mrs. Danske Dandridge's "Historic Shepherdstown," pp.88-89.)

OFFICERS.

Hugh Stephenson,.........Captain
William Henshaw, First Lieutenant
George Scott,...Second Lieutenant
Thomas Hite,....Third Lieutenant
Abraham Shepherd, Fourth Lieut.
William Pyle (or Pile),....Ensign
Samuel Finley,......First Sergeant
William Kelly,....Second Sergeant

Josiah Flagg,......Third Sergeant
Henry Bedinger,..Fourth Sergeant
John Crawford,.....First Corporal
David Miller,.....Second Corporal
Henry Barratt,.....Third Corporal
G. M. Bedinger,..Fourth Corporal
Garret Tunison,...........Surgeon

PRIVATES.

William Shepherd
Thomas Hutcheson
William Anderson
Duncan McFitrich
David Gray
William Blair
William Hunter
Richard Butcher
William Green
Thomas S. Williams
Arthur McCord
Jacob Fink
John Stewart
Adam Sheetz
David Smith
Henry McCartney
John Bodine
Benjamin Ardiger
Michael Engle
William Waller
John McDead
Robert Howard
Conway Oldham
James Wallace
Robert McCann
Nicholas Makin
George Tabb

Joseph Swearingen
William Hulse
James Neilson
James Wright
Edward Bennett
Benjamin Prime
William McCue
Francis Hickman
Joseph Carter
Nat Pendleton
James Yancey
George Benner
Ebenezer Allen
George Taylor
David Stedman
Charles Conner
John Curry
Peter Hill
Peter Mange
Peter Hanes
Patrick Vaughan
Peter Sever
Christian Brady
William Davis
Robert Eakins
Thomas Steer
John Beverley

Thomas Nelson
Josiah Swearingen
Adam Rider
Thomas Knox
John Millikin
Charles Murray
James Roberts
Robert White
John Smoote
John Cole
Stephen Varden
    (drummer boy)
Aaron Tullis
Philip Waggoner
Jacob Winn
Michael Tullis
William English
James Higgins
Richard Neal
William Logan
Battail Harrison
William Hickman
James Hamilton
John McGarah
John Medcalf (or Metcalf)
William Tabb
John Keys

AN OBSERVATION:—No sooner did it appear that the drama of the Revolution was at hand, than the patriotic sons of Berkeley county, then embracing the present county of Jefferson, organized for the fray. More than a hundred of them became members of a Company of Berkeley County Riflemen. For their uniform they adopted home-spun hunting-shirts, made of linsey-woolsey, fringed around the neck and down the front, leather leggings and moccasins. Hugh Stephenson was elected Captain, and then these gallant men held themselves in readiness to march at their country's call. The order came, when, on the 14th of June, 1775, the Continental Congress resolved that two companies of expert riflemen should be immediately raised in Pennsylvania; two in Maryland and two in Virginia, and that each should march as soon as ready. Captain Stephenson obeyed the summons with alacrity; Morgan's Spring, near Shepherdstown, now in Jefferson county, was designated as the place of rendezvous, and on the 17th of July, fixed as the day of departure. That morning having partaken of a frugal meal and reverently received the blessing of a holy Man of God, they, "not a man missing" took a "bee-line" for Boston, six hundred miles away, which they reached on the 10th of August, after a march of twenty-four days. On the arrival at the American Camp, at Cambridge, Captain Stephenson introduced the Company as being "from the right bank of the Potomac." General Washington knew some of these men personally, and passing along the line, shook the hand of every man in it. No other company rendered more faithful service in the war for independece. Fifty years passed away and brought July 17, 1825—the fiftieth anniversary of the departure from Morgan's Spring. Then but four of these volunteer riflemen were alive. These were Major Henry Bedinger, of Berkeley county; his brother Michael George Bedinger, of Blue Licks, Kentucky; Peter Lauck, of Winchester, Virginia; and William Hulse, of Wheeling, West Virginia.

THE VIRGINIA-MARYLAND RIFLE REGIMENT.

(*Source*—Company Organization of the Regiment supplied by Hon. Braxton D. Gibson, of Charles Town, Jefferson County, West Virginia.)

Captain Hugh Stevenson, returned from Boston in the spring of 1776, and together with Captain Moses Rawlings, organized the Virginia-Maryland Rifle Regiment, of which he became colonel, and Rawlings lieutenant-colonel. It was composed of Virginians from the counties of Berkeley and Hampshire; and of men from Western Maryland. It consisted of eight companies, 1st, 2d, 5th, 6th, and 7th, from Virginia; and the 3d, 4th, and 8th, from Maryland. The official organization of the Virginia Companies were as follows:—

FIRST COMPANY,

Abraham Shepherd, Captain,
Samuel Finley,......First Lieut.,
William Kelley,.....Second Lieut.,
Henry Bedinger,.....Third Lieut.

SECOND COMPANY.

Philemon Griffith, Captain,
Thomas Hussy Lucket, Lieutenant,
....,
....,

FIFTH COMPANY.

Thomas West, Captain,
William George,....First Lieut.,
Thomas Warman,...Second Lieut.,
Edward Smith,.....Third Lieut.

SIXTH COMPANY

Gabriel Long, Captain,
Nathan. Pendleton, First Lieut.,
Philip Slaughter,...Second Lieut.,
James Hanson,......Third Lieut.

SEVENTH COMPANY.

William Brady, ...Captain,
William Pile, ...First Lieutenant,
Christopher Brady, ...Second Lieutenant,
Battle Harrison, ...Third Lieutenant.

Any one acquainted with the family names in the Eastern Pan-Handle of West Virginia, will at once recognize those of these officers as being Berkeley and Hampshire county names.

AN ABSTRACT OF THE PAY DUE OFFICERS AND PRIVATES OF THE COMPANY OF RIFLEMEN COMMANDED BY CAPTAIN ABRAHAM SHEPHERD, RAISED IN BERKELEY COUNTY, VIRGINIA, (NOW WEST VIRGINIA), AND BEING THE FIRST COMPANY IN THE VIRGINIA-MARYLAND RIFLE REGIMENT ORGANIZED BY COLONEL HUGH STEPHENSON AND, AFTER HIS DEATH, COMMANDED BY COLONEL MOSES RAWLINGS IN THE CONTINENTAL SERVICE FROM JULY 1, 1776, TO OCTOBER 1, 1778.

(*Source*—Printed from original roll, loaned to the State Department of Archives and History, by Colonel Henry B. Davenport, of Clay, Clay county, West Virginia.)

NAMES.	RANK.	DATE OF ENLISTMENT.	KILLED OR DIED.	WHEN TAKEN PRISONER.	TERM OF SERVICE.		PAY	
					MONTHS.	DAYS.	IN DOLLARS.	CONT'L CURRENCY.
Abraham Shepherd	Lieutenant	July 1, 1776		Nov. 16, 1776		9	5⅜	£ 1:12:4
" "	Captain	July 9, 1776			22	21	908	272:08:0
" "	"	June 1, 1778			4		240	72:00:0
Samuel Finley	Lieutenant	July 1, 1776		Nov. 16, 1776	23		628⅔	188:12:0
" "	"	June 1, 1778			4		149⅓	44:16:0
William Kelley	"	July 9, 1776			5	22	156⅔	47:00:3
Henry Bedinger	"	July 9, 1776		Nov. 16, 1776	22	21	620⅜	186:02:6
" "	"	June 1, 1778			4		149⅓	44:16:0
John Crawford	1st Sergeant	July 1. 1776		Nov. 16, 1776	27		216	64:16:0
John Kerney	2d Sergeant	August 2, 1776		Nov. 16, 1776	25	29	207⅔	62:06:4
Robert Howard	3d Sergeant	July 1, 1776	Died		24	17	169¼	58:19:0
Dennis Bush	4th Sergeant	August 1, 1776		Nov. 16, 1776	26		208	62:08:0
John Jeaburn	1st Corporal	August 2, 1776	Died	Nov. 16, 1776	5	13	39 5-6	11:19:0
Everet Hogland	2d Corporal	August 18, 1776			25	12	186¼	55:15:7
Thomas Knox	3d Corporal	July 1, 1776		Nov. 16, 1776	6	20	48⅞	14:13:4
Jonathan Gibbons	4th Corporal	July 29, 1776	Died	Nov. 16, 1776	6	12	46 5-6	14:01:7
Stephen Vandine	Drummer	July 1, 1776		Nov. 16, 1776	27		198	59:08:0
Thomas Cook	Fifer	" "	Died		12	14	91⅜	27:08:6
William Anderson	Private	" "		Nov. 16, 1776	6	20	44 5-12	13:06:8
Jacob Wine	"	" "		Nov. 16, 1776	7	15	50	15:00:0
Richard Neal	"	" "			1	10	8 5-6	2:13:4
Peter Hill	"	" "	Killed		4	16	30¼	9:01:4
William Waller	"	" "	Died	Nov. 16, 1776	7	15	50	15:00:0
Adam Shirtz	"	" "			6		40	12:00:0
James Hamilton	"	" "			7		46⅔	14:00:0
George Taylor	"	" "				9	2	12:0
Adam Ryder	"	" "			6		40	12:00:0

Patrick Vaughn	Private	July 1, 1776	Died		4	13	29⅓	8:17:4
Peter Hanes	"	July 10, 1776			26	20	177¾	53:06:8
John Malcher	"	July 15, 1776	Died	Nov. 16, 1776	6	26	45¾	13:14:8
Peter Snyder	"	July 20, 1776			6	26	45¾	13:14:8
Daniel Bedinger	"	" "			26	11	175¾	52:14:8
John Barger	"	" "			1	9	8⅔	2;12:0
William Hickman	"	" "			1	9	8⅔	2:12:0
Thomas Pollock	"	" 21, "			5	10	35⅓	10;13:4
Bryan Timmons	"	" "			5	10	35⅓	10:13:4
Thomas Mitchell	"	" "			5	10	35⅓	10:13;4
Conrad Rush	"	" 24, "		Nov. 16, 1776	6	22	44 5-6	13:09:4
David Harmon	"	" "		Nov. 16, 1776	6	22	44 5-6	13:09:4
James Aitken	"	" "		Nov. 16, 1776	1	5	7¾	2;06;8
William Wilson	"	" "		Nov. 16, 1776	6	22	44 5-6	13;09;4
John Wilson	"	" "		Nov. 16, 1776	6	22	44 5-6	13:09:4
Moses McComesky	"	" 25, "			10	20	71 1-12	21:06:8
Thomas Beatty	"	" 26, "		Nov. 16, 1776	6	20	44 5-12	13:06:8
John Gray	"	" 27, "	Killed		5		33⅓	10:00:0
Valentine Fritz	"	" "			5	4	34⅓	10:05:4
Zechariah Butt	"	" 28, "			5	4	34⅓	10:05:4
William Moredock	"	" "		Nov. 16, 1776	6	18	44	13:04:0
Charles Collins	"	" 30, "	Died		5	20	38¾	11:06:8
Samuel Davis	"	" "		Nov. 16, 1776	6	16	43⅓	13:01:4
Conrad Cabbage	"	August 1, 1776	Died	Nov. 16, 1776	5	7	36 5-6	10:09:4
John Cummins	"	" "	Died	Nov. 16, 1776	5	27	39⅓	11:16:0
Gabriel Stevens	"	" "	Died	Nov. 16, 1776	7	1	46 5-6	14:01;1
Michael Wolf	"	" "		Nov. 16, 1776	26		173⅓	52:00;0
John Lewis	"	" "				28	6¾	1:17:4
William Donnally	"	" "	Died		5	10	35⅓	10:13:4
David Gilmore	"	" "	Died	Nov. 16, 1776	5	26	39 1-9	11:14:8
John Cassady	"	" "		Nov. 16, 1776	6	15	43⅓	13:00:0
Samuel Barnet	"	" "	Died		6	26	45¾	13:14:8
Peter Good	"	" "		Nov. 16, 1776	6	15	43⅓	13:00:0
George Helm	"	" "		Nov. 16, 1776	26		173⅓	52:00:0
William Bogle	"	" "	Died	Nov. 16, 1776	7		46⅔	14:00:0
John Nixon	"	" "		Nov. 16, 1776	6	15	43⅓	13:00:0
Anthony Blackhead	"	" "			3	15	23⅓	7:00:0
Christian Penninger	"	" "		Nov. 16, 1776	6	15	43⅓	13:00:0
Charles Jones	"	" "		Nov. 16, 1776	3	15	23⅓	7:00:0
William Case	"	" "	Died	Nov. 16, 1776	7	15	50	15:00:0
Casper Myre	"	" "	Died		6	16	43⅓	13:01:9
George Brown	"	" 3, "		Nov. 16, 1776	25	28	172 5-6	51:17:4
Benjamin McKnight	"	" 4, "			6	11	42 5-12	12:14:8
Anthony Larkin	"	" "			1	11	9 1-12	2:14:8
William Seaman	"	" "	Died		11	26	79 1-9	23:14:8
Charles Snowden	"	" 5, "	Died		5	2	33¾	10:02:8
John Boulden	"	" "				24	5⅓	1:12:0
John Blake	"	" "				24	5⅓	1:12:0
Nicholas Russell	"	" 6. "		Nov. 16, 1776	25	25	172⅓	51:13:4
Benjamin Hughes	"	" "		Nov. 16, 1776	25	25	172⅓	51:13:4

Abstract of Pay Due Officers and Privates of Company Commanded by Capt. Abraham Shepherd.—Continued.

Names.	Rank.	Date of Enlistment.	Killed or Died.	When Taken Prisoner.	Term of Service.		Pay	
					Months.	Days.	In Dollars.	Cont'l Currency.
James Brown	Private	August 6, 1776	Died	Nov. 16, 1776	25	25	172½	51:13:4
James Fox	"	" 7, "			8	25	58 5-6	17:13:4
William Hix	"	" " "			4	24	32	9:12:0
Patrick Connell	"	" " "				22	4 5-6	1:09:4
John Holmes	"	" 10, "	Died		5	10	35½	10:13:4
Thomas Mountsfield	"	" " "	Died		5	26	39 1-9	11:14:8
Isaac Price	"	" " "	Died		5	26	39 1-9	11:14:8
Samuel Brown	"	" 12, "	Killed		13	14	89½	26:18:8
John McSwame	"	" " "		Nov. 16, 1776	6	3	40½	12:04:0
James Griffith	"	" 16, "		Nov. 16, 1776	5	29	39½	11:18:8
Patrick Murphy	"	" " "			6	15	43½	13:00:0
James Aitkens	"	January 1, 1777			21		140	42:00:0
James Roberts	Armorer	July 20, 1776			4	17	91½	27:08:0
							$8,349.94	£2505:10:10

Memoranda.

	Compensation	
	Dollars.	Continental Currency.
Total Amount paid Captain Abraham Shepherd	1153.33	346:00:4
" " " 3 Lieutenants	1704.33	511:06:9
" " " 4 Sergeants	828.16	248:09:4
" " " 4 Corporals	321.66	96:09:6
" " " 2 Drummer & Fifer	289.33	86:16:6
" " " 72 Privates	3961.80	1189:00:5
" " " 1 Armorer	91.33	27:08:0
	$8,349.94	£2505:10:10

ABRAHAM SHEPHERD, Captain.

ROSTER OF CAPTAIN URIAH SPRINGER'S COMPANY FROM MONONGALIA COUNTY, WEST VIRGINIA, ON SERVICE AT PITTSBURG IN 1781.

OFFICERS.

Uriah Springer,	Captain.
John Harrison,	Lieutenant.
Joseph Winlock,	Ensign.
John Gibson,	do.
John Williams,	Sergeant.
Thomas Tannehill,	do.
Thomas Moore,	do.
William Evans,	Corporal.
James Adams,	do.
John Hagerty,	Corporal, from January 1, 1781.
Isaac Horsfield,	do.
John Smith,	Drummer.
Thomas Whealy,	do
John Hinds,	Fifer.

PRIVATES.

James Cumberford,	Philip Henthorn,	Thomas Craigg,
John Burnett,	Edward Paul,	James Duffy,
Garrett Cavener,	Samuel Smith,	James Gossett,
William Barr,	James Seavell,	Charles Evans,
John Britton,	Nicholas Carter,	Michael Kairns,
Thomas Hailey,	Robert Hughes,	William Bailey,
Alexander McIntosh,	Henry Squires,	Richard Sparrow,
William Harbert,	John Ross,	David Dunnagan,
Richard Roach,	Pat Baity,	Christopher Carpenter.
Hyatt Lazier,	William Hansford,	John Finney,
Roderick McDaniel,	Edward Mcdonald,	Robert McCarney,
Richard Carter,	James Smith,	Matthew Hurley,
William Smith,	Jacob Conrad,	Francis Smith,
James Reynolds,	Henry Vann,	Michael Smith,
William Craig,	Samuel Osburn,	Joseph Row.
Benjamin Broomes,		

Roster of Captain Benjam.n Bigg's Company from Ohio County, West Virginia, on Service at Pittsburg in 1781.

OFFICERS.

Benjamin Biggs,	Captain.
Jacob Springer,	Lieutenant.
John Mills,	Ensign.
Alexander Fraser	Sergeant.
John Hull,	do.
Moses Ward,	do.
John Barnett,	do. (Joined Feb. 1, 1781.)
Samuel Cruswell,	Corporal.
William Johannes,	do. (Joined Jan. 1, 1781.)
Thomas McIlwain.	Fifer.

PRIVATES.

Jonathan Welsh,
Samuel McCord,
William Overline,
John Rooke,
Robert Bacon,
Thomas Jackson,
John Guttery,
Samuel Lemon,
James Amberson,
James Carr,
John Robeson,
Thomas Buites,
Stephen Winters,
John Shea,
Pat Thornton,
James Stackpole,
Michael Murphy,
John Riley,
Alex. McAdams,
John Rock,
Peter McCarthy,
James Low,

John English,
William Cloyd,
Henry Skinner,
Charles Robinson,
Joseph Fowler,*
John Conner,
William Brumagem,
John Morrison,
William Connolly,
William Martin,
David Clark,
John Phillips,
Samuel Reaves,
Clement Gillihan,
Joseph Woods,
John Godfrey,
James Hoorish,
Jacob Adams,
John Cordonas,
William Love,
Isaac Devore,

John Ritchie,
Jacob Buher,
Jacob Rhodes,
Charles Morgan,
John Bean,
Thomas Jones
John Dougherty,
John Vilet,
John Richardson,
William Woods,
Joseph Denison,
Isaac Halfpenny,
Dennis Selavan,
John Berry,
James Johnson,
James Parlor,
Rueben Abbett,
James Beham,
Edward Walker,
William Brazer,
John Woodman.

A RETURN OF PART OF THE RECRUITS RAISED BY CAPTAIN HENRY BEDINGER OF BERKELEY (NOW JEFFERSON) COUNTY, UNDER THE ACT OF THE GENERAL ASSEMBLY IN OCTOBER, 1780, FOR THE STATE'S QUOTA OF TROOPS TO SERVE IN THE CONTINENTAL ARMY.

(*Source*—Copy supplied to the State Department of Archives and History by Hon. Braxton D. Gibson, of Charles Town, Jefferson County, West Virginia.)

NAMES.	AGE.	HEIGHT.	OCCUPATION.	RESIDENCE.	NATIVITY.	DRAFTED OR ENLISTED.
William Cruse	30	5 ft. 7 in.	Turner	Fort Pitt	England	Enlisted.
Alexander Denny	37	5 ft. 3 in.	Weaver	York, Pennsylvania	Ireland	do
Thomas Williams	45	5 ft. 4 in.	Farmer	Berkeley County	England	do
Samuel Earle	21	6 ft.	do	Frederick County	Virginia	do
William Jacobs	21	6 ft.	do	do	do	do
Thomas Mathews	21	5 ft. 4 in.	Painter	Maryland	Ireland	Drafted.
Lewis Wills	40	5 ft. 4 in.	Farmer	Frederick County	Germany	Enlisted.
John Bazel	18	5 ft. 8 in.	Shoemaker	Berkeley County	Pennsylvania	do
Joseph Whipple	18	5 ft. 4 in.	Wagonmaker	Frederick County	Germany	do
William Bedinger	23	5 ft. 6 in.	Farmer	do	Pennsylvania	Drafted.
George Bougher	20	5 ft. 7 in.	do	do	Virginia	Enlisted.
Walter Hooper	21	5 ft. 7 in.	do	do	do	

NAMES.	DATE OF ENLISTMENT.	TERM OF SERVICE.	REMARKS.
William Cruse	April 1, 1781	For the War	Well made; marked with small-pox. Left at Winchester.
Alexander Denny	do	do	Well made; fresh complexion; yellow hair.
Thomas Williams	do	For 16 months	Well made; brown complexion.
Samuel Earle	do	do	Very well made; brown hair.
William Jacobs	April 19, 1781	do	Well made; fair hair.
Thomas Mathews	do	do	Well made; brown hair.
Lewis Wills	April 23, 1781	For 18 months	Well made; reddish complexion.
John Bazel	May 3, 1781	do	Slender; fair complexion; brown hair.
Joseph Whipple	April 1, 1781	do	Brown complexion; well made.
William Bedinger	do	do	Brown complexion; well made.
George Bougher	do	do	Chunky made; fair complexion.
Walter Hooper	April 1, 1781	For the War	Well made; fair complexion; brown hair.

MISCELLANEOUS NOTES.

In the oldest burying ground at Wellsburg, in Brooke county, stands a neat monument having thereon the following inscription:

CAPTAIN OLIVER BROWN.[10]

Of the Massachusetts Line in the Revolutionary War.

BORN AT LEXINGTON, MASS., IN 1752.

"HE STOOD IN FRONT OF THE FIRST CANNON FIRED BY THE BRITISH ON THE AMERICANS IN THE AFFRAY AT LEXINGTON; WITNESSED THE "TEA PARTY" IN BOSTON HARBOR; WAS AT THE BATTLE OF BUNKER HILL; COMMISSIONED BY CONGRESS THE 16TH DAY OF JANUARY, 1776; COMMANDED THE VOLUNTEER PARTY THAT BORE OFF THE LEADEN STATUE OF KING GEORGE FROM THE BATTERY OF NEW YORK, AND MADE IT INTO BULLETS FOR THE AMERICAN ARMY; BORE A CONSPICUOUS PART IN COMMAND OF THE ARTILLERY AT THE BATTLE OF WHITE PLAINS, HARBOR HEIGHTS, PRINCETON, TRENTON, GERMANTOWN AND MONMOUTH.

DIED FEBRUARY 17, 1846.

In full assurance of a never-ending peace."

THE DAVENPORT BROTHERS.

(*Source*—Letter from Hon. Braxton D. Gibson, of Charles Town, Jefferson County, West Virginia, preserved in the State Department of Archives and History.)

Abraham Davenport came from St. Mary's or Charles County, Maryland, to Berkeley County, Virginia, now West Virginia, in the year 1775, bringing with him four sons all of whom rendered service in the Revolutionary Army. These were:

John, a private in the 6th Virginia Regiment, and later, in the 7th.
Adrian, a private in Captain Thomas Beall's Company in Colonel Moses Rawling's Virginia-Maryland, Rifle Regiment.
Abram, a Sergeant in Captain Thomas Beall's Company.
Anthony S., a private in a Company of a Virginia Regiment. His pension papers do not contain the name of his commanding officer.
Captain James Strode commanding a company of militia in Berkeley county was fifty years of age when the war began; served as a recruiting officer throughout its continuance.

---
10. Newton's "History of the Pan-Handle," p. 324.

BERKELEY AND JEFFERSON COUNTY MEN WITH GENERAL GEORGE ROGERS CLARK IN HIS CONQUEST OF THE ILLINOIS COUNTRY.

Letter from Colonel Joseph Crockett to Governor Thomas Jefferson, regarding the wants of troops intended for Clark's Expedition.

(*Source*—"Calendar of Virginia State Papers," Vol. I, p. 572.)

We have seen that a number of Greenbrier County men were with General George Rogers Clark in his Conquest of the Illinois Country. How many were with him from the Eastern Pan Handle, we do not know, but certain it is that there were at least one company. Of this, witness the following:

Shepherdstown, Virginia,
March 14, 1781.

To his Excellency, Governor Jefferson:

SIR:

By Orders received from Col: Clark, we have just Return'd from Frederick Town to this place, in hopes to get the Regt: equip'd for the Western expedition.

I must beg leave once more to mention to your Excellency the great distrefs the Regiment is in for want of cloathing, the Soldiers being almost naked for want of linen, and entirely without shoes. Col: Clark informs me he expects a considerable quantity of Linen at Winchester, of which we shall have a part; as for shoes, I know not where to apply.

This will be handed to your Excellency by Capt: Cherry, paymaster to the Western Battalion, who will wait on the Treasurer for a sum of money due the Officers, agreeable to a late Act of Afsembly, and also will with cheerfulnefs obey any commands your Excellency may please to lay on him, in order to serve the Regiment in forwarding cloathing, money, &c.

I have the Honor to be,
Your Excellency's most obdt
and very Humble Servant."
JOSEPH CROCKETT.

EARLY PENSION LEGISLATION BY CONGRESS—NAMES OF WEST VIRGINIANS ON THE PENSION ROLLS OF THE REVOLUTIONARY WAR.

Prior to the year 1818, Congress passed no pension laws, except for the relief of those officers and soldiers who were disabled in the service; consequently, all those who were not disabled, and died between the close of the Revolutionary War and the year 1818, could receive no pension, for all the pension laws require that the soldier "shall be living at the date of the passage of the law."

ACT APPROVED MARCH 18, 1818.

This Act of Congress provided that every commissioned officer, non-commissioned officer, musician, and private soldier who served in the War of the Revolution, to the end thereof; or who served for a term of nine consecutive months, or longer, at any period of the war on Continental Establishment (no matter how many terms were served, one must have been for nine months), and who was then or thereafter, by reason of his reduced circumstances in life, and shall be in need of assistance from his Country for support, and shall have substantiated his claim to a pension in the manner prescribed by this Act, shall receive a pension from the United States. Before the veteran could obtain a pension under this law he must show (1) that he had served in the War of the Revolution to the end thereof; (2) or for a term of nine consecutive months, or longer at some one period of the War, on Continental Establishment; (3) must yet be a resident of the United States; (4) and be in such destitute circumstances in life as to need the assistance of his country for support. Soon after the passage of this Act, applications for pensions, numbering about eight thousand (how many from West Virginia, I do not know), had accumulated. This alarmed Congress to such an extent that further pension legislation was speedily enacted.

ACT APPROVED MAY 1, 1820.

In this act it was provided that no person should be entitled to the further benefits under the law of 1818; "unless he shall have exhibited to some court of record, in the county, city, or borough. in which he resides, *a schedule, subscribed by him,* containing his

whole estate and income. Being poor, yet possessing too much
of the spirit of 1776, to permit their "goods and chattels" to be
thus exposed to the gaze of the public, many worthy men (some
of them in West Virginia) refused a compliance with the provisions of this Act; and still others, possessed of some estates,
could not affirm that they stood in "need of the assistance of their
country for a support." Many of these whose names had been
admitted to the pension rolls, now made out the Schedules as required, but, in the opinion of the Secretary of War, a large number of those who did this, were not entitled to the "assistance of
their country for support," and were subsequently dropped from
the rolls and ceased to be pensioners. A knowledge of these facts
brought forth from Congress further legislation.

ACT APPROVED MARCH 1, 1823.

This act authorized the Secretary of War" to restore to the
list of pensioners the name of any person who may have been or
may hereafter be, stricken therefrom, if such person has heretofore furnished, or hereafter shall furnish, evidence that he is
in such indigent circumstances as to be unable to support himself
without the assistance of his country, and that he has not dis-
posed of, or transferred, his property, or any portion thereof,
with a view to obtain a pension. After the passage of this act,
and after so many of the old soldiers had been "driven off the
field," the Secretary became more liberal in his opinions with
respect to the "schedules," and large numbers of them were by
degrees restored to the rolls.

ACT APPROVED MAY 15, 1828.

This act was provided without regard to any "property qualifi-
cations; and being provided on the half-pay acts of the Continental Congress and the Gratuity Act of May 15, 1778, no one
could claim its provisions, unless he was adjudged to be entitled
to "commutation" per act of March 22, 1783, or to the gratuity
of eighty dollars per act of May 15, 1778. Though precisely a
half century had rolled between the passage of the acts of May
15, 1778, and May 15, 1828, yet several hundreds of time-worn
and old non-commissioned officers, musicians and privates come
forth to receive the last token of their country's regard under the

latter act; many of whom had been "dropped" by the "Alarm" act of May 1, 1820.

ACT APPROVED JUNE 7, 1832.

Congress by this act provided "That each of the surviving officers, non-commissioned officers, musicians, soldiers, and Indian spies, who shall have served in the Continental Line, or State Line, volunteers, or militia, *at one or more terms, a period of two years,* during the War of the Revolution, and who are not entitled to any benefit under the act for the relief of certain survivors and soldiers of the Revolution, passed May 15, 1828, be authorized to receive a pension proportional to length of time served, but no pension should be granted to any one having served less than six months. How unjust this was, will appear when it is known that much of the most meritorious service was rendered, and fiercest battles of the war waged, by *four and six months' men.*

ACT APPROVED JULY 4, 1836.

It was declared in this act, "That if any person who served in the War of the Revolution, in the manner specified in the act passed June 7, 1832, have died, leaving a widow whose marriage took place *before the expiration* of the last period of his service, such widow shall be entitled to receive, during the time she may remain unmarried, the annuity or pension which might have been allowed to her husband, by virtue of the act aforesaid, if living at the time it was passed. A widow who, on her own application, has been divorced from her husband, has no claim to a pension. All persons applying for pensions under this act, must prove that their parents were legally married." The marriage of a widow does not destroy her claim to pension under this act, provided she was a widow a second time on the day of its passage.

ACT OF JULY 7, 1838.

This act provided, "That if any person who served in the War of the Revolution in the manner specified in the act passed June 7, 1832, have died, leaving a widow, *whose marriage took place after the expiration of the last period of his service, and before January* 1, 1796, such widow shall be entitled to receive, for and during the term of *five years from the 4th day of March*, 1836, the annuity or pension which might have been allowed to her husband, by virtue of the said act, if living at the time it was passed: *Provided,* That in the event of the marriage of such widow, said annuity or pension shall be discontinued. All widows whose husbands served in the Revolutionary War, as stated in the act, and who were married after the *last term* of his service, and prior to January 1, 1794, can claim pension under this act, provided they were widows at the passage thereof.''

OTHER PENSION LEGISLATION.

There was other pension legislation relating to the volunteers of the Revolution, chiefly in the years 1843, 1844, 1848, but it consisted of annulments to the acts above cited. It was by their provisions that survivors of the Revolution, their widows and orphans residing in West Virginia, were chiefly affected in the matter of pensions.

A STATEMENT SHOWING THE NAMES, RANK, &c. OF INVALID PENSIONERS RESIDING IN WEST VIRGINIA IN 1835; AS SHOWN BY THE REPORT OF JAMES L. EDWARDS, COMMISSIONER OF PENSIONS, MADE IN COMPLIANCE WITH RESOLUTIONS OF THE UNITED STATES SENATE THAT YEAR.

Names and Counties.	Rank.	Annual Allowance.	Sums Received	Description of Service.	When Placed on the Pension Roll.	Commencement of Pension.	Laws Under Which Inscribed. Increased and Remarks.
BERKELEY. David Blew	Private	$40 00	$	1 reg't of levies under Wayne	Sept. 6, 1792	Dec. 29, 1790	June 7, 1785.
do	do	64 00				April 24, 1816	April 24, 1816. Increased under this law. Transferred to Kentucky.
John Bayan	Corporal	48 00		Maryland militia		May 9, 1825	September 25, 1824. Transferred from Maryland.
James Campbell	Lieut.	100 00		Virginia volunteers	Nov. 13, 1788	Jan. 1, 1786	June 7, 1785.
do	do	120 00				April 24, 1816	April 24, 1816. Increased under this Law.
Angus McEver	Private	60 00	1,590 00			March 4, 1789	June 7, 1785. Transferred from Pennsylvania.
do	do	96 00	1,722 66			April 24, 1816	April 24, 1816. Increased under this law.
BROOKE. Joseph Biggs	Ensign	108 00		Virginia rangers	June 29, 1791	June 24, 1791	March 23, 1790.
do	do	140 40				April 24, 1816	April 24, 1816. Increased under this law. Transferred to Ohio.
William Guthrie	Private	24 00	224 03	Towson's artillery	Sept. 3, 1816	May 2, 1816	Acts military establishment. Transferred from Maryland.
Patrick Gass	do	96 00	1,798 12	1st r. U. S. Inf'y	Oct. 21, 1816	June 11, 1815	Acts military establishment.
Elijah Hedges	do	60 00		Frontier rangers		Sept. 4, 1796	June 7, 1785.
do	do	96 00				April 24, 1816	April 24, 1816. Increased under this law. Transferred to Ohio.
FAYETTE. Basel Brown	Private	40 00		Virginia militia	July 28, 1789	Jan. 1, 1786	June 7, 1785.
do	do	64 00				April 24, 1816	April 24, 1816. Increased under this law. Transferred to Pennsylvania.
GREENBRIER. Thomas Donnally	Private	72 00	376 03	20th reg. U. S. Inf	Feb. 18, 1817	June 11, 1814	Acts military establishment.
do	do	48 00	484 13			Sept. 4, 1819	March 3, 1819. Reduced under this law.
do	do	72 00	314 20			Oct. 10, 1829	March 3, 1819. Raised to this rate on account of increased disability.
Jacob Price	do	40 00	1,085 00	7th Virginia reg't	Feb. 21, 1796	March 4, 1789	June 7, 1785.

STATEMENT OF INVALID PENSIONERS IN WEST VIRGINIA—Continued.

Names and Counties.	Rank.	Annual Allowance.	Sums Received.	Description of Service.	When Placed on the Pension Roll.	Commencement of Pension.	Laws Under Which Inscribed, Increased and Reduced; and Remarks.
GREENBR'R—*Con'd* Jacob Price	Private	64 00	1,052 37			April 24, 1816	April 24, 1816. Increased under this law.
HAMPSHIRE. George Hill	Private	39 00		3d reg. Va. drag		Feb. 25, 1813	August 12, 1813.
do	do	62 00				April 24, 1816	April 24, 1816. Increased under this law. Transferred to Ohio.
John Newman	do	36 00	479 40	3d Maryland reg	March 17, 1803	Jan. 1, 1803	
do	do	57 60	120 18			April 24, 1816	April 24, 1816. Increased under this law. Relinquished for benefits of act March 18, 1818.
do	do	96 00	117 30		Nov. 27, 1819	May 25, 1818	March 18, 1818. Dropped under act of May 1, 1820.
do	do	57 60	308 40		June 26, 1827	March 4, 1820	May 1, 1820. Restored to invalid roll. Died July 26, 1826.
HARRISON. James Corbin	Private	48 00	345 46	Budd's co. of Inf	Jan. 24, 1827	Dec. 23, 1826	Acts military establishment.
James Jarvis	do	72 00	830 40	27th reg. U. S. Inf	April 10, 1816	August 22, 1814	Acts military establishment. Transferred from Ohio.
Patrick Sullivan	do	96 00	917 29	12th reg. U. S. Inf	Feb. 15, 1825	August 13, 1824	Acts military establishment.
JEFFERSON. William Eaty	Private	15 00	25 29	1st regt. riflemen	March 22, 1816	August, 17, 1814	Acts military establishment.
do	do	24 00	416 66			April 24, 1816	April 24, 1816. Increased under this law.
John McDonald	do	96 00	862 93	1st reg. U. S. Inf	Dec. 9, 1816	March 8, 1815	Acts military establishment.
Wm. D. Phielding	do	48 00	792 00	Va. vol. riflemen	Dec. 17, 1817	Sept. 12, 1817	Acts military establishment.
Hugh McDonald	do	96 00	957 60	Humphrey's Va. vol	April 19, 1824	April 13, 1824	April 24, 1816.
LEWIS. Jessie Cunningham	Private	96 00		Virginia militia	Sept. 1, 1834	Jan. 1, 1831	March 2, 1833.
William Stanley	do	20 00	37 69	12th reg. U. S. Inf	Jan. 3, 1816	June 4, 1814	Acts military establishment.
do	do	32 00	519 62			April 24, 1816	April 24, 1816. Increased under this law.
do	do	96 00	24 00			June 5, 1832	Raised to this rate on account of increased disability.
MASON. Samuel Hayes	Private	64 00	355 91			Feb. 11, 1814	Acts military establishment. Transferred from New York.

STATEMENT OF INVALID PENSIONERS IN WEST VIRGINIA.—Continued.

Names and Counties.	Rank.	Annual Allowance.	Sums Received.	Description of Service.	When Placed on the Pension Roll	Commencement of Pension.	Laws Under Which Inscribed Increased and Reduced, and Remarks.
MASON—Continued. Samuel Hayes	Private	42 60	450 05			Sept. 4, 1819	March 3, 1819. Reduced under this law.
do	do	64 00	196 25			August 9, 1830	March 3, 1819. Raised to this rate on account of increased disability.
Andrew Lewis	do	60 00	1,290 00			Sept. 4, 1793	June 7, 1785.
Charles Love	do	96 00				August 11, 1815	Acts military establishment. Transferred to Ohio.
George Lemasters	do	96 00	223 46	6th regt. U. S. inf	June 5, 1824	Nov. 6, 1823	Acts military establishment.
do	do	72 00	288 00			March 4, 1826	March 3, 1819. Reduced under this law.
do	do	64 00	224 00			March 4, 1830	March 3, 1819. Reduced under this law.
MONONGALIA. David Scott	Captain	100 00	314 92	13th Virginia reg	Dec. 5, 1798	Jan. 1, 1786	June 7, 1785.
do	do	240 00	795 33			May 18, 1814	April 30, 1816. Increased under this law.
Henry Williams	Private	60 00	1,856 50	2d Jersey regt	July 20, 1787	May 3, 1785	June 7, 1785. Transferred from New Jersey.
do	do	96 00	1,652 66			April 24, 1816	April 24, 1816. Increased under this law.
Henry J. Williams	do	96 00		10th r. U. S. Inft'y	Dec. 30, 1816	May 29, 1816	Acts military establishment. Transferred to West Tennessee.
Patrick Glasson	do	40 00	1,065 55			Sept. 4, 1789	June 7, 1785.
do	do	64 00	124 36			April 24, 1816	April 24, 1816. Increased under this law.
MONROE. John Davis	Sergeant	37 50		2d con. reg't S. C.		Sept. 4, 1789	June 7, 1785. Transferred to Alabama.
do	do	60 00				April 24, 1816	April 24, 1816. Increased under this law.
Samuel Hunt	Private	60 00	1,818 84	2d do Virginia reg	August 11, 1787	Jan. 1, 1766	June 7, 1785.
do	do	96 00	1,570 66			April 24, 1816	April 24, 1816. Increased under this law.
OHIO. John Charmichael	Private	60 00				Dec. 1, 1808	March 3, 1809. Increased under this law.
do	do	96 00				April 24, 1816	April 24, 1816. Transferred to Ohio.

STATEMENT OF THE NAMES OF THE HEIRS OF NON-COMMISSIONED OFFICERS AND PRIVATES WHO DIED IN THE UNITED STATES SERVICE; AND WHO OBTAINED FIVE YEARS' HALF-PAY IN LIEU OF BOUNTY LAND, UNDER THE SECOND SECTION OF THE ACT OF APRIL 16, 1816, AND WHO RESIDED IN WEST VIRGINIA COUNTIES.

Names of the Original Claimants.	Rank.	Description of Service.	Time of Decease.	Names of Heirs.	Annual Allowance.	Sums Received.	When Placed on Roll.	Commencement of Pension.	Ending of Pension.
				JEFFERSON.					
Van Butt	Private	1st reg. riflemen	May 10, 1813	Richard and Van Butt.	$48 00	$240 00	Jan. 9, 1822	Nov. 7, 1821	Nov. 7, 1826
George Jackson	do	12th reg. Infantry	Dec. 18, 1813	Eliza and William Henry Harrison Jackson	48 00	240 00	Aug. 15, 1817	Feb. 17, 1815	Feb. 17, 1820
				LEWIS					
John Flenner	do	3d reg. riflemen	Oct. 24, 1814	Washington, Emanuel and Elizabeth Flenner	48 00	240 00	Mar. 5, 1819	Feb. 17, 1815	do
				MONONGALIA.					
John Fairchild	do	12th r. infantry	Nov. 30, 1813	Morris Williams, Irene and Uri Tuttle.	48 00	240 00	Dec. 21, 1819	Feb. 17, 1815	do
Joshua Jones	do	12th r. do	Nov. ..., 1813	John, James, Henry, Joshua, Prudence and Jane Jones.	48 00	240 00	do	do	do
Thomas Murdoch	do	4th r. riflemen	Dec. 21, 1814	Elizabeth, David, Jane, John and Thomas Murdoch	48 00	240 00	Sept. 21, 1819	Feb. 17, 1819	Feb. 17, 1824
Selee, or Seley, Sayres	do	12th r. infantry	Jan. 3, 1815	John, Nicklin and Selee Sayres	48 00	240 00	Dec. 21, 1819	Feb. 17, 1815	Feb. 17, 1820
				OHIO.					
John Hardy	Corporal	12th r. infantry	Nov. 11, 1813	Barbara Hardy	60 00	300 00	Sept. 24, 1817	do	do
David Love	Private	do	Jan. 2, 1814	Mary Ann, and Jane Love	48 00	240 00	do	do	do
Arch Robinson	do	17th r. artillery	June 25, 1814	John, Wood, & James Robinson	48 00	240 00	Nov. 7, 1817	do	do

71

STATEMENT SHOWING THE NAMES, RANK, AND OTHER DATA RELATING TO PERSONS RESIDING IN WEST VIRGINIA COUNTIES, WHO WERE INSCRIBED ON THE PENSION LIST UNDER THE ACT OF CONGRESS, PASSED MARCH 18, 1818.

Statement of Berkeley County, West Virginia.

NAMES.	Rank.	Annual Allowance.	Sums Received.	Description of Service.	When Placed on the Pension Roll.	Commencement of Pension.	Ages.	Laws Under Which Inscribed, Increased, and Reduced; and Remarks.
Jacob Anderson	Private	$96 00	$1,397 06	Virginia line	June 28, 1819	Feb. 15, 1819	78	Died August 18, 1825.
Barruch Butt	do	96 00	701 44	Maryland line	Oct. 28, 1818	Apr. 28, 1818	79	Died July 10, 1825.
William Godman	Captain	240 00	1,724 51	Maryland line	Sept. 28, 1818	May 4, 1818	71	Suspended under Act May 1, 1820.
John Hixon	Private	96 00	177 83	Virginia line	Sept. 15, 1818	Apr. 28, 1818	91	
James Husband	do	96 00	508 15	do	Sept. 6, 1819	do	76	Died August 13, 1823.
Robert Johnson	do	96 00	1,327 11	Pennsylvania line	June 20, 1819	Jan. 29, 1819	81	Died December 10, 1832.
John Kibler	do	96 00	840 00	Maryland line	Oct. 28, 1818	Apr. 28, 1818	74	Died June 27, 1827.
John Lessley	do	96 00	685 86	Pennsylvania line	Sept. 28, 1818	Apr. 13, 1818	90	Died June 4, 1825.
Peter Marlatt	do	96 00	225 06	New York line	Oct. 13, 1818	May 1, 1818	74	
Thomas Russell	do	96 00	596 56	Virginia line	June 16, 1818	June 10, 1818	68	Died August 27, 1824.
William Somerville	Sergeant	96 00	756 38	Pennsylvania line	July 3, 1819	May 2, 1818	70	Died March 18, 1826.
William Smith	Private	96 00	1,127 46	Maryland line	Mar. 26, 1819	Sept. 30, 1818	83	Died June 27, 1830.
David Spong	do	96 00	376 36	Virginia line	July 21, 1819	Apr. 26, 1819	81	
William Scot	do	96 00	1,098 89	do	Feb. 15, 1819	Nov. 9, 1822	84	
James Wilson	do	96 00	178 36	do	Feb. 11, 1819	Apr. 28, 1818	84	Dropped under Act May 1, 1820.
do	do	96 00	262 89	do	June 10, 1831	June 9, 1831	94	

Statement of Brooke County, West Virginia.

NAMES.	Rank.	Annual Allowance.	Sums Received.	Description of Service.	When Placed on Pension Roll.	Commencement of Pension.	Ages.	Laws Under Which Inscribed, Increased, and Reduced; and Remarks.
Oliver Brown	Capt. & Lieut.	$240 00	$3,788 38	Massachusetts line	Feb. 1, 1819	May 23, 1818	81	
John Brownlee	Private	96 00	822 77	Pennsylvania line	June 26, 1818	Feb. 9, 1820	80	Transferred from Pennsylvania from Sept. 4, 1827.
Joseph Fowler	do	96 00	1,515 35	Virginia line	Feb. 1, 1819	May 23, 1818	70	
John Gallegher	do	96 00	1,515 35	Maryland line	May 1, 1819	do	77	
Thomas Graham	do	96 00	672 51	New Jersey line	Sept. 30, 1819	do	74	Died May 24, 1825.
Jeremiah Hawkins	do	96 00	522 09	Pennsylvania line	May 7, 1828	Mar. 28, 1828	80	
James Ledlee	do	96 00	292 18	do	Feb. 1, 1819	May 23, 1818	70	Died June 7, 1821.
William Linton	Captain	240 00	1,999 33	North Carolina line	Jan. 16, 1819	Nov. 2, 1818	69	Transferred from North Carolina from March 4, 1826. Died February 28, 1827.
Elijah Moore	Private	96 00	1,241 10	New Jersey line	July 14, 1819	Sept. 22, 1818	84	Transferred from Ohio, Pittsburg agency from Sept. 4, 1827. Died August 26, 1831.
Samuel Ogden	do	96 00	787 68	do	Mar. 16, 1826	Mar. 7, 1826	82	Died August 6, 1829.
Artemas Reed	do	96 00	787 86	Massachusetts line	Feb. 1, 1819	May 23, 1818	87	Dropped under Act May 1, 1820. Rest'd commencing Oct. 27, 1823.
Richard Roberts	do	96 00	788 41	Virginia line	Sept. 30, 1819	Apr. 27, 1818	78	

Statement of Cabell County, West Virginia.

NAMES.	Rank.	Annual Allowance.	Sums Received.	Description of Service.	When Placed on Pension Roll.	Commencement of Pension.	Ages.	Laws Under Which Inscribed, Increased, and Reduced; and Remarks.
Thomas Chandler	Private	$96 00	$ 591 22	Virginia line	Apr. 21, 1828	Jan. 8, 1828	72	
Larose, or Rosey Marrett	do	96 00	1,257 97	do	Sept. 28, 1820	June 23, 1818	82	Died July 30, 1831
Robert Rutherford	do	96 00	1,135 60	do	Apr. 23, 1819	July 2, 1818	77	Transferred from Ohio. Dropped under Act May 1, 1820. Restored commencing January 25, 1825.
William Steel	Corporal	96 00	1,146 56	North Carolina line	Mar. 11, 1820	Feb. 29, 1820	86	Transferred from North Carolina March 4, 1820. Died February 8, 1832.

Statement of Fayette County, West Virginia.

NAMES.	Rank.	Annual Allowance.	Sums Received.	Description of Service.	When Placed on Pension Roll.	Commencement of Pension.	Ages.	Laws Under Which Inscribed, Increased, Reduced; and Remarks.
Edward Burgess	Private	$96 00	$ 911 48	Maryland line	May 29, 1823	Mar. 1, 1823	80	Transferred from Pennsylvania from March 4, 1825. Died Aug. 29, 1825.
Thomas McGee	do	96 00	1,365 41	Pennsylvania line	May 30, 1820	Dec. 14, 1819	82	Dropped under Act May 1, 1820. Restored commencing April 16, 1823. Transferred from Ohio April 16, 1823.

Statement of Greenbrier County, West Virginia.

NAMES.	Rank.	Annual Allowance.	Sums Received.	Description of Service.	When Placed on Pension Roll.	Commencement of Pension.	Ages.	Laws Under Which Inscribed, Increased, Reduced; and Remarks.
John Neal Blair	Private	$96 00	$ 736 70	Virginia line	Dec. 1, 1818	June 23, 1818	84	Died February 23, 1824.
Robert Buchanan	do	96 00	1,371 16	New Jersey line	Jan. 26, 1820	Nov. 23, 1819	82	
Archibald Butt	do	96 00	238 00	North Carolina line	Feb. 7, 1820		58	Died May 14, 1822.
Jno. Crookshanks, Inv	do	30 00	190 33	Virginia line		Dec. 20, 1809		April 27, 1810.
do	do	48 00	88 27	do		Apr. 24, 1816		April 24, 1816.
do	do	96 00	388 80	do		June 4, 1818	67	Died June 21, 1822.
William Cart	do	96 00	122 63	Pennsylvania line	Feb. 11, 1819	Nov. 25, 1818	84	Dropped under Act May 1, 1820. Transferred from Ohio, from March 4, 1828.
Zachariah Cook	do	96 00	349 15	Virginia line	July 16, 1820	July 16, 1820	83	
Martin Delany	do	96 00	876 12	Pennsylvania line	Feb. 4, 1819	May 26, 1818	66	Died July 10, 1827.
John Jobbins	do	96 00	1,315 43	do	Jan. 26, 1820	June 22, 1819	87	Died April 11, 1833.
George Dougherty	do	96 00	586 32	do	Mar. 5, 1824	Jan. 27, 1824	81	Died June 4, 1831.
Abraham Griffiths	do	96 00	130 32	do	Dec. 1, 1818	Oct. 1, 1818	82	
Reuben Huffman	do	96 00	120 31	Virginia line		July 28, 1818	76	
William Henson	do	96 00	388 80	do	do	do	69	Died February 9, 1824.
Thomas Perry	do	96 00	1,474 32	Maryland line	Oct. 27, 1818	Oct. 27, 1818	76	Suspended under Act May 1, 1820.
James Smith, 1st	do	96 00	162 89	Virginia line	June 24, 1819	June 24, 1819	71	Suspended under Act May 1, 1820.
John Spencer	do	96 00	26 89	do	Jan. 26, 1820	Nov. 24, 1819		Transferred from New York from March 4, 1821.
Reuben Samons or Simons	do	96 00	1,059 12	New Jersey line	Oct. 1, 1819	Aug. 24, 1819	72	

75

Statement of Hampshire County, West Virginia.

NAMES.	Rank.	Annual Allowance.	Sums Received.	Description of Service.	When Placed on Pension Roll.	Commencement of Pension.	Ages.	Laws Under Which Inscribed, Increased, and Reduced; and Remarks.
Thomas Alby	Private	$96 00	$148 61	Virginia line	Mar. 6, 1819	Aug. 18, 1818	74	Suspended under Act May 1, 1820.
Richard Addison	do	96 00	1,418 32	do	Oct. 12, 1821	May 27, 1818	81	
John Bond	Serge'nt	96 00	946 60	Maryland line	Nov. 4, 1822	Oct. 26, 1818	72	
Gustavus Croston	Private	96 00	165 59	Virginia line	Oct. 24, 1818	June 15, 1818	63	Dropped under Act May 1, 1820.
John Dailey	do	96 00	1,131 38	do	July 31, 1820	May 23, 1818	72	
George Eskridge	Ensign	240 00	3,731 61	do	Sept. 15, 1819	Aug. 18, 1818	78	
Stephen Ferryman	Private	96 00	1,512 49	do	Dec. 2, 1818	June 3, 1818	84	
Andrew Gwin	do	96 00	302 95	do	July 15, 1819	Oct. 26, 1818	61	Died December 21, 1821.
Sampson Henderson	do	96 00	100 74	do	Feb. 2, 1819	Feb. 10, 1819	61	Dropped under Act May 1, 1820.
John J. Jacob	Lieut.	240 00	303 30	Maryland line	Feb. 11, 1819	May 31, 1818	63	Suspended under Act May 1, 1820.
William Mail	Private	96 00	1,514 32	Virginia line	Sept. 21, 1818	May 27, 1818	80	
Hugh Malone	do	96 00	878 18	Maryland line	July 21, 1819	Oct. 19, 1818	72	Died December 11, 1828.
Rees Pritchard	Ensign	240 00	2,058 24	Virginia line	do	May 28, 1818	90	Dropped under Act May 1, 1820. Reinstated April 25, 1822. Died Sept. 25, 1830.
George Payne	Private	96 00	434 57	do	Sept. 2, 1820	Aug. 26, 1820	76	Dropped under Act May 1, 1820. Reinstated July 21, 1821.
Francis Ravenscroft	do	96 00	436 64	Virginia line	Mar. 6, 1819	Aug. 18, 1818	74	
John Robinson	do	96 00	602 86	Pennsylvania line	May 20, 1819	May 25, 1818	70	June 7, 1785.
Robert Williams, Inv	do	96 00	1,357 04	Virginia line		Mar. 4, 1789		April 24, 1816.
do	do	80 00	167 33	do		Apr. 24, 1816		
do	do	96 00	1,514 57	do	June 22, 1818	May 26, 1818	92	
James White	do	96 00	399 47	do	Mar. 5, 1819	May 25, 1818	86	Died July 22, 1832.
Isaac Welch	do	96 00	343 03	do	Oct. 9, 1819	Aug. 21, 1819	80	Dropped under Act May 1, 1820. Restored commencing February 4, 1831.

Statement of Harrison County, West Virginia.

Names.	Rank.	Annual Allowance.	Sums Received.	Description of Service.	When Placed on Pension Roll.	Commencement of Pension.	Ages	Laws Under Which Inscribed, Increased, and Reduced and Remarks.
Jonathan Adams	Private	$96 00	$117 32	Virginia line	Jan. 29, 1819	June 15, 1818	63	Suspended under Act May 1, 1820.
John Byrns	do	96 00	1,525 83	do	Oct. 8, 1818	Apr. 13, 1818	84	
John Bunnell	do	96 00	470 19	New York line	Jan. 28, 1819	May 19, 1818	62	Died April 1, 1823.
James Cochran	Ensign	240 00	2,982 40	Virginia line	Mar. 12, 1819	July 20, 1818	79	Died November 13, 1830.
Valentine Clapper	Private	96 00	1,451 73	Maryland line	May 8, 1819	Apr. 22, 1818	88	Died June, 1833.
Michael Cary	do	96 00	1,284 12	do	June 4, 1819	Oct. 20, 1818	76	
John Cottrill	do	96 00	873 03	Virginia line	Feb. 11, 1825	Feb. 1, 1825	71	
Dabney Ford	do	96 00	1,500 12	do	Mar. 11, 1819	July 20, 1818	70	
Henry Farence	do	96 00	1,500 12	do	do	do	73	
Stephen Flecharty	do	96 00	626 31	Maryland line	July 7, 1819	Apr. 22, 1818	79	Died January 28, 1825.
Matthias Hite	Lieut.	240 00	1,131 80	do	Jan. 28, 1819	July 20, 1818	73	Died January 9, 1823.
Joseph Hall	Private	96 00	636 12	do	Mar. 11, 1819	May 20, 1818	83	
Adam Hickman	do	96 00	1,320 18	Pennsylvania line	Mar. 19, 1819	May 18, 1818	91	Dropped under Act May 1, 1820. Reinstated. Died February 16, 1833.
James Hanlon	do	96 00	876 50	Virginia line	May 14, 1819	Nov. 17, 1818	75	Died January 3, 1829.
Richard Jones, 2d	do	96 00	404 52	Pennsylvania line	Jan. 29, 1819	June 15, 1818	82	Died September 1, 1822.
Jacob Keyser	Serg'nt	96 00	1,231 43	Virginia line	July 13, 1819	May 20, 1818	78	Dropped under Act May 1, 1820. Restored February 21, 1823.
Aaron Lockhart	Private	96 00	179 43	Pennsylvania line	Jan. 28, 1819	Apr. 22, 1818	87	Suspended under Act May 1, 1820.
Walter Linsey	do	96 00	172 38	do	Jan. 28, 1819	May 18, 1818	77	Suspended under Act May 1, 1820.
John R. Miloy	do	96 00	1,327 34	Massachusetts line	July 8, 1819	May 18, 1819	80	Died November 14, 1832.
John Obert	do	96 00	1,301 32	New Jersey line	Nov. 28, 1818	Nov. 27, 1818	70	Transferred from New York from March 4, 1820. Died June 16, 1832.
George Pritchard	do	96 00	385 32	Virginia line	Jan. 29, 1819	June 15, 1818	86	Died June 19, 1822.
Moses Rollins	do	96 00	1,509 29	do	Sept. 22, 1820	Jan. 12, 1819	71	
John Roe, or Row	do	96 00	1,022 22	do	Nov. 21, 1820	July 6, 1818	70	
Nicholas N. Ryland	Lieut.	240 00	2,709 35	do	Apr. 15, 1819	Aug. 23, 1818	83	Transferred from Pennsylvania from Mar. 4, 1820. Dropped from roll July 6, 1821 Deserted.
Giles Read	Private	96 00	147 35	New Jersey line			69	
John Row	do	98 00	383 21	do	June 30, 1818	May 18, 1818	66	Dropped under Act May 1, 1820. Restored December 26, 1822.
John Stackhouse	do	96 00	172 68	Virginia line	Jan. 28, 1819	May 19, 1818	77	Died June 20, 1827.
John Sharp	do	96 00	1,228 64	Pennsylvania line	Mar. 19, 1819	May 18, 1818	78	
William Shingleton	do	96 00	1,492 90	Virginia line	Sept. 6, 1819	Aug. 17, 1818	80	
Joseph Selman	do	96 00	351 73	do	July 8, 1830	July 6, 1830	84	
Jacob Thompson	do	96 00	1,509 29	do	Jan. 28, 1819	May 18, 1818	74	
Robert Wadsworth	do	96 00	508 67	do	do	do	84	Suspended under Act May 1, 1820. Reinstated.
Joseph White, 2d	do	98 00	943 99	Maryland line	June 4, 1819	July 20, 1818	73	Died May 19, 1828.
John Westfall	do	98 00	623 35	Virginia line	July 21, 1819	June 15, 1818	64	Died December 12, 1824.

Statement of Hardy County, West Virginia.

NAMES.	Rank.	Annual Allowance.	Sums Received.	Description of Service.	When Placed on Pension Roll.	Commencement of Pension.	Ages.	Laws Under Which Inscribed, Increased, and Reduced; and Remarks.
John Berry	Private	$96 00	$1,518 70	New Jersey line	Nov. 17, 1819	May 11, 1819	83	
Elihu Chilcott	do	96 00	610 83	Virginia line	Jan. 19, 1825	Jan. 15, 1825	74	Died May 25, 1831.
John Jenkins	do	96 00	1,030 63	do	July 9, 1823	June 10, 1823	76	
Hugh Milligan	do	96 00	422 42	Pennsylvania line	Oct. 10, 1820	Aug. 9, 1820	90	Died January 2, 1825.
Michael McKnight	do	96 00	367 22	Virginia line	Nov. 1, 1820	May 8, 1818	85	
George Nipper	do	96 00	1,518 96	do	July 21, 1819	May 9, 1818	82	
John Redman	do	96 00	1,030 36	do	July 9, 1823	June 11, 1823	71	
Richard Redman	do	96 00	485 31	do	April 24, 1829	Feb. 14, 1829	75	
James Tasker	do	96 00	1,226 32	do	July 31, 1820	May 27, 1818	75	

Statement of Jefferson County, West Virginia.

NAMES.	Rank.	Annual Allowance.	Sums Received.	Description of Service.	When Placed on Pension Roll.	Commencement of Pension.	Ages.	Laws Under Which Inscribed, Increased, and Reduced; and Remarks.
Robert Avis	Private	$96 00	$ 130 12	Virginia line	Mar. 26, 1832	Mar. 24, 1832	79	Died February 5, 1824.
Daniel Brian	do	96 00	561 90	Maryland line	Feb. 11, 1819	Apr. 21, 1818	71	
James Crutcher	do	96 00	702 72	Pennsylvania line	Sept. 21, 1818		69	
Henry Frank	Dragoon	96 00	1,232 32	Washington lf. g'd line	June 2, 1819	Apr. 13, 1818	74	Died February 12, 1831.
William Gilpin	Private	96 00	1,514 83	Maryland line	Nov. 6, 1818	May 25, 1818	82	
Peter Hains	do	96 00	1,523 60	Va. and Md. line	Sept. 21, 1818	Apr. 21, 1818	80	
Thomas Johnson, 1st	do	96 00	1,295 50	Virginia line	Nov. 4, 1818	do	82	Died October 19, 1831.
George Johnson	do	96 00	1,131 72	do	Sept. 22, 1818	Apr. 22, 1819	90	
Boston Medlar	do	96 03	1,375 30	Maryland line	Feb. 11, 1819	Apr. 24, 1818	74	Died August 19, 1832.
Andrew McCarty	do	96 00	176 89	Pennsylvania line	May 4, 1819	Dec. 28, 1818	70	Suspended under Act May 1, 1820.
John Pierce	do	96 00	18 06	Virginia line	Oct. 8, 1818	Apr. 28, 1818	66	Dropped under Act May 1, 1820.
Philip Richcreek	do	96 00	122 60	Pennsylvania line	Mar. 5, 1819	Apr. 28, 1818	58	Suspended under Act May 1, 1820.
George Shaner	do	96 00	1,048 37	Virginia line			83	Dropped under Act May 1, 1820. Restored, commencing February 19, 1825.

Statement of Lewis County, West Virginia.

NAMES.	Rank.	Annual Allowance.	Sums Received.	Description of Service.	When Placed on Pension Roll.	Commencement of Pension.	Ages.	Laws Under Which Inscribed, Increased, and Reduced0 and Remarks.
Solomon Collins	Private	$96 00	$1,520 25	Pennsylvania line	July 9, 1819	May 4, 1818	74	
Peter McCune	do	96 00	1,291 35	Virginia line	Mar. 5, 1819	Aug. 3, 1818	84	Died January 15, 1832.
Samuel Oliver	do	96 00	71 20	Delaware line	Mar. 22, 1819	Sept. 7, 1818		Died June 3, 1819.
Jonathan Sheppard	do	96 00	378 98	Maryland line	Jan. 31, 1822	May 7, 1821	67	Died April 17, 1825.
Joseph Wilson	do	96 00	814 62	Virginia line	May 24, 1820	Oct. 5, 1818	70	Dropped under Act May 1, 1820. Restored commencing April 10, 1826.

Statement of Mason County, West Virginia.

NAMES.	Rank.	Annual Allowance.	Sums Received.	Description of Service.	When Placed on Pension Roll.	Commencement of Pension.	Ages.	Laws Under Which Inscribed, Increased, and Reduced; and Remarks.
Isaac Jackson	Private	$96 00	$ 211 73	Virginia line	Oct. 10, 1822	Sept. 16, 1822	82	Died November 29, 1824.
James McDade	do	96 00	1,435 09	do	Mar. 5, 1819	Aug. 19, 1818	86	Died July 30, 1833.

Statement of Monongalia County, West Virginia.

Names.	Rank.	Annual Allowance.	Sums Received.	Description of Service.	When Placed on Pension Roll.	Commencement of Pension.	Ages.	Laws Under Which Inscribed, Increased and Reduced; and Remarks.
Stephen Archer	Mariner	$96 00	$ 572 89	Delaware line	June 30, 1818	May 25, 1818	82	Transferred from Pennsylvania from March 4, 1820. Died May 12, 1824.
Richard T. Atkinson	Private	96 00	802 39	Maryland line	April 9, 1821	Apr. 16, 1819	82	
Joseph Bonner	do	96 00	800 35	Virginia line	Jan. 7, 1819	May 27, 1818	80	
Ezekiel Burrows	do	30 00	177 83	Delaware line	do	Apr. 28, 1818	61	Suspended under Act May 1, 1820.
Benj. Chesney	do	90 00	154 32	Virginia line	Jan. 21, 1819	July 27, 1818	57	Dropped under Act May 1, 1820.
Asaph Colegate	do	96 00	1,498 32	Maryland line	Nov. 21, 1819	do	71	
Henry F. Floyd	do	96 00	1,108 63	Virginia line	Mar. 21, 1820	May 30, 1818	73	Died December 16, 1829.
Jesse Gaskins	do	96 00	314 60	do	Jan. 7, 1819	May 26, 1818	79	
Youst Heck	do	96 00	170 32	Pennsylvania line	do	May 27, 1818	71	Dropped under Act May 1, 1820.
Edward Haymond	do	96 00	123 16	do	May 13, 1820	Nov. 23, 1818	65	Suspended under Act May 1, 1820.
Richard Johnston	do	96 00	1,178 35	Virginia line	July 29, 1819	May 27, 1818	82	Died April 3, 1819.
Daniel Lee	do	96 00	81 31	New York line	Feb. 2, 1819	May 30, 1818	62	Dropped under Act May 1, 1820. Restored February 16, 1821. Died March 15, 1822.
Christian Madera	do	96 00	281 41	Pennsylvania line	Jan. 7, 1819	Apr. 28, 1818	65	Dropped under Act May 1, 1820.
Zadock Morris	do	96 00	177 83	Delaware line	April 8, 1818	do	59	Died November 27, 1820.
Thomas Malone	do	96 00	81 00	Maryland line	Dec. 29, 1820	Jan. 25, 1820	76	
Joseph Sapp	do	60 00	1,521 19	Delaware line	do	Mar. 4, 1795		June 7, 1785. Invalid. Relinquished for benefits of Act of March 1818. Transferred from Pennsylvania Invalid roll July 12, 1821; and dropped July 10, 1824. Restored commenc'g March 22, 1826.
do	do	96 00	1,151 25	do	Jan. 5, 1822	June 27, 1820	74	
Gabriel Williams	Sergeant	97 31	977 31	Maryland line	Jan. 7, 1819	Apr. 28, 1818	80	
Stephen Watkins	Private	96 00	1,507 43	do	Sept. 7, 1819	June 22, 1818	81	Died July 2, 1828.

Statement of Monroe County, West Virginia.

NAMES.	Rank.	Annual Allowance.	Sums Received.	Description of Service.	When Placed on Pension Roll.	Commencement of Pension.	Ages.	Laws Under Which Inscribed, Increased, and Reduced; and Remarks.
Augustine Comer	Private	$96 00	$576 50	Virginia line	July 6, 1819	July 21, 1818	67	Died July 22, 1824.
Abraham Dehart	do	96 00	1,508 23	Pennsylvania line	Jan. 29, 1819	June 19, 1818	79	
Isaac Fisher	do	96 00	556 15	Virginia line	Mar. 5, 1819	Aug. 19, 1818	71	Died June 5, 1824.
James Foster	do	96 00	532 12	do		do	77	Died March 3, 1824.
John Ford	Serge'nt	96 00	812 67	Maryland line	Aug. 19, 1824	Mar. 16, 1824	80	
Solomon Jarrell	Private	96 00	100 15	Virginia line	Mar. 8, 1819	Aug. 20, 1818	86	Dropped September 4, 1819. Not Continental.
James Larkin	do	96 00	1,508 00	do	Jan. 29, 1819	June 17, 1818	81	
Francis Meadows	do	96 00	1,413 03	do	do	June 16, 1818	80	
John Males	do	96 00	1,133 92	Maryland line	Mar. 8, 1819	Oct. 20, 1821	87	Died August 11, 1830.
Thomas McDaniel	do	96 00	1,035 46	North Carolina line	Jan. 7, 1822	Nov. 22, 1821	81	
John Rains	do	96 00	1,516 38	Virginia line	Sept. 6, 1818	May 19, 1818	79	
James Smith, 2d	do	96 00	1,508 76	Delaware line	Mar. 17, 1819	June 17, 1818	86	

Statement of Nicholas County, West Virginia.

NAMES.	Rank.	Annual Allowance.	Sums Received.	Description of Service.	When Placed on Pension Roll.	Commencement of Pension.	Ages.	Laws Under Which Inscribed, Increased, and Reduced; and Remarks.
William Foster	Private	$96 00	$539 61	Virginia line	Aug. 3, 1826	July 22, 1826	73	
Isaac Rose	do	96 00	24 46	do	Jan. 26, 1820	Sept. 7, 1819	79	Died April 4, 1822.

Statement of Ohio County, West Virginia.

NAMES.	Rank.	Annual Allowance.	Sums Received.	Description of Service.	When Placed on Pension Roll.	Commencement of Pension.	Ages.	Laws Under Which Inscribed, Increased, and Reduced; and Remarks.
James Byrnes	Private	$96 00	$ 591 67	Pennsylvania line	Sept. 16, 1820	May 4, 1818	69	Died July 1, 1824.
Samuel Bowman	do	96 00	999 73	New York line	Jan. 14, 1824	Oct. 6, 1823	74	
John Cummings	do	96 00	1,303 48	Virginia line	Sept. 7, 1820	Aug. 7, 1820	85	Transferred from Connecticut from March 4, 1820. Died September 1, 1823.
George Gordon	Corporal	96 00	510 19	Connecticut line	June 23, 1819	May 9, 1818		
John O'Neal	Private	96 00	176 25	Pennsylvania line	Mar. 31, 1820	Mar. 4, 1818	89	
James Salter	do	96 00	629 67	Virginia line	Aug. 24, 1827	Aug. 14, 1827	90	
John Sockman	do	96 00	906 31	Pennsylvonia line	Feb. 11, 1819	July 4, 1818	74	Died December 12, 1827.

Statement of Pendleton County, West Virginia.

NAMES.	Rank.	Annual Allowance.	Sums Received.	Description of Service.	When Placed on Pension Roll.	Commencement of Pension.	Ages.	Laws Under Which Inscribed, Increased, and Reduced; and Remarks.
Henry Douberman	Private	$96 00	$970 95	Pennsylvania line	June 30, 1818	May 5, 1818	74	Died June 15, 1827.
William Eagle	do	96 00	274 88	Virginia line	Apr. 24, 1830	Apr. 24, 1830	86	
David Fulk	do	96 00	1,383 73	Pennsylvania line	Sept. 30, 1819	Oct. 6, 1818	83	Died January 16, 1832.
Reuben George	do	96 00	299 34	Virginia line	Mar. 13, 1819	Dec. 4, 1818	66	Died December 13, 1822.
Christian Hoffman	do	96 00	203 06	Pennsylvania line	Mar. 9, 1820	Nov. 2, 1819	67	Dropped under Act May 1, 1820. Restored commencing August 11, 1826.
Wm. Lawrence	do	96 00	742 43	Maryland line	Jan. 8, 1820	Jan. 5, 1819		
John P. Long	do	96 00	65 38	Pennsylvania line	Feb. 18, 1831	Feb. 16, 1831	80	Died October 22, 1831.
Jacob Schreader	do	96 00	1,400 51	do	Nov. 26, 1819	Aug. 3, 1819	83	
John Stonkard	do	96 00		do	Jan. 15, 1824	Jan. 8, 1824		
Henry Wymer	do	96 00	87 69	do	July 26, 1819	Apr. 6, 1819	74	Suspended under Act May 1, 1820.

Statement of Preston County, West Virginia.

NAMES.	Rank.	Annual Allowance.	Sums Received.	Description of Service.	When Placed on Pension Roll.	Commencement of Pension.	Ages.	Laws Under Which Inscribed, Increased, and Reduced; and Remarks.
William Webb	Private	$96 00	$1,232 79	Virginia line	July 3, 1820	Nov. 2, 1818	78	

Statement of Randolph County, West Virginia.

NAMES.	Rank.	Annual Allowance.	Sums Received.	Description of Service.	When Placed on Pension Roll.	Commencement of Pension.	Ages.	Laws Under Which Inscribed, Increased, and Reduced; and Remarks.
Abraham Burner	Private	$96 00	$ 34 83	Virginia line	Nov. 27, 1819	Oct. 25, 1819		Suspended under Act May 1, 1820.
Wm. Shrieves	do	96 00	1,514 83	do	Jan. 30, 1819	May 25, 1818	73	
Fortunatius Sydnor	do	96 00	122 33	do	Sept. 23, 1822	May 27, 1822	68	

Statement of Tylor County, West Virginia.

NAMES.	Rank.	Annual Allowance.	Sums Received.	Description of Service.	When Placed on Pension Roll.	Commencement of Pension.	Ages.	Laws Under Which Inscribed, Increased, and Reduced; and Remarks.
Patrick Hanlin	Private	$96 00	$ 725 16	Pennsylvania line	Mar. 5, 1819	Aug. 12, 1818	82	Suspended under Act May 1, 1820. Died February 28, 1826.
John Harris, 2d	do	96 00	1,389 56	Virginia line	May 14, 1819	Sept. 14, 1818	78	
David Jacobs	do	96 00	1,518 44	Pennsylvania line	Sept. 29, 1819	May 11, 1818	75	

Statement of Wood County, West Virginia.

Names.	Rank.	Annual Allowance.	Sums Received.	Description of Service.	When Placed on Pension Roll.	Commencement of Pension.	Ages.	Laws Under Which Inscribed, Increased, and Reduced; and Remarks.
Samuel B. Bell	Lieut.	$240 00	$2,366 44	Maryland line	May 7, 1819	May 18, 1818	65	Transferred to the District of Columbia, from March 4, 1820; and from District of Columbia, from March 4, 1826. Died March 28, 1828.
Benj. Crutchly	Private	$96 00	$1,487 43	do	May 13, 1819	Sept. 7, 1818	90	
Francis Langfit	do	96 00	671 72	Virginia line	May 13, 1819	Sept. 6, 1826	72	Died January 1, 1831.
Matthew Maddox	do	96 00	1,003 34	do	Sept. 21, 1820	July 20, 1820	79	Died February 2, 1821.
James Neal	Captain	240 00	840 08	do	June 8, 1820	June 3, 1818	84	
Bailey Rice	Private	96 00	1,392 76	do	Nov. 27, 1819	Sept. 2, 1819	77	
Caleb Wiseman	do	96 00	563 03	Pennsylvania line	July 19, 1830	Jan. 1, 1828	78	

A STATEMENT SHOWING THE NAMES, RANK, AND OTHER DATA RELATING TO PERSONS RESIDING IN WEST VIRGINIA COUNTIES, WHO HAVE BEEN INSCRIBED ON THE PENSION LIST UNDER THE ACT OF CONGRESS PASSED ON THE 7TH OF JUNE, 1832.

Statement of Berkeley County, West Virginia.

Names.	Rank.	Annual Allowance.	Sums Received.	Description of Service.	When Placed on Pension Roll.	Commencement of Pension.	Ages.	Laws Under Which Inscribed. Increased and Reduced; and Remarks.
George Everhart	Private	$60 66	$181 98	Penn. militia	Mar. 20, 1833	Mar. 4, 1831	79	
James Foster	do	20 00	60 00	do	Apr. 1, 1833	do	77	
Erasmus Gault	Cornet	160 00	480 00	Maryland militia	May 28, 1834	do	75	
Isaac Krolson	Private	60 00	120 00	Virginia con'l	May 10, 1833	do	80	
John Stevens	do	40 00	120 00	Virginia militia	June 28, 1833	do	76	
John Shober *alias* Shover	Pr. & ma.	53 33	159 99	Maryland militia	Sept. 26, 1833	do	74	
Paul Taylor	Private	80 00	240 00	Virginia militia	Apr. 9, 1834	do	86	
Charles Young	Private of art'y	100 00	300 00	do	Apr. 21, 1834	do	77	

Statement of Brooke County, West Virginia.

Names.	Rank.	Annual Allowance.	Sums Received.	Description of Service.	When Placed on Pension Roll.	Commencement of Pension.	Ages.	Laws Under Which Inscribed, Increased and Reduced; and Remarks.
William Baxter	Pr. & Sgt	$61 66	$119 98	Virginia contin'l	Mar. 22, 1833	Mar. 4, 1831	76	
Moses Congleton	Music'n	88 00	264 00	Virginia militia	Feb. 18, 1833	do	70	
Robert Cummins	Private	56 68	169 98	do	Dec. 26, 1832	do	82	
Adam Casner	do	30 00	90 00	Penn. militia	May 9, 1833	do	86	
Richard Criswell	do	30 00	90 00	Virginia militia	May 20, 1833	do	86	
Samuel Corey	do	60 00	180 00	New Jersey militia	July 13, 1833	do	71	
George Cox	Ensign	60 00	180 00	Va. State troops	July 18, 1833	do	85	
Thomas Hutson	Private	30 00	90 00	Penn. militia	May 4, 1833	do	75	
Isaac Linton	do	50 00	150 00	Md. State line	do	do	70	
Robert McIntyre	do	22 55	67 65	Va. State troops	Dec. 26, 1832	do	73	
Richard Mathews	do	40 00	120 00	Penn. contin'l	May 20, 1833	do	80	
Samuel Miller	do	30 00	90 00	Maryland militia	Feb. 5, 1833	do	79	
Thomas Peterson	do	60 00	180 00	Virginia militia	June 18, 1833	do	77	
Abraham Rogers	do	50 55	151 65	do	July 13, 1833	do	73	
Wm. Stevens	Pr. of art	62 50	187 50	Penn. contin'l	Dec. 26, 1832	do	81	
John Sherman	do	80 00	240 00	N. J. State troops	Dec. 7, 1833	do	77	
John Vanasdall	do	35 00	117 40	Virginia contin'l	Jan. 17, 1834	do	71	
Joachan Wilkoff	do	60 00	180 00	New Jersey militia	Dec. 3, 1832	do	84	
Simeon Woodroe	do	28 88	86 65	Penn. militia	May 20, 1833	do	78	
David Work	do	28 00	84 00	do	Oct. 29, 1833	do	91	

Statement of Cabell County, West Virginia.

NAMES.	Rank.	Annual Allowance.	Sums Received.	Description of Service.	When Placed on Pension Roll.	Commencement of Pension.	Ages.	Laws Under Which Inscribed, Increased, and Reduced; and Remarks.
Jas. Anderson, alias Asha Crockett.	Private	$80 00	$240 00	Virginia militia	May 21, 1833	Mar. 4, 1831	77	
Valentine Bloss	do	26 66	79 88	do	May 21, 1833	do	77	
Daniel Davis	do	47 77	143 31	do	Nov. 7, 1833	do	76	
Thomas Laidley	Gun, &c	36 00	108 00	do	Jan. 29, 1834	do	79	
John McComas	Private	36 66	91 65	do	Dec. 14, 1833	do	77	
Henry Payton	do	40 00	120 00	do	Jan. 6, 1834	do	75	
Thomas Roberts	do	50 00	125 00	do	Nov. 6, 1833	do	73	
Isaac Roberts	do	40 00	120 00	do	Apr. 21, 1834	do	74	
Allen Rice	do	60 00	180 00	Penn. militia	Sept. 16, 1833	do	75	
John Stephenson	do	30 00	90 00	Virginia militia	Nov. 7, 1834	do	71	
Nathaniel Scales	do	34 66	103 98	N. Carolina militia	Apr. 9, 1834	do	75	
James Turley	do	80 00		Va. State troops	May 9, 1834	do	80	

Statement of Fayette County, West Virginia.

NAMES.	Rank.	Annual Allowance.	Sums Received.	Description of Service.	When Placed on Pension Roll.	Commencement of Pension.	Ages.	Laws Under Which Inscribed, Increased, and Reduced; and Remarks.
William Brooks	Private	$26 66	$ 66 65	Va. State troops	June 21, 1833	Mar. 4, 1831	82	
Barnabus Cooper	do	80 00	147 10	Virginia militia	Aug. 9, 1833	Mar. 4, 1833	74	Died January 6, 1833.
Moses Fleshman	do	20 00	40 00	do	Feb. 21, 1834	do	74	
Benj. Johnson	do	80 00		Maryland militia	June 12, 1834	do	76	
John Kincaid	do	33 33		Virginia militia	Apr. 21, 1834	do	73	
Abraham Vandall	do	80 00	240 00	do	Dec. 11, 1833	do	76	

87

Statement of Greenbrier County, West Virginia.

NAMES.	Rank.	Annual Allowance.	Sums Received.	Description of Service.	When Placed on Pension Roll.	Commencement of Pension.	Ages.	Laws Under Which Inscribed, Increased, and Reduced; and Remarks.
Thomas Blake	Private	$30 00	$90 00	Virginia cont'l	May 20, 1833	Mar. 4, 1831	74	
Anthony Courtner	Pri. & ser	53 77	107 54	do	Feb. 6, 1833	do	94	
Samuel Day	Private	30 00	90 00	do	May 30, 1833	do	90	
John Fryer	do	80 00	240 00	do	May 13, 1833	do	83	
James Gregory	do	50 00	150 00	do	Jan. 6, 1834	do	83	
Samuel Gwinn	do	60 00		Virginia militia	Feb. 22, 1834	do	82	
George Hull	do	40 00	100 00	do	Sept. 11, 1833	do	76	
Berryman Jones	do	60 00	180 00	Virginia cont'l	Aug. 5, 1833	do	77	
Thomas Jones	Pri. cav	100 00	300 00	do	Aug. 26, 1833	do	86	
Joseph McMilliam	Private	20 00		Virginia militia	Apr. 9, 1834	do	71	
Elias Perkins	do	61 88	185 64	Virginia cont'l	Nov. 29, 1832	do	75	
Jacob Price	do	80 00	240 00	Va. State troops	Mar. 22, 1833	do	84	
Wm. Richmond	do	80 00	240 00	N. Carolina cont'l	Aug. 31, 1833	do	82	
John Sammons	do	56 66	169 98	Virginia militia	Aug. 5, 1833	do	75	
Corn. Vandersdell	do	36 10	108 30	Virginia cont'l	Sept. 26, 1833	do	76	

Statement of Hampshire County, West Virginia.

Names.	Rank.	Annual Allowance.	Sums Received.	Description of Service.	When Placed on Pension Roll.	Commencement of Pension.	Ages.	Laws Under Which Inscribed, Increased and Reduced; and Remarks
Henry Brinker	Lieut. & private	$115 00	$345 00	Virginia militia	May 9, 1833	Mar. 4, 1831	73	
John Brown, 4th	Serge'nt	120 00	360 00	Virginia cont'l	Feb. 28, 1834	do	72	
William Berry	Private	30 00	90 00	Virginia militia	Apr. 28, 1834	do	84	
John Cundiff	do	33 33	99 99	Virginia cont'l	Nov. 6, 1833	do	90	
Henry Cump	do	30 00	90 00	Virginia militia	Feb. 28, 1834	do	75	
Samuel B. Davis	do	22 00	66 00	Penn. State troops	Feb. 2, 1833	do	77	
Spencer Davis	do						77	
William Herin	Ser., cor. & priv	63 33	189 99	Virginia militia	Oct. 16, 1833	do	73	
John Hawkins	Private	97 97	293 91	do	Mar. 2, 1833	do	72	
John Harisbrough	do	20 00	60 00	do	May 2, 1833	do	84	
Christian Haas	do	33 33	99 99	Va. State troops	May 10, 1833	do	72	
Siras Hamrick	do	20 00	60 00	Penn. militia	June 28, 1833	do	78	
William Hook	P1, & ser	48 33	144 99	Virginia militia	Feb. 28, 1834	do	75	
Isaac James	Private	30 00	90 00	do	Apr. 4, 1834	do	81	
George Little	Fifer	43 33	120 99	Virginia cont'l	Apr. 9, 1834	do	72	
John Mallck	Private	26 66	79 98	New Jersey militia	May 8, 1833	do	79	
John Peters		28 66	85 98	Virginia militia	May 11, 1833	do	72	
James Parker	do	28 33	84 99	do	May 8, 1833	do	80	
Henry Purgett	do	21 55	64 65	do	Aug. 3, 1833	do	74	
Henry Powelson	do	53 33	159 00	do	Oct. 21, 1833	do	81	
John Queen	do	50 00	125 00	S. C. militia	Nov. 29, 1833	do	76	
John Rosebrough	do	80 00	240 00	Penn. cont'l	Aug. 3, 1833	do	79	
Asa Simmons	do	80 00	240 00	Virginia cont'l	Aug. 9, 1833	do	90	
Daniel Taylor	Serge'nt	110 00	330 00	do	Aug. 30, 1833	do	75	
Thomas Taylor	Private	20 21	84 63	do	Mar. 15, 1833	do	76	
Wm. Vandevin	do	20 00		Va. State troops	May 11, 1833	do	74	
					May 10, 1833	do	72	

Statement of Hardy County, West Virginia.

Names.	Rank.	Annual Allowance.	Sums Received.	Description of Service.	When Placed on Pension Roll.	Commencement of Pension.	Ages.	Laws Under Which Inscribed, Increased, and Reduced; and Remarks.
Anthony Baker	Private	$20 00	$50 00	Virginia cont'l	Sept. 16, 1833	Mar. 4, 1831	71	
Adam Bolener	do	20 00	60 00	Virginia militia	Jan. 17, 1834	do	67	
John E. Bills	do	50 00	150 00	do	Feb. 28, 1834	do	71	
Jacob Fisher	do	32 50	81 25	do	Sept. 16, 1833	do	77	
Joseph George	do	20 00	60 00	do	Feb. 28, 1834	do	73	
Christop'r Goodnight	do	20 00	60 00	do	do	do	72	
William Heath	do	30 00	75 00	Va. State troops	Sept. 16, 1833	do	76	
Henry Jones	do	23 33	69 99	Virginia cont'l	Feb. 28, 1834	do	83	
Daniel Ketterman	do	30 00	90 00	Va. State troops	do	do	73	
Benj. Marshall	do	20 00	60 00	Virginia militia	Apr. 9, 1834	do	79	
Searchman Our	do	20 00	60 00	Va. State troops	Mar. 15, 1833	do	78	
Archibald Roberts	do	38 90	97 25	Maryland militia	Sept. 3, 1833	do	70	
David Real	do	20 00	60 00	N. Carolina militia	Feb. 28, 1834	do	69	
Jacob Randall	Priv. & Ensign	60 00	180 00	Virginia militia	Mar. 15, 1834	do	75	
Jos. Vanmeter	Ensign & Serg'nt	193 19	483 50	do	Jan. 24, 1834	do	90	
Joseph Walker	Private	46 66	116 65	Penn. militia	Sept. 16, 1833	do	82	
Jacob Yoskhum or Yoskham	do	30 00	75 00	Virginia cont'l	do	do	80	

89

Statement of Harrison County, West Virginia.

NAMES.	Rank.	Annual Allowance.	Sums Received.	Description of Service.	When Placed on Pension Roll.	Commencement of Pensionn.	Ages.	Laws Under Which Inscribed, Increased, and Reduced; and Remarks.
John Ashcroft	Private	$ 40 00	$120 00	Virginia militia	Nov. 19, 1832.	Mar. 4, 1831	97	Suspended.
Joseph Britton	do	80 00	240 00	Va. State troops	Feb. 27, 1833.	do	72	do
Joseph Barnett	do	40 00	120 00	Penn. militia	Nov. 19, 1832.	do	73	do
Michael Bock	do	66 66	199 98	Virginia cont'l	May 22, 1833.	do	77	do
Richard Bell	In. spy	80 00	240 00	do	Nov. 7, 1833.	do	..	do
John Brake	do	40 00	120 00	Virginia militia	Feb. 25, 1834.	do	..	do
Joseph Baley	Private	20 00	60 00	do	Mar. 24, 1834.	do	..	do
Anthony Coon	do	80 00	240 00	Virginia cont'l	Oct. 4, 1832.	do	79	do
Leonard Critzer	do	63 33	188 99	New Jersey militia	Nov. 19, 1832.	do	75	do
Anderson Corbin	do	40 00	120 00	Va. State troops	Nov. 24, 1832.	do	69	do
Walter Cunningham	do	20 00	60 00	Virginia militia	Feb. 2, 1833.	do	85	do
Jesse Cornet	do	80 00	223 33	Virginia cont'l	June 28, 1833.	do	71	Died December 19, 1833.
Harman Crim	do	20 00	60 00	Virginia militia	Sept. 11, 1833.	do	84	Suspended.
Benjamin Coplin	do	80 00	240 00	do	Sept. 16, 1833.	do	92	do
John Carn	do	50 00	150 00	do	Jan. 7, 1834.	do	70	do
Josiah Davidson	do	20 00	60 00	do	Nov. 19, 1833.	do	73	do
Samuel Davis	do	88 00	264 00	New Jersey militia	Mar. 1, 1833.	do	78	do
John Davis	Drum'r	63 33	189 99	do	July 18, 1833.	do	76	do
William Davis	Private	27 22	....	Virginia militia	do	do	73	do
Jacob Davis	do	80 00	240 00	do	Apr. 9, 1834.	do	..	do
Jonah Davidson	do	56 66	96 15	Virginia cont'l	Feb. 23, 1833.	do	79	Died November 15, 1832.
Ebenezer Fisher	Lieut.	120 00	263 23	Virginia militia	Nov. 13, 1832.	do	90	Died May 14, 1833.
James Fleming	Private	40 00	120 00	do	Mar. 6, 1833.	do	74	Suspended.
Job Goff	do	80 00	172 38	Virginia cont'l	Feb. 23, 1833.	May 19, 1818	76	March 18, 1818. Suspended May 1, 1820.
John Greathouse	do	80 00	200 00	do	Jan. 28, 1819.	Mar. 4, 1831	76	Again pensioned under Act, June 1832. Suspended.
do	do	..	..	..	Mar. 22, 1833.	..	..	
John Goodwin	do	80 00	240 00	Virginia militia	Oct. 29, 1833.	do	72	Suspended.
Edward Goodwin	do	20 00	60 00	Virginia cont'l	Jan. 24, 1834.	do	70	do
Jonathan Humphrey	do	20 00	60 00	Penn. militia	Feb. 2, 1833.	do	75	do
William Haddox	In. spy	66 66	199 98	Virginia militia	Mar. 5, 1833.	do	76	do
Sotha Hickman	do	46 66	139 98	do	May 7, 1833.	do	86	do
Jacob Harrow	do	33 33	99 99	do	July 8, 1833.	do	79	do
Samuel Harbert	do	40 00	120 00	Virginia cont'l	Sept. 11, 1833.	do	74	do
Moses Husstead	do	80 00	240 00	Virginia militia	Oct. 29, 1833.	do	86	do
Edward Harbert	do	80 00	240 00	do	Mar. 27, 1833.	do	72	do
Joshua Jones	Private	58 33	174 99	Penn. militia	Nov. 24, 1833.	do	74	do
Peter Knight	do	20 00	60 00	Virginia militia	Nov. 13, 1832.	do	74	Dead.
William Keys	do	20 00	35 33	do	Apr. 4, 1834.	do	78	Suspended.
Joseph Kester	do	30 00	90 00	do	Nov. 19, 1832.	do	81	do
John Latham	do	80 00	240 00	Virginia cont'l	do	do	70	do

Name	Rank			Service	Date		Age
William Martin	do	90 00	240 00	Maryland militia	Feb. 19, 1833	do	72
Enock Moore	do	20 00	60 00	Va. State troops	Nov. 13, 1832	do	76
John Middleton	do	20 00	60 00	Va. State troops	Mar. 1, 1833	do	73
William McRee	do	20 00	60 00	Virginia militia	July 17, 1833	do	78
William Martin	Ass. com	480 00	1,140 00	do	Nov. 5, 1833	do	70
Christopher Nutter	Private	30 00	90 00	do	Feb. 23, 1833	do	74
John Nay	do	60 00	180 00	Virginia cont'l	Jan. 17, 1834	do	84
William Pepper	do	24 10	72 30	Virginia militia	May 8, 1833	do	73
John Patton	do	26 66	79 98	Va. State troops	Aug. 25, 1833	do	84
Rhodam Rogers	do	26 66	79 98	Virginia militia	Nov. 19, 1832	do	84
James Randall	do	20 00	60 00	do	do	do	73
John Romine	do	20 00	43 04	Va. State troops	May 2, 1833	do	73
Isaac Richards	do	73 33	219 99	Maryland militia	May 17, 1833	Died April 29, 1833.	75
James Robinson	do	80 29	240 87	Va. State troops	May 20, 1833	Suspended.	87
Jacob Riffee	In. spy	80 00	240 00	Virginia militia	Oct. 29, 1833	do	73
John Read	Private	40 00	120 00	do	Jan. 24, 1834	do	89
Caleb Stout	do	20 00	60 00	New Jersey cont'l	Nov. 20, 1832	do	88
Charles Shaw	do	40 00	100 00	Va. State troops	Feb. 25, 1833	do	76
John Smith	do	60 00	180 00	Maryland militia	July 16, 1833	do	74
Daniel Smith	do	22 66	68 65	Virginia militia	Oct. 12, 1833	do	78
Michael Seas	do	80 00	240 00	Penn. militia	Oct. 29, 1833	do	70
Thomas Stout	In. spy	80 00	240 00	Virginia militia	do	do	83
Isaac Shinn	Private	56 66	169 98	do	Dec. 31, 1833	do	74
John Sweger	In. spy	80 00	240 00	do	Feb. 5, 1834	do	74
John Tucker	Private	30 00	90 00	do	Feb. 2, 1833	do	91
David Tichanal	do	26 66	53 32	do	Mar. 6, 1833	do	70
Henry Tucker	do	79 00	237 00	Virginia cont'l	Feb. 2, 1833	do	90
Arthur Trader	do	80 00	240 00	Virginia militia	Jan. 17, 1834	do	87
Evan Thomas	do	29 34	88 02	N. Y. State troops	Jan. 24, 1834	do	81
John T. Waldo	do	20 00	60 00	Va. State troops	Feb. 2, 1833	do	72
John Welch	do	80 00	240 00	do	Mar. 6, 1833	do	84
William Wamsley	do			do	June 7, 1833	do	74

Statement of Jackson County, West Virginia.

NAMES.	Rank.	Annual Allowance.	Sums Received.	Description of Service.	When Placed on Pension Roll.	Commencement of Pension.	Ages.	Laws Under Which Inscribed, Increased, and Reduced; and Remarks.
Constantia O'Neale	Private	$80 00	$240 00	Virginia militia	Sept. 3, 1833	Mar. 4, 1831	81	
Joseph Parsons	Ind. spy	80 00	200 00	do	Dec. 31, 1833	do	79	
Michael Rader	Prt. cav.	70 00	175 00	do	Nov. 15, 1833	do	83	
Charles Smith	Private	60 00		do	Feb. 28, 1834	do	70	

Statement of Jefferson County, West Virginia.

NAMES.	Rank.	Annual Allowance.	Sums Received.	Description of Service.	When Placed on Pension Roll.	Commencement of Pension.	Ages.	Laws Under Which Inscribed, Increased, and Reduced, and Remarks.
Daniel Folck	Private	$80 00	$180 00	Va. State troops	Feb. 28, 1834	Mar. 4, 1831	74	
Peter Staley	do	20 00	60 00	Virginia militia	Mar. 12, 1834	do	80	

Statement of Kanawha County, West Virginia.

NAMES.	Rank.	Annual Allowance.	Sums Received.	Description of Service.	When Placed on Pension Roll.	Commencement of Pension.	Ages.	Laws Under Which Inscribed, Increased, and Reduced; and Remarks.
Isham Bailey	Private	$25 97	$	Virginia militia	Sept. 16, 1833	Mar. 4, 1831	79	
William Bailey	do	80 00	200 00	do	do	do	80	
Marshall Bowman	do	30 00	75 00	Virginia cont'l	Nov. 15, 1833	do	74	
John Casey	do	80 00	200 00	do	Feb. 21, 1833	do	70	
Robert Christian	do	23 33	58 32	Virginia militia	May 9, 1833	do	70	
Peter Grass	do	43 33	129 99	do	Nov. 29, 1833	do	79	
Rush Millam	do	30 00	90 00	do	May 20, 1833	do	75	
Job Martin	do	80 00	200 00	Virginia cont'l	Oct. 16, 1833	do	81	
Alexander Thompson	do	20 00	....	Virginia militia	Sept. 16, 1833	do	71	
Joseph Thomas	do	43 33	....	Virginia cont'l	Nov. 21, 1833	do	75	
John Young	do	46 66	139 98	Virginia militia	Sept. 16, 1833	do	74	

Statement of Lewis County, West Virginia.

Names.	Rank.	Annual Allowance.	Sums Received.	Description of Service.	When Placed on Pension Roll.	Commencement of Pension.	Ages.	Laws Under Which Inscribed, Increased, and Reduced; and Remarks.
John Brown	Pr. & en	$146 66	$439 98	Virginia militia	May 10, 1833	Mar. 4, 1831	69	Suspended.
James Brown	Private	80 00	240 00	do	May 16, 1833	do	78	do
Jacob Bush	do	50 00	137 33	do	Oct. 18, 1833	do	78	Died November 22, 1832.
Peter Bonnett	In. spy	80 00	240 00	Virginia militia	July 19, 1833	do	70	Suspended.
Lewis Bonnett	do	80 00	240 00	Va. State troops	do	do	72	do
Levin Benson	Private	80 00	240 00	Virginia cont'l.	Aug. 2, 1833	do	79	do
Jacob Bonnett	do	23 33	240 00	Va. State troops	Aug. 26, 1834	do	73	do
Thomas Bibb	do	80 00		Virginia militia	Mar. 19, 1834	do	80	do
Isaac Cox	Serge'nt	100 00	320 00	New Jersey militia	Dec. 15, 1832	do	91	do
William Clarke	Private	50 00	150 00	Virginia cont'l.	Apr. 23, 1833	do	73	do
John Cuthright	do	80 00	240 00	Virginia militia	May 16, 1833	do	80	do
George Collins	do	85 00	255 00	New Jersey militia	do	do	78	do
John Carlinton	do	80 00	240 00	Virginia militia	do	do	70	do
Thomas Coteral	do	80 00	240 00	do	Sept. 6, 1833	do	72	do
Peter Coper	do	80 00	240 00	Virginia cont'l.	Sept. 11, 1833	do	81	do
Philip Cox	do	70 00	210 00	Virginia militia	Oct. 12, 1833	do	71	do
Thomas M. Call	Pr. & ser	106 66	319 98	Virginia militia	do	do	76	do
John Cain	Ind. spy	80 00	240 00	do	Oct. 16, 1833	do	74	do
William Gardner	Private	80 00	240 00	Virginia cont'l.	Jan. 17, 1834	do		do
William Davis	do	80 00	240 00	Virginia militia	May 14, 1833	do	76	do
William Davis	do	80 00	240 00	do	Oct. 23, 1833	do	84	do
Adam Flesher	do	80 00	240 00	do	Dec. 31, 1833	do	81	do
Nicholas Gibson	do	80 00	240 00	Virginia cont'l.	Feb. 19, 1833	do	77	do
John Hazle	do	70 22	210 66	Virginia militia	Oct. 12, 1833	do	78	do
Aaron Holbert	Ind. spy	80 00	240 00	do	Oct. 29, 1833	do	75	do
Jacob Hyre	do	80 00	240 00	Penn. militia	Nov. 6, 1833	do	79	do
Hezediah Hess	Prl. & Li	189 99	569 97	Virginia militia	Oct. 12, 1833	do	77	do
Samuel Z. Jones	Ind. spy	80 00	240 00	do	May 29, 1833	do	74	do
Isaac Mace	Private	73 33	219 99	Virginia cont'l.	May 16, 1833	do	72	do
Christoph. McVancy	do	95 00	285 00	do	June 17, 1833	do	75	do
Henry McWhorter	Prl. & ser	80 00	240 00	Virginia cont'l.	Aug. 5, 1833	do	73	do
John Mitchell	Ind. spy	80 00	240 00	do	Oct. 12, 1833	do	82	do
Patrick McCan	Private	76 66	229 98	Virginia cont'l.	Jan. 6, 1834	do	76	do
Tunis Mucklewaine	do	66 66	199 98	Virginia militia	Sept. 11, 1833	do	73	do
John Mace	do	31 66	94 98	do	Mar. 25, 1833	do	78	do
John Neely	Prl. & ser	80 00	240 00	do	Sept. 16, 1833	do	78	do
Leavin Nicholas	Ind. spy	80 00	240 00	do	Oct. 26, 1833	do	74	do
Zephaniah Nichols	do	80 00	240 00	do	Feb. 29, 1833	do		do
Henry Persinger	Private	80 00	240 00	do	Feb. 21, 1833	do		do
William Powers	Ind. spy	80 00	240 00	do	Oct. 16, 1833	do	69	do

Name	Rank			Service	Date		No.
John Rains	Private	80 00	240 00	Virginia cont'l	Oct. 18, 1832	do	78
Wm. Ratcliffe	do	80 00	240 00	Virginia militia	May 16, 1833	do	74
Philip Regar	do	20 00	60 00	do	May 20, 1833	do	67
George Richards	Ind. spy	80 00	240 00	do	Oct. 16, 1833	do	75
Bazel Right	Private	53 00	159 99	do	Feb. 28, 1834	do	70
David W. Sleeth	do	80 00	240 00	do	Oct. 18, 1832	do	72
John Schoolcraft	do	80 00	240 00	do	Sept. 6, 1833	do	76
Geo. P. Smith	do	80 00	240 00	do	Oct. 12, 1813	do	77
Mark Smith	Ind. spy	80 00	240 00	do	do do	do	71
Sam. Stalmacker	do	80 00	240 00	do	Nov. 18, 1833	do	75
Paul Shaver	do	80 00	240 00	do	Oct. 28, 1833	do	79
John Sims	Private	80 00	240 00	do	Nov. 6, 1833	do	83
Thomas Smith	do	80 00	240 00	do	Feb. 28, 1834	do	82
John Waggoner	do	80 00	240 00	do	May 16, 1833	do	86
John Wingrove	do	75 66	229 98	do	June 20, 1833	do	74
Alexander West	do	66 66	199 98	do	July 18, 1833	do	69
James Warmsley	Ind. spy	80 00	240 00	N. Carolina militia	July 19, 1833	do	74
George Wilson	do	80 00		Virginia militia	do do		
David Warmsley	do				Oct. 26, 1833		

95

Statement of Logan County, West Virginia.

NAMES.	Rank.	Annual Allowance.	Sums Received.	Description of Service.	When Placed on Pension Roll.	Commencement of Pension.	Ages.	Laws Under Which Inscribed, Increased, and Reduced; and Remarks.
Philip Ballard	Private	$80 00	$168 00	Virginia cont'l	Dec. 24, 1833	Mar. 4, 1831	77	Died April 13, 1833.
John Cook	do	80 00	137 08	New York militia	Nov. 30, 1833	do	80	Died November 21, 1832.
William Davis	do	80 00	200 00	Virginia cont'l	May 23, 1833	do	87	
William Davis	do	80 00	240 00	Va. State troops	May 19, 1834	do	78	
William Meade	do	80 00		Virginia militia	Apr. 28, 1834	do	72	
Ralph Stewart	do	20 00		do	do	do	84	
Robert White	do	20 00	240 00	Va. State troops	Nov. 21, 1833	do	79	
Oliver Walker	do	20 00	60 00	Virginia militia	Apr. 4, 1834	do	89	

Statement of Mason County, West Virginia.

NAMES.	Rank.	Annual Allowance.	Sums Received.	Description of Service.	When Placed on Pension Roll.	Commencement of Pension.	Ages.	Laws Under Which Inscribed, Increased, and Reduced; and Remarks.
John C. Aleshire	Private	$30 00	$90 00	Virginia cont'l	Apr. 9, 1834	Mar. 4, 1831	78	
Andrew Akerd	do	20 00		Va. State troops	Apr. 21, 1834	do	76	
David Bumgardner	do	20 00	50 00	Virginia cont'l	Oct. 23, 1833	do	76	
Luman Gibbs	do	26 66	66 65	Virginia militia	Sept. 11, 1833	do	69	
John Hereford	Pr. & adj	120 00	300 00	Va. State troops	May 31, 1833	do	76	
William Hawkins	Private	20 00		Virginia militia	June 18, 1833	do	69	
Robert Love	do	20 00		do	Mar. 24, 1834	do	71	
Peter Peck	do	30 00		do	May 18, 1834	do	79	
Jonas Rouch	do	20 00		do	May 20, 1833	do	71	
Thomas Waddle	Pr. & ser	25 00	62 50	do	Sept. 11, 1833	do	75	

Statement of Monongalia County, West Virginia.

Names.	Rank.	Annual Allowance.	Sums Received.	Description of Service.	When Placed on Pension Roll.	Commencement of Pension.	Ages.	Laws Under Which Inscribed, Increased, and Reduced; and Remarks.
Peter Bertrugg	Private	$80 00	$240 00	Virginia militia	Oct. 26, 1833	Mar. 4, 1831	84	
John Burdin	do	40 00		New York militia	May 17, 1834	do	78	
Solomon Chalfin	do	80 00	240 00	Virginia militia	Dec. 5, 1832	do	82	
Elisha Clayton	do	80 00	240 00	do	June 18, 1833	do	77	
James Collins	do	30 00	90 00	Va. State troops	Apr. 4, 1834	do	73	
John Dent	Lieut.	320 00	960 00	Virginia cont'l	Nov. 28, 1832	do	79	
Henry Dorton	Private	40 00	120 00	do	May 10, 1833	do	86	
Samuel Dudley	do	50 00	150 00	do	May 17, 1833	do	72	
James Devers	do	39 56	118 68	Virginia militia	Apr. 20, 1834	do	79	
Simeon Everly	Ind. spy	30 00		do	Dec. 11, 1833	do	71	
John Evans	Colonel	150 00	450 00	do	May 6, 1833	do	95	
William Ford	Private	80 00	200 00	Va. State troops	Feb. 19, 1833	do	71	
Caleb Farbee	do	80 00	240 00	Virginia militia	Jan. 17, 1834	do	82	
Stephen Gapen	do	73 33	219 99	Penn. St. line	Nov. 28, 1832	do	73	
Jacob Holland	Corps of Drag's	120 00	360 00	Penn. cont'l	Nov. 20, 1832	do	81	
Peter Hammer	Private	50 00	150 00	Penn. militia	Mar. 23, 1833	do	75	
Peter Heught	do	40 00	120 00	Virginia militia	June 4, 1833	do	78	
Purnell Houston	do	28 33	84 99	do	May 14, 1833	do	80	
William Hull	Pr. & ser	100 00	300 00	do	Sept. 16, 1833	do	81	
George Keller	Private	65 00	195 00	do	May 10, 1833	do	73	
Peter Miller	do	40 00	120 00	do	Mar. 20, 1833	do	74	
Jackouill Morgan	do	25 89	77 67	do	Apr. 23, 1833	do	76	
Amos Morris	do	80 00	240 00	do	June 17, 1833	do	75	
Evan Morgan	do	56 22	168 66	Virginia cont'l	Jan. 17, 1834	do	81	
Richard Price	do	53 33	159 99	Virginia militia	Mar. 21, 1832	do	78	
Zachariah Piles	do	36 66	109 98	New Jersey militia	Aug. 29, 1833	do	77	
Isaac Reed	do	23 33	69 99	do	May 14, 1833	do	76	
James Scot	Music'n	88 00	264 00	Virginia cont'l	Nov. 28, 1832	do	68	
John Stone	Private	40 00	120 00	do	May 2, 1833	do	81	
Charles Simpkins	do	30 00	90 00	Virginia militia	June 21, 1833	do	78	
Henry Stone	do	26 66	79 98	do	May 14, 1834	do	72	
Philip Smell	do	20 00	60 00	Penn. militia	May 9, 1834	do	76	
George Tucker	do	20 00	40 00	Virginia militia	May 11, 1833	do	72	
James Troy	Surgeon	55 00	165 00	do	May 27, 1833	do	75	
Richard Thralls	Private	80 00	240 00	Virginia cont'l	Aug. 5, 1833	do	81	
Henry Williams	do	80 00	240 00	New Jersey militia	May 23, 1833	do	74	
George Wade	do	40 00	120 00	Virginia militia	June 17, 1833	do	73	
John Wells	do	20 00	60 00	Maryland militia	May 14, 1833	do	77	
William Wilson, 2d	do	25 11	65 33	Virginia militia	Sept. 10, 1833	do	74	
Henry Yoho	do	80 00	240 00	do	Apr. 10, 1833	do	82	

Statement of Monroe County, West Virginia.

Names.	Rank.	Annual Allowance.	Sums Received.	Description of Service.	When Placed on Pension Roll.	Commencement of Pension.	Ages.	Laws Under Which Inscribed. Increased. and Reduced; and Remarks.
Henry Arnot	Private	$33 33	$99 99	Virginia militia	Sept. 25, 1833	Mar. 4, 1831	73	
Samuel Allen	do	60 00	180 00	Virginia cont'l	Dec. 3, 1832	do	88	
Thomas Alderson	do	20 00	50 00	Va. State troops	Aug. 28, 1833	do	90	
Jacob Arnbute	do	73 33	219 19	Virginia militia	Sept. 25, 1833	do	74	
Jesse Bland	do	80 00	240 00	Virginia cont'l	Feb. 21, 1833	do	78	
Patrick Boyd	do	80 00	240 00	do	Sept. 10, 1833	do	72	
John Boon	do	80 00	240 00	Virginia militia	Nov. 21, 1833	do	79	
Samuel Clark	do	50 00	125 00	Virginia militia	Dec. 28, 1832	do	70	
William Carter	do	33 33	99 99	Virginia cont'l	Apr. 22, 1833	do	75	
Robert Chambers	Serge'nt	120 00	360 00	Virginia militia	May 13, 1832	do	90	
William Canafax	Ind. spy	40 00	120 00	do	Apr. 28, 1831	do	75	
James Ellison	Private	40 00	120 00	do	June 18, 1833	do	77	
John Foster	Private	80 00	240 00	Virginia cont'l	Mar. 22, 1833	do	75	
Nathaniel Garter	do	30 00	90 00	Virginia cont'l	May 7, 1834	do	74	
John Hutchinson, sr	do	40 00	120 00	Virginia cont'l	Nov. 13, 1832	do	79	
Christopher Hand	Serge'nt	40 00	100 00	do	May 24, 1833	do	76	
do	do	40 00	100 00	Virginia militia	Jan. 20, 1824	do	73	
James Jones	Pr. art'l	100 00	300 00	Virginia cont'l	Nov. 13, 1832	do	73	
Field Jarvis	Private	21 11	63 33	Virginia militia	July 5, 1833	do	77	
Godrell Lively	Pr. ln							
	cav.							
Benjamin Morgan	Private	98 32	294 96	Armond's Legion	Nov. 6, 1833	do	71	
Christian Peters	Pr. cor.	20 00	60 00	Virginia militia	Dec. 10, 1832	do	73	
	ser.							
John Robinson	Private	40 33	120 99	Va. State troops	June 18, 1833	do	73	
Jonathan Roach	do	20 00	60 00	Virginia militia	Apr. 1, 1833	do	85	
Samuel Sams	do	80 00	240 00	do		do	73	
Joseph Wiseman	do	40 00	120 00	do	Nov. 13, 1832	do	75	
Henry Winkleblack	do	40 00	120 00	Penn. militia	Dec. 10, 1832	do	76	
Thomas Walker	do	60 00	180 00	Virginia militia	Apr. 23, 1833	do	79	
William Willis	do	41 91	80 00	Virginia cont'l	Apr. 26, 1833	do	69	
Robert Wilson	do	20 00	83 98	Virginia militia	May 20, 1833	do	75	
					May 27, 1833	do	74	

Statement of Morgan County, West Virginia.

NAMES.	Rank.	Annual Allowance.	Sums Received.	Description of Service.	When Placed on Pension Roll.	Commencement of Pension.	Ages.	Laws Under Which Inscribed, Increased, and Reduced; and Remarks.
Christian Crouse	Private	$20 00	$60 00	Penn. militia	Apr. 22, 1833	Mar. 4, 1831	81	
David Catlett	do	30 00	90 00	Virginia cont'l	Mar. 12, 1834	do	78	
John Easter	do	30 00	75 00	Virginia militia	Oct. 16, 1833	do	74	
Nicholas Henry	do	33 33	99 99	do	Sept. 1, 1832	do	74	
John Johnson	do	80 00	240 00	do	Sept. 5, 1833	do	100	
John Miller	do	20 00	60 00	do	do	do	75	
Christian Shank	Pr. & cor	83 00	249 00	do	Nov. 24, 1832	do	83	
Elijah Sutton	Private	46 66	139 98	New Jersey militia	May 18, 1833	do	79	
Jacob Smith	do	20 00	60 00	Maryland militia	Sept. 16, 1833	do	76	
Michael Widmeyer	do	20 00	40 00	Virginia militia	Apr. 23, 1833	do	74	
Zachariah Wharton	do	21 10	63 30	do	Sept. 5, 1833	do	75	

Statement of Nicholas County, West Virginia.

NAMES.	Rank.	Annual Allowance.	Sums Received.	Description of Service.	When Placed on Pension Roll.	Commencement of Pension.	Ages.	Laws Under Which Inscribed, Increased, and Reduced; and Remarks.
Jesse Carpenter	Private	$80 00	$240 00	Virginia militia	Sept. 6, 1833	Mar. 4, 1831	74	
Jacob Chapman	do	20 00		do	Apr. 21, 1834	do	81	
Abraham Duffield	do	20 00	60 00	do	Dec. 30, 1833	do	71	
Jonathan Dunbar	do	40 00		do	Apr. 21, 1833	do	72	
Jacob Fisher	do	30 00	75 00	Virginia cont'l	Sept. 11, 1833	do	71	
Benjamin Hamrick	do	80 00	240 00	do	Dec. 1, 1832	do	77	
Benjamin Lemasters	do	80 00	240 00	Va. State troops	Sept. 10, 1833	do	78	
Jeremiah Odell	do	30 00	75 00	Virginia militia	Oct. 16, 1833	do	73	
James Sims	do	30 00		do	Apr. 21, 1833	do	79	

Statement of Ohio County, West Virginia.

NAMES.	Rank.	Annual Allowance.	Sums Received.	Description of Service.	When Placed on Pension Roll.	Commencement of Pension.	Ages.	Laws Under Which Inscribed, Increased, and Reduced; and Remarks.
Abisha Blodgett	Private	$80 00	$180 00	Connecticut cont'l	Feb. 6, 1834	Mar. 4, 1831	71	
John Caldwell	do	80 00	240 00	Virginia militia	Mar. 20, 1833	do	81	
John Curtiss	do	80 00	240 00	Penn. militia	May 7, 1834	do	81	
Robert Humphrey	do	80 00	240 00	Penn. cont'l	Nov. 20, 1832	do	83	
James Holliday	do	51 66	154 98	do	June 18, 1833	do	80	
John Hoffman	do	80 00	240 00	Virginia cont'l	Oct. 29, 1833	do	72	
Edward Kearney	do	60 00	180 00	Virginia militia	May 22, 1833	do	81	
Abraham McCullock	do	41 66	124 98	do	Mar. 26, 1833	do	72	
John Millingan	do	63 33	189 99	do	Sept. 11, 1833	do	83	
Thomas Mills	do	30 00	90 00	do	Sept. 26, 1833	do	70	
Jonathan Purdy	do	80 00	240 00	New York militia	Aug. 5, 1833	do	75	
Robert Pyatt	do	80 00	240 00	Penn. cont'l	Nov. 5, 1833	do	80	
Samuel White	do	31 66	94 98	Va. State troops	Aug. 26, 1833	do	79	

101

Statement of Pendleton County, West Virginia.

NAMES.	Rank.	Annual Allowance.	Sums Received.	Description of Service.	When Placed on Pension Roll.	Commencement of Pension.	Ages.	Laws Under Which Inscribed, Increased and Reduced; and Remarks.
Charles Blechhynden	Private	$40 00	$120 00	Virginia militia	May 11, 1833	Mar. 4, 1831	76	
Charles Borer	do	30 00	75 00	do	Sept. 11, 1833	do	74	
Burton Blizzard	do	30 00	90 00	do	Jan. 10, 1834	do	77	
John Devericks	do	20 00	60 00	do	Jan. 29, 1833	do	79	
Henry Huffman	do	33 33	99 99	do	Jan. 11, 1833	do	77	
Michael Hoover	do	20 00	60 00	do	do	do	81	
Palser Hammer	do	30 00	90 00	Penn. militia	Feb. 27, 1833	do	71	
Thomas Hoover	do	30 00	90 00	Virginia cont'l	Oct. 18, 1833	do	83	
Jacob Hoover	do	20 00	60 00	Virginia militia	Jan. 10, 1834	do	70	
Thomas Kinhead	do	30 00	60 00	Virginia cont'l	Jan. 11, 1833	do	75	
Henry Mallows	do	23 33	73 32	Virginia militia	Jan. 31, 1833	do	70	
Edward Morton	do	20 00	50 00	do	Jan. 11, 1833	do	73	
Zachariah Rexrode	do	30 00	60 00	do	July 24, 1834	do	81	
George Rymer	do	41 00	82 00	Virginia cont'l	Feb. 10, 1833	do	82	
William Smith	do	21 66	54 15	Virginia militia	Feb. 27, 1833	do	90	
John Simmons	do	26 66	79 98	Maryland cont'l	Jan. 17, 1834	do	74	
John Smith	do	30 00	90 00	Virginia militia	Jan. 7, 1833	do	79	
Eli B. Wilson	do							

102

Statement of Pocahontas County, West Virginia.

NAMES.	Rank.	Annual Allowance.	Sums Received.	Description of Service.	When Placed on Pension Roll.	Commencement of Pension.	Ages.	Laws Under Which Inscribed. Increased, Reduced; and Remarks.
Adam Arboghast	Private	$20 00	$60 00	Virginia militia	Mar. 5, 1833		74	
John Bradshaw	Ind. spy	80 00	240 00	do	June 21, 1833		75	
Isaac Hawk	Private	20 00	60 00	do	Nov. 6, 1833	Mar. 4, 1831	75	March 18, 1818. Suspended under Act of May 1, 1820.
John Slaven	do	96 00	51 35	Virginia cont'l	Feb. 15, 1822	Aug. 23, 1819		
do	do	80 00	240 00	do	Nov. 29, 1832	Mar. 4, 1831	74	Again pensioned under Act of June 7, 1832.
Thomas Tucker	do	30 00	90 00	Virginia militia	May 11, 1833	do	77	
Joseph Woodell	Pr. & Li.	60 00	220 00	do	Jan. 17, 1834	do	83	
John Young	Private	80 00	240 00	do	Apr. 1, 1833	do	74	

Statement of Preston County, West Virginia.

NAMES.	Rank.	Annual Allowance.	Sums Received.	Description of Service.	When Placed on Pension Roll.	Commencement of Pension.	Ages.	Laws Under Which Inscribed. Increased, Reduced; and Remarks.
Thomas Brown	Private	$20 00	$50 00	Virginia militia	Dec. 1, 1832	Mar. 4, 1831	74	
Leonard Cupp	do	23 33	69 99	Penn. militia	May 14, 1832	do	79	
Nicholas Casey	Prl. cav	25 00	58 32	Virginia militia		do	80	
Levi Hopkins	Private	23 33	60 00	do	Sept. 9, 1833	do	80	
Jacob Hartzell	do	20 00	60 00	Penn. militia	May 14, 1833	do	83	
John Hartman	do	50 00	150 00	Virginia militia	do	do	77	
Andrew Johnson	do	22 33	66 99	Virginia cont'l	Feb. 5, 1834	Mar. 4, 1831	73	
Isaac Matthews	do	40 00	121 98	New Jersey militia	Mar. 6, 1833	do	76	
Robert McMillen	do	33 33	99 99	Virginia militia	May 8, 1833	do	76	
Thomas McGee	do	50 00	150 00	Maryland militia	Jan. 6, 1834	do	72	
Abner Messenger	do	20 00	50 00	Virginia militia	July 16, 1833	Mar. 4, 1831	93	
John Orr	do	30 00	90 00	Virginia militia	July 17, 1833	do	84	Died March 18, 1833.
Thomas Renchart	do	30 00	163 11	Penn. militia	May 9, 1833	do	90	Dead.
Jacob Wagner	do	66 66	95 90	Penn. cont'l	June 26, 1834	do		
John Wilson	do							

Statement of Randolph County, West Virginia.

NAMES.	Rank.	Annual Allowance.	Sums Received.	Description of Service.	When Placed on Pension Roll.	Commencement of Pension.	Ages.	Laws Under Which Inscribed, Increased and Reduced; and Remarks.
Henry Farnster	Private	$21 55	$64 65	Virginia cont'l	Feb. 28, 1833	Mar. 4, 1831	73	
Simon Harris	do	20 00	60 00	do	do	do	73	
Jacob Kittle	do	47 66	119 15	New Jersey militia	Sept. 11, 1833	do	77	
Barney Karren	do	80 00	240 00	Virginia cont'l	Feb. 28, 1833	do	83	
Ambrose Lipscomb	do	23 33	69 99	Virginia militia	Sept. 16, 1833	do	82	
David Munier	do	80 00	240 00	do	Feb. 28, 1834	do	70	
John Neville	do	20 00		Va. State troops	May 1, 1833	do	60	
John Ryan	do	41 66	124 98	Virginia cont'l	Oct. 12, 1833	do	75	
James Tenney	do	80 00	240 00	Mass. cont'l	Jan. 15, 1833	do	68	
John Wolford	do	20 88	62 64	do	Sept. 16, 1833	do	80	
Matthew Whitman	do			do	Oct. 12, 1833	do	74	
Henry Whiteman	do	50 00	150 00	Penn. militia	Mar. 5, 1833	do	75	

Statement of Tylor County, West Virginia.

NAMES.	Rank.	Annual Allowance.	Sums Received.	Description of Service.	When Placed on Pension Roll.	Commencement of Pension.	Ages.	Laws Under Which Inscribed, Increased and Reduced; and Remarks.
William Bennett	Private	$80 00	$240 00	New York cont'l	May 6, 1833	Mar. 4, 1831	88	
Richard Dotson	Ind. spy	60 00	180 00	Virginia militia	July 18, 1833	do	82	
David Heysham	Private	80 00	240 00	do	Mar. 27, 1834	do	71	
Jacob Lewis	do	43 33	129 99	do	July 18, 1834	do	78	
William McKay	do	78 33	234 99	do	Apr. 20, 1834	do	74	
Thomas Rhodes	do	80 00	240 00	Virginia cont'l	July 18, 1833	do	78	
Charles Swann	Pri. cav	100 00	300 00	do	Nov. 14, 1832	do	81	
Duckett Wells	Private	33 33	70 31	Maryland cont'l	May 6, 1833	do	81	Died April 13, 1833.
Samuel Wheeler	do	30 00	90 00	Md. State troops	May 21, 1833	do	73	
Jeremiah Williams	do	48 33	144 99	Penn. militia	May 6, 1833	do	73	
Thomas Weekly	do	40 00	120 00	Md. State troops	do	do	79	
Hezekiah Wade	Ind. spy	80 00	240 00	Virginia militia	Oct. 26, 1833	do	80	

Statement of Wood County, West Virginia.

NAMES.	Rank.	Annual Allowance.	Sums Received.	Description of Service.	When Placed on Pension Roll.	Commencement of Pension.	Ages.	Laws Under Which Inscribed, Increased, and Reduced; and Remarks.
Samuel Barrett	Private	$80 00	$240 00	Virginia cont'l	Mar. 26, 1833	Mar. 4, 1831	76	
Patrick Board	do	80 00	240 00	do	June 17, 1833	do	84	
John Brookover	do	60 00	180 00	Virginia militia	Aug. 3, 1833	do	74	
William Cunningham	do	23 33	63 32	do	Mar. 1, 1833	do	71	
William Congreve	do	20 00	60 00	Virginia cont'l	Apr. 21, 1834	do	81	
Adam Deem	do	30 00	75 00	do	May 9, 1834	do	72	
James Holder	do	108 00	324 00	do	Oct. 29, 1833	do	72	
George Leach	Bomb'rd	30 00	75 00	Virginia militia	Sept. 19, 1832	do	77	
Thomas Leach	Private	63 33	126 63	Virginia cont'l	Oct. 29, 1833	do	70	
Richard Nicholls	do	43 33	129 99	Penn. militia	May 20, 1833	do	75	
Jacob Swisher	do	46 66	116 65	Virginia militia	May 10, 1833	do	82	
Patrick Sennett	do				Aug. 31, 1833	do	81	
John Sheets	do	20 00	50 00	Penn. militia	Oct. 26, 1833	do	81	

STATEMENT SHOWING THE NAMES, RANK, AND OTHER DATA RELATING TO PERSONS RESIDING IN THE STATE OF WEST VIRGINIA, WHO HAVE RECEIVED THE BENEFITS OF THE ACT OF CONGRESS PASSED MAY 15, 1828.

NAMES AND COUNTIES.	Rank.	Annual Allowance.	Sums Received.	Description of Service.	When Placed on Pension Roll.	Names of Agents or Representatives.	Remarks.
BERKELEY. Henry Bedinger	Captain	$480 00	$3,840 00	5th reg. Va. line	June 9, 1828	Philip C. Pendleton, agent	
FAYETTE. Peter Boyer	Matross	100 00	900 00	Proctor's artillery	Aug. 3, 1829	William Hays, agent	
GREENBRIER. Thomas Butts	Musician	88 00	615 75	reg. Md. line	Aug. 3, 1829	William Hays, agent, Mary Butts, widow	Died March 1, 1833.
HAMPSHIRE. Gustavus Crosston	Private	80 00	720 00	reg. Va. line	May 21, 1829	Christ'r Helskell, agent	Paid as Lieutenant to January 1, 1830.
John J. Jacob	Lieut.	340 00	1,224 02	reg. Md. line	Sept. 23, 1828		Increased to this rate by Act of May 29, 1830, commencing January 1, 1830.
do	Captain	480 00	2,482 66	do	do		
HARRISON. Jonathan Adams	Dragoon	100 00	913 32	reg. Pa. cav	Nov. 18, 1828	J. R. Nourse, agent, Margaret Adams, widow	Died April 21, 1835.
Peter Johnson	Private	80 00	720 00	8th reg. Pa. line	May 23, 1829	David Mann, agent	Died April 14, 1835.
JEFFERSON. Wm. Broadus	Lieut	320 00	1,479 11	reg. Va. line	Mar. 6, 1830	Wm. Broadus. adm'r	Died October 7, 1830.
MONONGALIA. Ebenezer Blackshire	Private	80 00	630 74	Delaware line	Nov. 29, 1828	Chas. S. Morgan, agent	Died October 22, 1834.
Benjamin Chesney	Dragoon	100 00	850 00	Lee's legion	Oct. 22, 1828		
Zadock Morris	Private	80 00	680 00	Delaware line	do		
MONROE. John Wright	Dragoon	100 00	900 00	Armand's corps	Feb. 27, 1829	James McDowell, jr., & John Floyd, agents	
OHIO. Archibald McDonald	Musician Lieut.	88 00 320 00	748 00 2,471 11	1st reg. Pa. line 7th reg. Va. line	July 29, 1828 Nov. 18, 1828	Z. Jacob, agent. John White, agent, Ruth Mills, widow	
John Mills							Died November 23, 1833.
William Wilson	Private	80 00	640 00	reg. Md. line	Apr. 26, 1830		
PRESTON. Daniel Martin	Private	80 00	720 00	1st reg. N. J. line	Oct. 6, 1828	Thomas P. Ray, agent	

NAMES OF PENSIONERS OF THE REVOLUTIONARY WAR, WHO WERE LIVING IN WEST VIRGINIA IN 1840; TOGETHER WITH THEIR AGES AND NAMES OF THE HEADS OF FAMILIES WITH WHOM THEY WERE RESIDING ON JUNE 1ST, OF THAT YEAR.

(*Source*—Special Report, United States Census for 1840.)

Counties.	Names.	Ages.	Names of Heads of Families with whom Pensioners Resided June 1, 1840.
BERKELEY	Charles Young	84	Charles Young.
	Catharine McKeeven, (widow)	84	Elizabeth McKeeven.
	Erasmus Gant	81	Erasmus Gant.
	Paul Taylor	90	Paul Taylor.
	Basil Lucas	83	Basil Lucas.
	Henry Bedinger	86	Henry Bedinger.
	Susan Shober, (widow)	70	Susan Shober.
BRAXTON	Jacob Fisher	77	William Cutlip.
BROOKE	Joachim Wicoff	90	Robert Moore.
	David Craig	58	David Craig.
	Samuel Corey	86	Elijah Corey.
	Daniel Corkle	93	William McConnell.
	Samuel Ogden	87	Samuel Ogden.
	William Baxter	91	William Baxter.
	Patrick Gass	70	Patrick Gass.
	Captain Oliver Brown	88	Stephen Colwell.
	Samuel Miller	85	Joseph Miller.
CABELL	John Everritt, Sr	87	John Everritt, Jr.
	Asher Crockett	81	Asher Crocket.
	Valentine Blose	82	Isaac Blose.
	John Stephenson	79	John Stephenson.
	Robert Rutherford	77	Thomas Rutherford.
	Thomas Roberts	78	Thomas Roberts.
	James Gellengwaters	74	John Gellengwaters.
	John Lesley	79	Milton Stratton.
	William Meade	78	Theophilus Goodwin.
	Adam Crom	85	Adam Crom.
	John Adkins, Sr	84	John Adkins.
	Peter Sullivan	85	Aaron Sullivan.
	Thomas Chandler	78	Thomas Chandler.
FAYETTE	Abraham Vandal	80	E. D. Vandal.
	John Reins	96	John Reins.
	William Richmond	80	Shadrick Martin.
GREENBRIER	John Pryor	81	John Pryor.
	Eli Perkins, Sr	82	Eli Perkins, Jr.
	Berryman Jones	78	Berryman Jones.
	James McLaughlin	58	James Scott.
	Thomas Perry	89	Thomas Perry.
HAMPSHIRE	George Little	84	George Little.
	John Mallick	78	John Mallick.
	John Queen	85	Stephen Queen.
	Henry Powelson	79	Henry Powelson.
	Asa Simons	81	Asa Simons.
	John Peters	86	John Peters.
	Christian Haas	88	Peter Haas.
	Thomas Shores	86	William Abernathy, Jr.
	Alexander Doran	80	Joseph Doran.
	John Hansbrough	75	John Hansbrough.
	Wilmore Male (colored)	84	Wilmore Male.
	Henry Kump	82	Henry Kump.
	Major Willm Heron	78	William Heron.
	Daniel Taylor	83	Daniel Taylor.
	Isaac James	78	Isaac James.
HARDY	John Rosebraugh	101	John Rosebraugh.
	Adam Bullinger	73	Adam Bullinger.
	Jacob Randall	81	Jacob Randall.
	Cichman Ours	85	Cichman Ours.

NAMES OF PENSIONERS OF THE REVOLUTIONARY WAR—Continued.

Counties.	Names.	Ages.	Names of Heads of Families with whom Pensioners Resided June 1, 1840.
	John Ebills	76	John Ebills.
	Christopher Goodnight	78	Christopher Goodnight.
	Daniel Ketterman	78	Daniel Ketterman.
	John Berry	96	John Berry.
	Richard Redman	84	John Martin.
HARRISON	Joshua Jones, Sen.	79	Joshua Jones, Sen.
	Job Goff, Sen.	79	Job Goff, Sen.
	Peter Knight	81	Peter Knight.
	Jacob Harrow	84	Jacob Harrow.
	Peter Johnson	88	Peter Johnson.
	William Shingleton	80	William Shingleton.
	John Waldo	79	John Waldo.
	Pamela Keyser (widow)	76	George Keyser.
	John Latham	74	John Latham.
	Susanna Roe (widow)	77	James Roe.
	Leonard Cutzer	81	Leonard Cutzer.
	William Martin	78	William Martin.
	John Bennet	61	John Bennet, Sen.
	John Nay	91	Oliver Nay.
	Jacob Thompson	80	Jacob Thompson.
	Elisha Gri...th	89	Charles McEntire.
	William Nichol	94	Kezin Fowler.
	Edward Stewart	84	Edward Stewart, Sen.
	Christopher Nutter	80	Christopher Nutter.
	Rhodam Rogers	84	Benjamin Harvey.
	Mary Lindsey (widow)	76	Mary Lindsey.
	William Davis	82	John Sutton.
	Jonathan Hughes	86	Robert Stutler.
	Henry McWhorter	90	Leonard S. Ward.
JACKSON	Thomas Good	82	Thomas Good.
	Andrew Welch	82	Andrew Welch.
	John McKown	83	John McKown.
	Samuel Carpenter	77	Samuel Carpenter.
	Elijah Runnion	78	Elijah Runnion.
	David Harris	71	David Harris.
	Henry Raburn	100	Weden Carney.
JEFFERSON	Peter Haines	90	John Avis.
	Daniel Folck	86	Daniel Folck.
KANAWHA	Benjamin Stone	80	Benjamin Stone.
LEWIS	John Waggoner	90	Samuel Waggoner.
	John Rains	83	William R. Sturcher.
	Jacob Hunt	85	John Hunt.
	Philip Reeger	73	Nathan Reeger.
	James Tenney	75	James Tenney.
	Jacob Hyse	83	Jacob Hyse.
	John Cutright	87	Christopher Cutright.
	John Davis	86	Benjamin Shammon.
	William Powers	75	William Powers.
	Joseph Wilson	83	Dolpheas D. Holbert.
	Peter Cogar	85	Adam Starcher.
	Phebe Cunningham, (widow)	80	Benjamin Hardman.
LOGAN	William Davis	96	William Davis.
	John S. Barsden	90	Edward Barsden.
	Samuel Mead	90	Samuel Mead.
MASON	John Hereford	83	John Hereford.
	Samuel Hayes	59	Samuel Hayes.
	James Harrison	85	George Chapman.
	George Lemastor	42	George Lemastor.
	John Kersey	78	John Kersey.
	Luman Gibbs	75	Luman Gibbs, Sr.
	William Hawkins	76	Nancy Hawkins.
	Robert Love	78	Robert Love.
	Andrew Eckard	80	Andrew Eckard.
MARSHALL	David Ferrel	75	David Ferrel.
	John Caldwell	90	Ezekiel Caldwell.

Names of Pensioners of the Revolutionary War—Continued.

Counties.	Names.	Ages.	Names of Heads of Families with whom Pensioners Resided June 1, 1840.
	John Cummins	95	John Cummins.
	John Fox	85	John Fox, Jr.
	Henry Yoho	58	Henry Yoho.
MERCER	Josiah Meadows	83	Green Meadows.
MONONGALIA	Evan Morgan	88	Evan Morgan.
	William Wilson	84	William Wilson.
	Isaac Reed	82	Isaac Reed.
	James Bevars	86	James Bevars.
	George Keller	81	John Keller.
	James Collins	85	James Collins.
	Charles Simkins	82	Charles Simkins.
	Benjamin Chesney	80	William Cole.
	James Scott	75	James Scott.
	John Dent	85	John Dent.
	Elisha Clayton	83	Elisha Clayton.
	Asaph M. Colegate	77	Asaph M. Colegate.
	Samuel Dudley	77	Samuel Dudley.
	Robert Derrah	71	Robert Derrah.
	Amos Morris	77	Amos Morris.
	Zadoc Morris	79	Zadoc Morris.
MONROE	John Wright	90	David G. Givins.
	John Foster	80	John Foster.
	Flora Smith, (widow)	95	Thomas Pritt.
	James Jones	79	James Jones.
	James Larkin	96	Robert Young.
	John Hutchinson	86	Isaac Hutchinson.
	James Boyd	81	James Boyd.
	Nathaniel Garlen	78	Nathaniel Garlen.
	Henry Arnott, Sen	80	Henry Arnott, Jr.
	Samuel Clarke	76	Samuel Clarke.
	William Kirby	81	Martin Kirby.
	Samuel Allen	95	George Allen, Sr.
	Thomas Walker	77	Thomas Walker.
MORGAN	Nicholas Henry	84	Peter Henry.
OHIO	James Holliday	86	James Holliday.
	Samuel Miller	85	Joseph Miller.
	John Curtis	89	James Darling.
PENDLETON	Charles Borror	83	Charles Borror.
	John Devericks, Sen	78	John Devericks, Sen.
	William Eagle	79	William Eagle.
	Michael Hoover	88	Michael Hoover.
	Thomas Kinkead	76	Thomas Kinkead.
	William Lawrence	73	William Lawrence.
	Edward Morton	75	Edward Morton.
	Zachariah Rexroad	79	Solomon Rexroad.
	George Rymer, Sen	90	George Rymer, Sen.
	Eli B. Wilson	84	Eli B. Wilson.
POCAHONTAS	John Young, Sen	79	John Young, Sen.
	Adam Arbegast, Sen	80	Adam Arbegast, Sen.
	John Webb	89	Martin Dilley.
PRESTON	Isaac Matthew	84	Isaac Matthew.
	John Jennings	90	Jonathan Jenkins.
	John Hartman	84	John Hartman.
	Daniel Martin	80	Daniel Hartman.
	Dabney Ford	80	Frederick K. Ford.
	Asa Wilson	78	Asa Wilson.
	Nathan Ashby	75	Elijah Hardesty.
	Abner Messenger	81	Samuel Messenger.
RANDOLPH	Mary Chenoweth, widow	78	Jehu Chenoweth.
	John Neville, Sen	75	John Neville, Sen.
	Henry Tansler	79	Andrew Tansler.
	Jacob Kittle	83	Jacob Kittle.
	Nancy Ann Hart, (widow)	83	Nancy Ann Hart.

NAMES OF PENSIONERS OF THE REVOLUTIONARY WAR.—Continued.

Counties.	Names.	Ages.	Names of Heads of Families with whom Pensioners Resided June 1, 1840.
TYLER	Charles Swan	86	Charles Swan.
	Thomas Weekly, Sen.	88	Thomas Weekly, Sen.
	William Bennet	94	William Bennet.
	Sarah Wells, (widow)	85	Eli Wells.
	Jacob Lewis	85	Jacob Lewis.
	Philip Miller	83	Philip Miller.
	Samuel Wheeler	80	Samuel Wheeler.
	Richard Dotson	88	James Dotson.
	James S. Ferrel, Sen.	78	James S. Ferrell, Sen.
	Jeremiah Williams, Sen.	79	Jeremiah Williams, Sen.
	John Burden, Sen.	81	John Burden, Sen.
	Temperance Cochran	79	Samuel Cochran.
WOOD	Thomas Leach	78	John Cooper.
	Bailey Rice	85	Bailey Rice.
	Patrick Sumett	83	George Sumett.
	William Cunningham	76	Willam Cunningham.
	Moses Rollins	76	Henry Rollins.

LIST OF THE NAMES OF PERSONS RESIDING IN WEST VIRGINIA WHOSE CLAIMS FOR PENSIONS FOR SERVICE IN THE REVOLUTION UNDER THE PROVISIONS OF THE ACTS OF CONGRESS OF JUNE 7, 1832; JULY 4, 1836; AND JULY 7, 1838, AND AMENDMENTS THERETO, WERE REJECTED, OR SUSPENDED, AWAITING FURTHER EVIDENCE.

H. H. Stuart, Secretary of the Interior, on February 23, 1852, transmitted to the U. S. Senate, a statement showing the names of all applicants for pensions under the acts of June 7, 1832, July 4, 1836, and July 7, 1838, respectively, and the acts amendatoroy thereof, whose claims have been rejected, or suspended, the grounds of such suspension or rejection, and the places of residence of such applicants, so far as the same could be given. This report he made February 16, 1850, and from it we have compiled the following relating to West Virginia pensioners of the Revolution, as to suspension or rejection of their claims. This data is shown in the following:

NAMES OF APPLICANTS.	RESIDENCE COUNTY.	REASONS FOR REJECTION OR SUSPENSION
John Shimp	Berkeley	Did not serve six months.
Peter Shaffer	"	For a more perfect narrative of his services.
Hezekiah Atkins	Cabell	For further proof and specification.
John Atkins	Fayette	For further proof and specification.
Hugh Caul	Greenbrier	Did not serve six months.
Henry Ebeli	"	Did not serve six months.
John McFerren	"	Did not serve six months.
Andrew Morrison	"	Did not serve six months.
James Gillelan	"	A Frontiersman.
George Hanger	"	Was a Wagon-Master.
David Hanna	"	Did not serve in any regularly organized corps.
Henry Hendrich	"	A Frontiersman.
Thomas Hughes	"	Neighborhood service against the Indians.
Joseph Hanna	"	Services at a neighboring Fort against the Indians.
Joseph McClintick	"	A Frontiersman engaged in garrison duty.
John Patton	"	Engaged in garrison duty exclusively.
John Pattison	"	Engaged in garrison duty exclusively.
David Williams	"	Did not serve in any regularly organized corps.
John Martin	"	Awaiting further proof.
Memucan Walker	"	Awaiting more perfect details of service.
Richard Williams, heirs of	"	Awaiting further proof.

LIST OF THE NAMES OF PERSONS RESIDING IN WEST VIRGINIA WHOSE CLAIMS FOR PENSIONS, ETC.—*Continued.*

NAMES OF APPLICANTS.	RESIDENCE COUNTY.	REASONS FOR REJECTION OR SUSPENSION
Isabella Hamilton, widow of William	Greenbrier	Awaiting further proof.
Elizabeth Boone, widow of John	"	Died before adoption of Joint Resolution of August 23, 1842.
Eleanor Gregory, widow of James	"	Was not a widow at date of the passage of the act of July 7, 1838.
Mary Cook, widow of John	"	Marriage admitted. The soldier who received the Department certificate for 12:5s :4d was of the same name, but other and more precise proof identity is required.
John Copsy	Hampshire	Further proof required.
John Walford	"	Awaiting further proof.
Elizabeth Little, widow of George	"	Suspended for proof of service and marriage.
Mary Tasker, widow of James	"	Proof of marriage not complete.
Philip Facks	"	For more direct proof.
Samuel Bonnafield	Harrison	Did not serve six months.
John Cole	"	Did not serve six months.
Elisha Griffin	"	Did not serve six months.
Christopher Knight	"	Did not serve six months.
John Conway	"	Services were against the Indians.
Joseph Davis	"	Services as a Walter.
Francis Goodwin	"	A Frontiersman.
John Hullerman	"	Service subsequent to the Revolution.
Thomas Lynott	"	Service as a Privateer.
Elijah Runion	Jackson	Did not serve six months.
Bazel Wright	"	Did not serve six months.
Thomas Hughes	"	Service in Indian Wars of 1777, 1778, 1779 and 1780.
Anna Parsons, formerly widow of John Heath	"	Awaiting further proof of service.
Fleming Cobb	Kanawha	Did not serve six months.
Thomas Smith	"	Did not serve six months.
Benjamin Johnston	"	Collecting beeves for Continental Army.
Jonathan Windsor	"	Did not serve in a military capacity.
Charles Young	"	Services in Indian Wars previous to 1775.
Samuel Martin	"	Awaiting further proof of service.
James S. Wilson	"	Did not serve six months in any regularly organized corps.
Mary Cook, widow of Peter	"	Suspended for further proof and papers withdrawn.
Edward Brown	Lewis	Did not serve six months.

List of the Names of Persons Residing in West Virginia Whose Claims for Pensions, Etc.—*Continued.*

NAMES OF APPLICANTS.	RESIDENCE COUNTY.	REASONS FOR REJECTION OR SUSPENSION
Robert Mean	Lewis	Did not serve six months.
David Wolff	"	Did not serve six months.
Henry Phillps	"	Service wholly against the Indians.
Isaac Phillps	"	Service wholly against the Indians.
Lawrence Hopkins	"	Awaiting further proof.
Benjamin Reynolds	"	Awaiting further proof and explanation.
John Mitchell	"	For further proof.
John Townsend	Logan	Did not serve six months.
William Lucas	"	Did not serve six months.
John Hamilton	"	For further proof and explanation.
Mary Biggs, widow of Joseph	Marshall	Married after January 1, 1794.
Elizabeth Edwards, widow of Michael	"	Did not serve six months in his first term, and his second requires additional proof.
Mary Lane, widow of Henry	"	Awaiting further proof.
Isaac Robinson	Mason	Did not serve six months.
William Arbuckle	"	For further evidence of service to be furnished.
Thomas Harmon	"	Awaiting further proof of service.
Obed Prewitt (Pruitt?)	"	Awaiting further proof of service.
John M. Roseberry	"	Awaiting further proof of service.
Joseph Davidson	Mercer	Did not serve in regularly organized corps.
Joseph Dunlop	Monongalia	Did not serve six consecutive months.
Hezekiah Summers	"	Did not serve six months.
Adam Ice	"	Frontier service in Indian Wars.
Thomas McElray	"	Was a Wagoner with the army.
Isaac Horner, widow of	"	For further proof and a return of original papers.
Samuel Hanaway	"	Awaiting further proof.
Aaron Luzader	"	Awaiting further proof.
Jacob Van Gilder	"	Awaiting further proof.
Achsa Chalfant, formerly widow of James Cotton	"	Rejected under act of July 4, 1836, but ordered to apply under act of July 7, 1838.
Rebecca Rose, widow of Charles	"	Period, length, localities and names of company and field officers must be set forth, and service verified by New Jersey records.
Thomas Steele	Monroe	Did not serve six months.
Isaac Nickel	"	Service was exclusively against the Indians.
John Dunn, Sr.	"	Not sufficient proof of evidence.
John Ellison	"	Claim for service as Indian Spy.
William Hutchinson	"	Claims for service in Indian Wars.
William Johnson	"	Awaiting further proof.

LIST OF THE NAMES OF PERSONS RESIDING IN WEST VIRGINIA WHOSE CLAIMS FOR PENSIONS, ETC.—Continued.

NAMES OF APPLICANTS.	RESIDENCE COUNTY.	REASONS FOR REJECTION OR SUSPENSION.
Jacob Cook	Monroe	Services were in Indian Wars from 1773 to 1779.
Valentine Miller	"	Proof of service required by two witnesses.
Isaac Nickell	"	For further proof.
John Robinson	"	For further proof.
Michael Swope	"	Awaiting further proof.
Sarah Lively, widow of Godfrell	"	Was not living August 23, 1842.
Flora Boyd, widow of James	"	The Special Act to claimant's husband granting a pension for twelve months' service is not regarded as conferring widows' rights under the general laws.
Jane Miller, widow of Robert	"	Period, length, and grade of service, and names of company and field officers wanting; also proof of marriage.
Thomas T. Rochold	Morgan	Awaiting further proof.
Ann Catlett, widow of David	"	Suspended, pending proof of date of marriage.
Peter Fisher	Nicholas	Did not serve six months.
Jonathan Windsor	"	Did not serve in any regularly organized corps.
Peter Anderson	Ohio	Did not serve in any regularly organized corps.
Alexander Hill	"	Evidence of two credible witnesses.
Archibald Woods	"	Did not serve six months.
Philip Eckle	Pendleton	For further proof and explanation.
Elizabeth Thompson, widow of David	"	Awaiting further proof.
William Sharp	"	Did not serve six months.
Richard Hill	Pocahontas	Services at a neighboring Fort.
Welden Baswell	"	Awaiting further proof.
William Boswell	Preston	For proof of two credible witnesses.
John Lap (Sap) widow of Susannah Cupp	"	Awaiting further proof.
Mary Feathers, widow of Leonard	"	For deficient proof of marriage.
Jacob	"	Awaiting further proof.
Elizabeth Orr, widow of John	"	No claim. Services of her husband were rendered after the Revolution.
Thomas Isner	Randolph	Service subsequent to the Revolution.
Valentine Stalnaker	"	Service before the Revolution.
Jonathan Smith	"	Services were not of a military capacity.
Michael Boyles	"	Awaiting further proof and specification.
Catharine Parsons, widow of William	"	Period, length and mode of service, and names of company and field officers wanting; also proof of marriage,

LIST OF THE NAMES OF PERSONS RESIDING IN WEST VIRGINIA WHOSE CLAIMS FOR PENSIONS, ETC.—*Continued.*

NAMES OF APPLICANTS.	RESIDENCE COUNTY.	REASONS FOR REJECTION OR SUSPENSION
Thomas Wells............	Tyler	Awaiting further proof.
John Williamson, widow	"	For further proof.
Margaret Hanlin, widow of Patrick........	"	Married after service, but previous to January 1, 1794—so she or her children can claim under act of July 7, 1838.
James Jones.............	"	Awaiting further proof.
Leonard Kelch...........	"	Awaiting further proof.
David McKankey.........	"	For further proof.
Elizabeth Sutherland, widow of Alexander....	Wayne	Service admitted—so far as the rolls show, a soldier of this name, as drummer, who served in Captain Strother Jones' Company, of Colonel Gist's regiment; and the bounty land, if traced, would be the best proof of identity at hand of the widow's claim to soldiers' service.
Jacob Deem.............	Wood	Services against the Indians on the frontier.
Jonathan Sarns..........	"	Services against the Indians after 1783.
Peter Anderson..........	"	For a more perfect setting forth of service.

DATA RELATING TO THE PENSION AGENCY AT WHEELING, WEST VIRGINIA, FOR THE PAYMENTS OF REVOLUTIONARY PENSIONS

March 26, 1838, the House of Representatives adopted a Resolution requesting the Secretary of War to communicate to that body the aggregate number of Pensioners then payable at the several agencies under his Department; with the aggregate amount of money required semi-annually to make payment at each agency, also the names of pensioners who have been added to the roll of each agent, and of all who have died or been dropped off by the Commissioner of Pensions, since the last report in August, 1834.

In compliance with this Resolution James L. Edwards, Comissioner of Pensions, made a report June 20, 1838, which filled a printed volume of 204 pages. From this the following data relative to the Revolutionary Pension Agency at Wheeling, West Virginia, is extracted. At this place Archibald Woods, himself an aged Revolutionary soldier, was the Pension Agent, through whom all the Pensioners belonging to the Wheeling Agency were paid, he having been appointed as such June 17, 1836. Here were paid, at this time, 20 Invalid Pensioners, their pensions granted prior to 1818; so under the act of March 18, 1818; 8 under the Act of May 15, 1828; 190 under the act of June 7, 1832. and 5 under the act of July 4, 1836,—a total of 285 pensioners.

NAMES OF REVOLUTIONARY PENSIONERS ADDED TO THE LIST PAID AT THE WHEELING AGENCY, FROM AUGUST, 1834, TO MARCH 26, 1838.

Jacob Rinehart	Invalid Pensioner.
David Baldwin	Act of June 7, 1838.
Leonard Coleman	do
Elisha Griffith	do
Thomas Jordan	do
Hugh McGavock	do
Tobias Moore	do
John Simmons	do
Joseph Tomlinson	do
Joseph Willis	do
Temperance Cochran, widow of James	Act of July 4, 1836.
Mary Chenoweth, widow of John	do
Mary Hupp, widow of Philip	do
Nancy Hart, widow of Edward	do
Mary McClure, widow of Abdiel	do

All were paid semi-annually, and this required at each payment, the sum of $9,701.00, or $19,402.00 yearly.

NAMES OF REVOLUTIONARY PENSIONERS PAID AT THE WHEELING AGENCY WHO DIED BETWEEN AUGUST —, 1834, AND MARCH 26, 1838.

Pensioned under Act of March 18, 1818.

John Byrns,
Jeremiah Hawkins,
Thomas Miner,
John O'Neal,
Robert Reynolds,
Joseph Sapp,
Stephen Watkins.

Pensioned under Act of May 15, 1828.

Archibald McDonald,
William Wilson.

Pensioned under Act of June 7, 1836.

Solomon Chaffin,
Harmon Cain,
Thomas Forshey,
Edward Greenlesh,
John Milligan,
John Middleton,
William McKay,
John Ripley,
William Stevens,
Matthew Whitman.

Pensioned under act of July 4, 1836.

Mary McClure, widow of Abdiel.

The history of the operations of the Wheeling Agency for the payment of Revolutionary Pensioners, from the time of its establishment until it was closed, would be of great interest to all West Virginians, and this may be compiled by some one hereafter—that is when the records of the Bureau of Pensions are printed.

NAMES OF SOME OF THE WEST VIRGINIANS WHO RECEIVED LANDS FROM VIRGINIA FOR SERVICES IN THE REVOLUTIONARY WAR.

(*Source*—Document 30, in Journal of the House of Delegates of Virginia, Session beginning December 2, 1833.)

Names.	Rank.	Line.	Number of Acres.	Date of Warrant.	Time of Service and Remarks.
Stephen Ashby	Captain	Continental	4,000	Dec. 21, 1784	Three years.
Mathew Arbuckle	do	do	4,000	Dec. 19, 1799	do
George Baylor	Colonel	do	6,666 2-3	Jan. 30, 1783	January 1777, to date of Warrant.
do	do	do	2,222	Jan. 29, 1784	7th and 8th years.
Robert Beale	Captain	do	4,666 2-3	March 26, 1784	February 10, 1776, to date of Warrant.
do	do	do	4,000	June 17, 1783	Three years.
do	do	do	1,055 1-2	April 27, 1808	Nineteen months.
do	do	do	555	Sept. 27, 1808	Ten months.
Benjamin Biggs	do	do	4,000	April 1, 1783	Three years ending December 27, 1779.
do	do	do	666 2-3	Nov. 1, 1783	Seventh year.
Henry Bedinger	do	do	4,000	April 5, 1783	Summer 1775, to November 1783.
do	do	do	1,330 1-3	Oct. 23, 1783	do
Daniel Bedinger	Lieutenant	do	2,666 2-3	May 9, 1821	Three years.
Rees Bowen	Ensign	do	2,666 2-3	March 9, 1783	For the war.
Joseph Crockett	Lieut.-Colonel	State	6,666 2-3	March 9, 1783	September 1775, to February 6, 1781.
do	do	do	2,443	Jan. 9, 1810	Two years and nine months.
Benjamin Casey	Captain	Continental	4,000	June 5, 1783	Three years.
William Crawford	Colonel	do	6,666 2-3	June 17, 1783	Three years.
William Cherry	Captain	do	4,000	Nov. 28, 1783	Three years.
do	do	do	2,666 2-3	March 19, 1832	Eighteen months.
Leonard Cooper	do	do	4,666 2-3	Oct. 18, 1784	Seven years.
do	do	do	6,666 2-3	Dec. 13, 1796	Seven years.
William Darke	Lieut.-Col.	do	1,111 1-3	March 5, 1790	February 1776, to December 1782.
do	do	do	883	March 2, 1810	Seventh year.
Horatio Gates	Major-General	do	17,500	June 13, 1783	Nine months.
Abraham Hite	Captain	do	4,000	April 7, 1783	May 1776, to date of Warrant.
do	do	do	611	Nov. 12, 1808	Three years.
Battle Harrison	Lieutenant	do	2,666 2-3	Nov. 28, 1796	Eleven months.
Joseph Hite	Ensign	do	4,000	Feb. 17, 1810	For the war.
Peter Johnson	Lieutenant	do	2,666 2-3	Feb. 29, 1784	End of war.
William McMechen	Surgeon	do	6,000	Oct. 20, 1783	Three years.
Cleon Moore	Captain	do	2,666 2-3	June 29, 1784	Resolution of House of Delegates.
Hugh McGavock	Lieutenant	State	666	Sept. 21, 1831	Three years.
Presley Neville	Colonel	Continental	7,000	Nov. 24, 1782	August 1775, to date of Warrant.
John Neville	do	do	7,777 2-3	June 20, 1783	August 1775, to date of Warrant.
do	do	do	1,388 3-4	Aug. 18, 1807	Fifteen months.

Names of Some of the West Virginians Who Received Lands from Virginia for Services in the Revolutionary War.—Continued.

Names.	Rank.	Line.	Number of Acres.	Date of Warrant.	Time of Service and Remarks.
James Neal	Captain	Continental	4,000	Dec. 9, 1806	Three years.
Alexander Parker	do	do	5,333 1-3	July 12, 1783	Eight years. Land on which Parkersburg, West Virginia, now stands.
Abraham Shepherd	do	do	4,000	April 5, 1783	Three years.
do	do	do	1,333 1-3	March 7, 1807	Seventh and eighth years.
do	do	do	277 1-3	August 22, 1807	Five months.
Joseph Swearingen	do	do	4,000	April 15, 1783	Three years.
do	do	do	666 2-3	April 19, 1789	Seventh year.
do	do	do	666 2-3	Jan. 23, 1805	Eighth year.
do	do	do	277	Nov. 19, 1807	Five months.
Charles Sims	Lieut.-Col.	do	6,000	April 17, 1783	Three years.
Ballard Smith	Lieutenant	do	2,666 2-3	March 26, 1783	June 11, 1777, to March 12, 1783.
do	do	do	185	May 22, 1811	Five months.
William Smith	do	do	2,666 2-3	Nov. 23, 1787	Three years.
Hugh Stephenson	Colonel	do	6,666 2-3	April 21, 1784	Three years.
Uriah Springer	Captain	do	4,000	April 1, 1783	Three years.
do	do	do	666	March 12, 1800	Seventh year.
Joseph Van Meter	Ensign	State	2,666 2-3	June 5, 1782	Three years.
William Vawter	Lieutenant	Continental	4,000	Jan. 21, 1783	
Thomas Warman	Captain	do	4,000	April 22, 1783	Three years.
Andrew Waggoner	Major	do	6,222	April 21, 1783	July 1775, to May 1783.
do	do	do	1,185	Nov. 20, 1807	Sixteen months.

CHAPTER V.

WEST VIRGINIANS IN THE INDIAN WARS AFTER THE REVOLUTION—THE LATER INDIAN WARS.

(From 1783 to 1795.)

The barbarian warfare which devastated the settlements west of the Alleghenies, after the close of the Revolution, was merciless in the extreme. The Indian nations occupying the region now embraced in the States of Ohio, Indiana, Illinois, and Michigan, who had been the allies of the British, not only refused to lay down their arms, but made powerful organizations to resist every force which could be sent against them. Great Britain refused to give up her western posts in compliance with the terms of the treaty of 1783, and her officers and garrisons fed the fires of Indian hate by their presence, their tender of protection, their supplies of guns, powder, and knives, and in many instances, by their actual participation in the war waged against the American frontier. This continued from 1783, until General Wayne broke forever the savage power at the battle of Fallen Timbers,—August 20, 1794,—a period of twelve years. During these border wars, more men, women and children perished at the hands of the barbarian foe, victims of the stake, rifle, tomahawk, and scalping-knife—in what is now West Virginia, than had died from similar causes in any other region of like extent in America.

These Indian wars on the frontier will be best understood, by having knowledge of the county organization of West Virginia during their continuance. At the close of the Revolution, (1783) the counties of Berkeley, Greenbrier, Hampshire, Monongalia, and Ohio had an existence; and Montgomery county extended to the Ohio and included all that part of West Virginia between the Great Kanawha and Big Sandy rivers. To these, during the continuance of the Indian Wars, were added Harrison county, formed from Monongalia in 1784; Hardy from Hampshire, in 1786; Randolph from Harrison, in 1787; Pendleton, from parts of Augusta, Hardy and Rockingham, in 1788; and Kanawha from parts of Greenbrier and Montgomery, in 1789. It was in these counties that the scenes of the Indian wars in West Virginia after the Revolution, are laid, and here their tragedies and dramas were enacted.

Further, that we may gain a correct knowledge of the Indian

wars in West Virginia after the Revolution, it is necessary that we be informed as to the military establishment of the Border at that time. By an Act of the Virginia Assembly passed at the October Session, it was provided that all free male persons—(other than those excepted between the ages of eighteen and fifty years should be enrolled and formed into Companies of three sergeants, three corporals, a drummer and a fifer, and not less than forty nor more than sixty-five rank and file; and these companies into Regiments of not more than one thousand nor fewer than five hundred men, if there be so many in the county. Each company shall be commanded by a captain, lieutenant and ensign; and each Regiment by a colonel, lieutenant-colonel, and a major; and the whole by a county-lieutenant.[1]

It is thus seen that in each county of the State there was a regimental organization. These were in turn, formed into brigades and Divisions. The Regiments in the West Virginia counties were all in the tenth and thirteenth brigades, and all in the Fourth Division. The military organization in West Virginia in the Indian wars is shown in the following:—

BERKELEY COUNTY—Fifty-fifth and Sixty-seventh Regiments, (completely organized): Sixteenth Brigade and Third Division. 2,126 free white males of 16 years and upwards.

GREENBRIER COUNTY—Seventy-ninth Regiment (organized) Thirteenth Brigade and Third Division. 732 free white males of 16 years and upwards.

HAMPSHIRE COUNTY—Seventy-seventh Regiment (completely organized) Tenth Brigade and Third Division, 1,662 free white males of 16 years and upwards.

HARDY COUNTY—Fourteenth Regiment (ten companies), Tenth Brigade and Third Division. 1,108 free white males of 16 years and upwards.

HARRISON AND RANDOLPH COUNTIES—Eleventh Regiment (one company of Light Infantry in Harrison and three in Randolph), Tenth Brigade and Third Division. 708 free white males of 16 years and upwards.

KANAWHA COUNTY—Eightieth Regiment, Thirteenth Brigade and Third Division. 731 free white males of 16 years and upwards.

MONONGALIA COUNTY—Seventy-sixth Regiment; Tenth Brigade and Third Division. 1,089 free white males of 16 years and upwards.

OHIO COUNTY—Fourth Regiment; Tenth Brigade and Third Division. 1,222 free white males of 16 years and upwards.

PENDLETON COUNTY—Forty-sixth Regiment (eight companies) Tenth Brigade and Third Division. 568 free white males of 16 years and upwards.[2]

---

1. Hening's "Statutes at Large," of Virginia, Vol. VII, pp. 9, 10, 11.
2. "Calendar of Virginia State Papers," Vol. VII. pp. 162, 163, 164, 165, 166, 167.

Each company was required to muster every two months at the call of the Captain; each Regiment once a year in April or May, on the call of the Colonel; and all at a general muster in October or November annually, on the call of the County-Lieutenant. In all counties east of the Blue Ridge the militia was required to be armed with muskets, but all to the westward of that mountain barrier, might be armed with rifles, and if any private made it to appear that he was unable to purchase a rifle, the County-Lieutenant, might buy it for him, paying for it out of militia fines in his hands. All regimental officers made reports within ten days after the general muster to the County-Lieutenant, who in turn within forty days after receiving these made his annual report to the Governor. December 15, 1788, it was enacted by the General Assembly that each militiaman in the counties on the Western Waters—those in West Virginia—should keep always ready a good musket or rifle, half a pound of good powder, and one pound of lead to be produced whenever called for by his commanding officer.[3]

3. Hening's "Statutes at Large," Vol. XII, p. 697.

A Pay Abstract of Captain John Whitzell's Company of Rangers from Monongalia County, Under the Command of Colonel Daniel McFarland, Ranging in Monongalia and Ohio Counties, from the 22nd Day of April to the 25th of July 1778, Both Days Included.

(*Source*—Printed from Original Roll in the possession of the State Department of Archives and History.)

Names.	Rank.	Commencing.	Ending.	Months.	Days.	Pay per Month.	Continental Currency.
John Whitzell	Captain	April 22.	July 25	3	5	40 dols.	£47:10:0
William Crawford	Lieutenant	do 27	do	3	..	27 "	30: 7:6
John Madison	Ensign	do 27	do	3	......	20 "	22:10:0
Peter Miller	Sergeant	do 22	do	3	5	8 "	9:10:0
Christian Copley	do	May 1	do	2	26	8 "	8:12:0
John Six	Private	April 28	do	2	29	25 "	27:16:3
Samuel Brown	do	do	do	2	29	25 "	27:16:3
Lewis Bonnell	do	May 1	do	2	26	25 "	26:18;4
Jacob Teusbaugh	do	do	July 14	2	15	25 "	23: 7:6
Joseph Morris	do	April 22	July 25	3	5	6⅔ "	7:18:4
Benjamin Wright	do	do	do	3	5	6⅔ "	7:18:4
William Hall	do	do	do	3	5	6⅔ "	7:18:4
Philip Nicholas	do	do	do	3	5	6⅔ "	7:18:4
John Nicholas	do	do	do	3	5	6⅔ "	7:18:4
Henry Yoho	do	do	do	3	5	6⅔ "	7:18:4
John Duncan	do	do	do	3	5	6⅔ "	7:18:4
Thomas Hargis	do	do	do	3	5	6⅔ "	7:18:4
John Province, Jr.	do	do	do	3	5	6⅔ "	7:18:4
Harvey Franks	do	do	do	3	5	6⅔ "	7:18:4
Nicholas Crousber	do	do	do	3	5	6⅔ "	7:18:4
Jacob Teusbaugh	do	do	April 30	.....	9	....	15:0
John Six	do	do	do	.....	9	....	15:0
Abram Eastwood	do	April 23	July 25	3	4	6⅔ "	7:16;8
Conrad Hur	do	do	do	3	4	6⅔ "	7:16:8
Mark Hare	do	do	do	3	4	6⅔ "	7:16:8
Martin Whitzell	do	do	do	3	4	6⅔ "	7:16:8
Enoch Enochs	do	April 26	do	3	3	6⅔ "	7:15:0
Jacob Riffle	do	April 24	do	3	3	6⅔ "	7:15:0
Valentine Lawrence	do	do	do	3	3	6⅔ "	7:15:0
John Andreuer	do	do	do	3	3	6⅔ "	7:15:0
John Smith	do	do	do	3	3	6⅔ "	7:15:0
William Gardiner	do	April 25	do	3	2	6⅔ "	7:15:0
David Casto	do	May 25	do	2	2	6⅔ "	5: 3:4
Joseph Yeager	do	May 21	June 21	1	2	6⅔ "	2:13:4
Philip Catt	do	May 25	June 17	....	24	6⅔ "	2: 0:0
George Catt	do	May 25	July 25	2	2	6⅔ "	5: 3:4
Joseph Coone	do	May 28	do	1	29	6⅔ "	4:18;4
Matthias Riffle	do	May 30	do	1	27	6⅔ "	4:15:0
Jacob Spangler	do	May 29	do	1	28	6⅔ "	4:16:8
Peter Goosey	do	June 26	July 3	.....	8	....	13:4
Philip Barker	do	April 30	May 17	...	24	6⅔ "	2:00:0
						....	£478;17:10

A PAY ROLL OF CAPTAIN WILLIAM CLENDENNIN'S COMPANY OF
RANGERS[4] FROM GREENBRIER COUNTY, ON SERVICE AT THE
MOUTH OF ELK RIVER, NOW CHARLESTON, ON THE
GREAT KANAWHA, IN 1788.

(*Source*—"Calendar of Virginia State Papers," Vol. IV. pp. 450, 451; and Vol. V. pp. 13, 14.)

OFFICERS.

William Clendenin, ... Captain.
George Shaw, ... Lieutenant.
Francis Watkins, ... Ensign.
Shaderick Harriman, ... Sergeant.
Reuben Slaughter, ... Sergeant.

PRIVATES.

John Tollypurt,	William Carroll,	William Turrell,
Samuel Dunbar,	Thomas Shirkey,	William Hyllard,
John Burns,	Nicholas Null,	John Cavinder,
Isaac Snedicer,	Archer Price,	Henry Morris,
William Miller,	Benjamin Morris,	Charles Young,
John Buckle,	Levi Morris,	William George,
James Edgar,	Joseph Burwell,	Alexander Clendenin,
Michael Newhouse,	William Boggs,	John Moore.
Robert Aaron,	William Morris,	

AUDITOR'S WARRANTS ISSUED IN 1789, TO PAY SCOUTS AND RANGERS
IN WESTERN VIRGINIA, AND PLACED IN THE HANDS OF JOHN
HENDERSON, SHERIFF OF OHIO COUNTY, VIZ:—

(*Source*—"Journal of the Virginia House of Delegates." Session beginning October 18, 1790, pp. 113, 114.)

	£ s. d.		£ s. d.
To William McCulloch	24 0 0	To Charles Williams	8 5 0
" James Williams	12 0 0	" Samuel Ogdin	4 19 0
" Joseph Huff	8 5 0	" Jacob Holmes	4 19 0
" William Sherrard	4 19 0	" Charles Sparks	8 5 0
" Edmund Baxter	8 5 0	" John Spencer	10 0 0
" William Layton	8 5 0	" William Johnson	8 5 0
" Joseph Eddington	21 0 0	" Michael Woodson	17 0 0
" Duncan McKenzie	8 5 0	" Daniel Pierce	4 19 0
" Michael Baker	7 0 0	" Edward Walling	8 5 0

To James Purseley .... £8 5s.

---

4. These were the men who in the summer of 1788 erected Fort Lee, on the site of Charleston, the Capital city of West Virginia.—V. A. L.

A Muster Roll of Scouts Ordered into Service by Governor Beverly Randolph for the Protection of the Settlements of Randolph County in the Year 1790.

(*Source*—"Calendar of Virginia State Papers," Vol. VIII, p. 243.)

NAMES.	When Entered.	When Discharged.	No. of Days in Service.	Age.	Size. Ft. In.	Nation.	Where Employed.	Wages per Day.	Amount of Pay. £ s. d.
Valentine Stalnaker	1790. March 1	April 30	61	30	5 9	Virginia	Randolph County	5s	15 5 0
Phineas Wells	" 1	" 30	61	30	5 9	New York	"	5s	15 5 0
Jas. Stewart Elliott	" 1	" 30	61	22	5 10	Virginia	"	5s	15 5 0
James Westfall	" 1	" 30	61	23	5 11	Virginia	"	5s	15 5 0
Jacob Reger	" 1	" 30	61	20	6	Virginia	"	5s	15 5 0
James Schoolcraft	" 1	" 30	61	20	5 8	Virginia	"	5s	15 5 0
									£91 10 0

MUSTER ROLL OF CAPTAIN JOHN MORRIS' COMPANY OF RANGERS OF KANAWHA COUNTY, CALLED INTO SERVICE BY GENERAL HENRY KNOX, SECRETARY OF WAR, COMMENCING MAY 1, AND ENDING SEPTEMBER 30, 1791.

(*Source*—"Calendar of Virginia State Papers," Vol. V., pp. 475, 476.)

OFFICERS.

John Morris,............................Captain.
George Shaw, ...Lieutenant.
Andrew Lewis, ...Ensign.
Alexander Clendenin,..................Ensign.
Joseph McBride, ...Sergeant.
William Morris, ...Sergeant.
John Handsford, ...Sergeant.
George Roberts, ...Sergeant.

PRIVATES.

Thomas Upton,
David Johnston,
John Buckle,
Larkin Stone,
James Hale,
Thomas Allsbury, Sr.,
James Hazleton,
Lewis Lloyd,
William Miller,
Edmund Newhouse,
Leonard Morris,
Edward Price,
John Moss,
Reuben Slaughter,
Adonijah Mathews,
Henry Morris,
Charles Young,
John Jones,
William Droddy,
John Tacket,
John Bailey, Jr.,
Nathaniel Huddleston,
William Smith.
Rowland Wheeler,
Philip Juon,
John Wheeler,
Ezekiel Droddy,
William Pryer,
John Windsor,
John Sheppard,

Michael Newhouse,
John Morris, Jr.,
Charles McClurg,
Henry Newhouse,
Edward McClurg,
James Spencer,
William Hall,
William McCullum,
Joseph Graham,
George Alderson,
William Griffith.
William Carroll,
William Morris, Jr.,
Jonathan Windsor,
Conrad Young,
Joseph Edwards,
Levi Morris,
Thomas Allsbury, Jr.,
Archibald Caisey,
John Cavender,
Roland Wheeler,
John Childers,
Samuel White,
William Hughes,
Davis Alderson,
John Jenkins,
Carroll Morris,
Charles Allsbury,
John Sharp,
William Crain,

William Neel,
Joseph Burwell,
Thomas Sammons,
John Carter,
Benjamin Johnston,
Patrick Cockhern
   Cochran?)
Pleasant Wede,
Reuben Simmons,
Abram Barker,
Joseph Carroll,
Francis Watkins,
John Bailey,
William Rider,
Matthias Young,
Lewis Tacket,
Benjamin Morris,
Lewis Tacket, Jr.,
Edward Hughes,
Joseph Clymer,
Henry Bailey,
Mathew Wheeler,
Robert Juon,
John Caseboll,
Samuel Peoples,
Thomas Hughes,
Thomas Shirkey,
Thomas Hughes, Jr.,
Gabriel Jones,
John Edwards.

A ROLL OF CAPTAIN JOHN MORRIS' COMPANY OF RANGERS, CALLED INTO SERVICE MARCH 15TH, IN THE YEAR 1792, AND CONTINUED THEREIN TILL THE FIRST DAY OF JANUARY, 1793, IN KANAWHA COUNTY.

(*Source*—"Calendar of Virginia State Papers," Vol. VI., pp. 237, 238, 239, 240.)

NAMES.	RANK.	REMARKS.
John Morris	Captain	Performed his duty at his own Fort.
John Young	Lieutenant	At Colonel George Clendenin's station; brought his family from the Town where he resided, and which is one quarter of a mile from the Battallon.
Alexander Clendenin	Ensign	At Colonel George Clendenin's; made his crop at William Clendenin's, one mile from the station—his family at the station.
Ezekiel Droddy	Sergeant	At Captain John Morris', now Alden Station, Kanawha county; no family.
Abram Baker	"	At Colonel George Clendenin's; made his crop at his own place, three miles from the station—his family at the station.
Jacob Caster	"	At William Morris'; at mouth of Kelly's Creek, Kanawha county; a family in Rockingham.
David Millburn	Corporal	At same; no family.
Thomas Ashbury	"	At Captain John Morris'; made a crop there—his family there also.
Roland Wheeler	"	At Allyn Pryor's; no family; made a crop there.
Leonard Morris	"	At his own station part of the time, and part at William Morris'; his people moving with him.
John Edwards	"	At Colonel George Clendenin's; his family there, and made his crops on his own lotts, one quarter mile from the station.
Thomas Upton	Private	At Colonel George Clendenin's where he had his family, and made a crop on the Colonel's land, five miles from his own place.
Larkin Stone	"	At Colonel George Clendenin's; a single man, previously hired to labor by William Clendenin, where he assisted in making a crop.
Thomas Upton, Jr.	"	At Colonel George Clendenin's, five miles from his place of residence.
Joseph Burwell	"	At Colonel George Clendenin's; his place of residence; a single man.
Andrew Hamilton	"	At Colonel George Clendenin's; his place of residence; a single man.
Michael Newhouse	"	At Colonel George Clendenin's; his family at the station; made his crop a mile & quarter from Station.
Lewis Tacket, Sen.	"	At Colonel George Clendenin's, his family at the station; made his crop on his Town lotts.
Lewis Tacket, Jr.	"	At Michael Lee's, at Point Pleasant, till after Lee's death, then at Colonel George Clendenin's; a single man.
Francis Tacket	"	At Colonel George Clendenin's; a single man.
Pleasant Wade	"	At Colonel George Clendenin's; a single man.
Francis Watkins	"	At Colonel Andrew Donnally's; his residence in the Town.
William Miller	"	At Colonel Andrew Donnally's; no family.

Name	Rank	Description
William Droddy	Private	At Colonel Andrew Donnally's with his family, and made a crop on his own place, one mile off.
Thomas Smith	"	At Colonel Andrew Donnally's with his family, and made a crop there.
John Carter	"	At Captain John Morris'; a single man; wounded 15th July—3 wounds; cured by Mrs. Allsbury.
Charles Allsbury	"	At Captain John Morris'; has a family; made crop at Morris', (John).
Thomas Allsbury	"	At Captain John Morris'; has no family; made a crop at Morris', (John).
George Alderson	"	At Colonel Donnally's, with his family; made a crop at home over the River, 1 mile above.
Thomas Haman	"	At Captain John Morris' & George Alderson', who was part of his time at home.
John Shepherd	"	At Colonel Donnally's part of the time—at George Alderson's part of the time; was shot through the thigh and hand—cured by Mrs. Allsbury.
Edward Price	"	At Leonard Morris' with his family, and made a crop there—his own place over the River.
Henry Newhouse	"	At Leonard Morris'; no family.
Robert Lewis	"	At Leonard Morris'; with his family; made a crop there.
William Lewis	"	At Leonard Morris'; no family; staid in the county as a soldier, having no other business.
Joseph Carrol	"	At his home and William Morris' alternately.
William Carrol	"	At his father's, Joseph Carrol's.
Davy Alderson	"	At Joseph Carrol's, two miles from his own place, where he attempted to make a crop and failed.
John Moss	"	At Joseph Carrol's, no wife's father; made a crop on his own land, one mile off.
Henry Bailey	"	At Joseph Carrol's, no family; was a hired laborer by J. Carrol.
John Wheeler	"	At William Morris'; no family; supposed to be taken by the Indians on the 16th of October.
Matthew Wheeler	"	At William Morris'; no family; killed 16th October, 1792.
Allen Rice	"	At William Morris'; with his family; made a crop there, three-quarters of a mile from his home.
Joseph Clymer	"	At William Morris'; no family.
William Smith	"	At William Morris' with his family; concerned in the Boat Building.
Jonathan Hendson	"	same with his family; made his crop on Morris' land.
William Morris, Jr.	"	his father's, William Morris'.
John Jones	"	his home; keeps a Boatyard, &c.; part of his time at William Morris'.
John Jenkins	"	Jones'; a family; made a crop at his own place, one and one-half miles off.
Edward Hughes	"	At Captain William Morris'; no family; made a crop there.
John Campbell	"	At John Jones'; no family; made a crop on William Morris' place.
John Hansford	"	At Captain William Morris'; his wife's father; made a crop over the River one and one-quarter miles off.
Levi Morris	"	At John Jones'; a family; made a crop at home, about three miles off.
Nathan Huddleston	"	At his father's.
Daniel Tawney	"	At Allyn Pryor's.
Henry Morris	"	At Peter's Creek until his children were killed, then at Jones'.
Robert Irwin	"	At John Jones'; no family.
Joseph Edwards	"	At Gauley Foyd until the death of Morris' children, then at Jones'.
Daniel Huddleston	"	At William Morris'; made a crop at his own place, 12 miles up the River; his wife in Bedford.
Jonathan Kindson, Jr.	"	At William Morris'; with his father; a little boy 14.
Benjamin Morris	"	At John Jones'; made a crop at home about four miles off.

A Roll of Captain John Morris' Company of Rangers.—Continued.

NAMES.	RANK.	REMARKS.
John Huddleston	Private	At his father's.
Carrol Morris	"	Son of William.
John Cavender	"	At William Morris'; no family; concerned in the Boat Building.
John Bailey	"	At William Morris'; no family; a hireling to Morris.
Thomas Castor	"	At William Morris'; no family.
Thomas Salmons	"	With Benjamin & Levi Morris; no family.
Gabriel Jones	"	Son of John Jones; no family; made a crop at Jones'.
William Morris, Sr	"	At his own Fort; was returned one month longer than he ought to have been which appears from his letter to Col. Clendenin.
Matthias Young	"	At Peter's Creek with Henry Morris.
Charles Young	"	At Peter's Creek with Henry Morris; no family.
John Buckle	"	At Peter's Creek with Henry Morris; no family.
Amos Attwater	"	At Colonel Clendenin's generally; no family.
James Robinson	"	At Peter's Creek with Henry Morris; no family.
Edward Newhouse	"	At Colonel Clendenin's; no family; assisted his brother in making a crop one and one-quarter miles from the station.
On the back of the Roll.		
Samuel White	"	At William Morris'; carried his family to Jackson's River, where continued part of the time from May to October; William Morris' negro, Dudley, his substitute.
Henry Young	"	At Peter's Creek, with Henry Morris.
John Nugent	"	At William Morris'; no family.
Nathan Wheeler	"	At William Morris'; no family; made a crop two and one-half miles off with his father.
William Pryor	"	At home and at William Morris' alternately; made his crop at home.
Isaac Jenkins	"	With his father; John Jenkin's; a little boy, 14.
Thomas Hughes, Jr	"	At John Jones; made a crop six miles off.
Roland Wheeler	"	With his father; a little boy, 15.
James Shicky	"	At Captain William Morris' & Carrol's alternately; was killed 16th October, a few days after he went from Morris'.
		At John Jones'; no family; made a crop at Jones'.

PAY-ROLL OF SCOUTS OF HARRISON, RANDOLPH, AND MONONGALIA COUNTIES, AS ORDERED INTO SERVICE IN 1792, BY HENRY LEE, GOVERNOR OF VIRGINIA.

(*Source*—"Calendar of Virginia State Papers," Vol. VII. p. 469.)

COUNTIES.	NAMES.	COMMENCEMENT OF SERVICE.	TIME WHEN DISCHARGED.	NUMBER OF DAYS.
Harrison	Ellis Hughes	March 15, 1792	December 1, 1792	262
do	Robert Lowther	do	do	do
do	David Carpenter	do	do	do
do	Jonathan Coburn	March 29, 1792	do	248
do	John Hall	May 28, 1792	do	188
do	Thomas Herbert	do	do	do
do	Watson Clark	June 22, 1792	do	163
do	William Haymond	do	do	163
do	Christopher Carpenter	June 20, 1792	do	165
do	Obediah Davisson	do	do	do
Randolph	Valentine Stalnaker	March 15, 1792	do	262
do	Charles Parsons	do	do	262
do	George Westfall	March 27, 1792	do	250
do	John Jackson	June 10, 1792	September 1, 1792	159
do	William Gibson	June 12, 1792	December 1, 1792	173
do	William Westfall	do	do	do
do	Thomas Carney	September 19, 1792	do	74
Monongalia	Edward Pindale	June 16, 1792	November 30, 1792	168
do	Morgan Morgan	do	do	do
				3,755

3,755 days at 5s. per day equals 938.15s.

ABSTRACT OF THE ROLL OF CAPTAIN HUGH CAPERTON'S COMPANY OF RANGERS, ON DUTY ON THE FRONTIERS OF GREENBRIER AND KANAWHA COUNTIES, AS IT WAS MAY 6, 1792.

(*Source*—"Calendar of Virginia State Papers," Vol. V., pp. 536, 537.)

OFFICERS.

Hugh Caperton, Captain, of Greenbrier County.

PRIVATES.

James Shelley,	on service on the Greenbrier and Kanawha Frontier.							
Thomas Thompson,	"	"	"	"	"	"	"	
Robert McKee,	"	"	"	"	"	"	"	
James Lacy,	"	"	"	"	"	"	"	
Joseph Abbott,	"	"	"	"	"	"	"	
Isaac Cole,	"	"	"	"	"	"	"	
Matthias Meadows,	"	"	"	"	"	"	"	
George Paul,	"	"	"	"	"	"	"	
Laban Booten,	"	"	"	"	"	"	"	
John Jamieson,	"	"	"	"	Greenbrier Frontier.			
Mathew Medley,	"	"	"	"	"	"		
William Medley,	"	"	"	"	"	"		
John Dunn,	"	"	"	"	"	"		
John Harvee,	"	"	"	"	"	"		
Isaac Smith,	"	"	"	"	"	"		
Mathew Lamb,	"	"	"	"	"	"		
William Storms,	"	"	"	"	"	"		
John Harvee,	"	"	"	"	"	"		
Robert Lee,	"	"	"	"	"	"		
Nimrod Smith,	"	"	"	"	"	"	; a boy.	
George Swope,	"	"	"	"	"	"		
William Lee,	"	"	"	"	"	"		
Samuel Peck,	"	"	"	"	"	"		
Francis Farley,	"	"	"	"	"	"		
Thomas Weatt,	"	"	"	"	"	"		
Thomas Fulton,	"	"	"	"	"	"	; at home.	
Samuel McClung,	"	"	"	"	"	"	; at home	
Andrew McClung,	"	"	"	"	"	"		
Edward Farley,	"	"	"	"	"	"		
Thomas Patterson,	"	"	"	"	Kanawha	"		
William Dock,	"	"	"	"	"	"		
John Scott,	"	"	"	"	"	"		
William Hamrick,	"	"	"	"	"	"		
Felix Williams,	"	"	"	"	"	"		
Reuben Solomon,	"	"	"	"	"	"		
John Woodrum,	"	"	"	"	"	"		
Francis Kelly,	"	"	"	"	"	"		

Francis Farley,   "   "   "   "   "   "
Philip Lacy,   "   "   "   "   "   "
Joel Sturgeon, a scout; place of service not given.
James Haynes, a scout; place of service not given.

ROSTER OF CAPTAIN HUGH CAPERTON'S COMPANY OF RANGERS FROM GREENBRIER, KANAWHA, MONTGOMERY, AND WYTHE COUNTIES, AS REVIEWED BY COLONEL JOHN STEELE, MAY 27, 1793, AT FORT LEE AT THE MOUTH OF ELK ON THE GREAT KANAWHA RIVER.—NOW CHARLESTON, WEST VIRGINIA.

(*Source*—"Calendar of Virginia State Papers," Vol. VI. pp. 382, 383, 384.)

OFFICERS.

Hugh Caperton, Captain, of Greenbrier county.
Moses Mann, Lieutenant, of Greenbrier county.
Robert McKee, Sergeant, of Rockbridge county.
Isaac Cole, Corporal, of Greenbrier county.
David Johnson, Corporal, of Montgomery county.
Andrew Hatfield, Corporal, of Montgomery county.
William Morris, Jr., of Kanawha county.
James Stuart, Fifer, of Montgomery county.

PRIVATES.

Samuel Henderson,	of Greenbrier county.			
James Kelley,	"	"	"	
James Sweeny,	"	"	"	on furlough (married 9th May) twenty days.
William Storms,	"	"	"	married.
Francis Travers,	"	"	"	a boy.
Michael Burk,	"	"	"	a boy.
William Lee,	"	"	"	....
William Wilson,	"	"	"	....
Robert Lee,	"	"	"	a little boy.
Patrick Wilson,	"	"	"	....
John Smith,	"	"	"	....
James Ingram,	"	"	"	....
John Neill,	"	"	"	....
Peter Neill,	"	"	"	....
Matthias Meadows,	"	"	"	....
Moses Massey,	"	"	"	at John Morris' residence.
Henry Massey,	"	"	"	at District Court as witness.
Mathew Farley,	"	"	"	appointed a scout by Colonel John Steele.
Francis Farley,	"	"	"	at home all the winter.
Joseph Hilliard,	"	"	"	at Captain William Morris' residence.
Drewry Farley,	"	"	"	at home all winter.
Edward Farley,	"	"	"	Licken Stone as substitute, at A. W. Clendenin's.
Isaac Calloway,	"	"	"	at Leonard Morris'.
John Hubbard,	"	"	"	....
Lewis Booten,	"	"	"	aged 53.

Andrew Johnson,				
David Marshall,				
Alexander Curry,	"	"	"	at Captain John Morris'; received June 6th.
John Jamieson,	"	"	"	Andrew Hamilton being his substitute.
Henry Dickson,	"	"	"	....
John Lewis,	"	"	"	at home all winter.
Felix Williams,	"	"	"	absent on furlough.
John Conner,	"	"	"	....
Abner Lewis,	"	"	"	....
John Scott,	"	"	"	his substitute being Patrick McCool.
Lawrence Bryant,	"	"	"	....
William Graham,	"	"	"	appointed a scout by Colonel John Steele.
David Graham,	"	"	"	never mustered.
James Abbott,	"	"	"	absent on ———— villainy here.
Thomas LeMaster,	"	"	"	absent on command.
James Graham,	"	"	"	never mustered; a little boy.
Enoch Attwater,	"	"	"	....
Martin Hammick,	"	"	"	a scout.
William Dick,	"	"	"	....
George Huzzard,	"	"	"	....
David Milburn,	"	Kanawha	"	....
William Morris, Jr.,	"	"	"	....
Thomas Allsbury,	"	"	"	....
Samuel Thomas,	"	"	"	at A. W. Clendenin's.
Edward Hughes,	"	"	"	at A. W. Morris'.
Andrew Donnally,	"	"	"	at Colonel Donnally's on furlough.
Thomas Upton,	"	"	"	....
John Bailey,	"	"	"	at Captain William Morris'.
James Starkey,	"	"	"	at Captain William Morris'.
Jesse Van Bibber,	"	"	"	....
Thomas Carter,	"	"	"	at Captain William Morris'.
John Carter,	"	"	"	....
William Carroll,	"	"	"	....
John Morris,	"	"	"	a scout.
Thomas Allsbury, Jr.,	"	"	"	a scout.
Jonas Hatfield,	"	Montgomery	"	....
John Rue,	"	"	"	....
John Burton,	"	"	"	....
Isaac Smith,	"	"	"	married.
William Smith,	"	"	"	sick.
George Swope,	"	"	"	a boy; sick in Greenbrier county.
John Cock,	"	"	"	on furlough since 14th May.
Thomas Cook,				a boy.
John Garrison,	"	"	"	at Alderson's.
Joseph Canterbury,	"	"	"	....
David French,	"	"	"	a scout.
Andrew Lewis,	"	Shenandoah Valley	....
John Cavenaugh,	"	"	"	at Captain William Morris' residence.
Richard Nugent,	"	"	"	....
Joseph Burwell,	"	"	"	....
George Abbot,	"	Wythe county	....
John Sellards,	"	"	"	....
Stephen Tow,	"	Campbell	"	at A. W. Morris'.
Henry Montgomery,	"	Bedford	"	at Leonard Morris'.

PAY AND MUSTER-ROLL OF SCOUTS ORDERED INTO SERVICE BY BRIGADIER-GENERAL BIGGS, OF OHIO COUNTY, IN 1795, AND ATTACHED TO CAPTAIN WILLIAM LOWTHER'S COMPANY OF HARRISON COUNTY RANGERS, AS A PROTECTION AGAINST THE INDIANS.

(*Source*—"Calendar of Virginia State Papers," Vol. VIII, p. 401.)

NAMES.	WHEN IN SERVICE.	WHEN DISCHARGED.
Robert Bartlett	1795	January 1, 1796
Moses Hall	do	do
Elias Hughes	do	do
Henry Brandenbery	do	do
Moses Hewett	do	October 24, 1795
Daniel Rowell	do	do
Bird Lockhart	do	do

AN OBSERVATION.

Such were some of the early military organizations of West Virginia, which more than a hundred years ago, withstood the storm of savage warfare. The names and deeds of the men who formed their rank and file should never be forgotten. When the Indian wars were ended, these men went forth to conquer, not with the rifle, but with the axe, that they might subdue the wilderness, and thus not only found for themselves a home of peace, but a rich inheritance for their posterity. Their sons, many of them, served in Virginia Regiments in the Second War with England; and their grandsons, some of them, were with Scott and Taylor in Mexico. By the last census of the United States it was shown that of all the States, West Virginia had the highest per cent of native born population; thus showing that the descendants chose to remain where a soldier ancestry sleeps,—an ancestry largely representative of the people of the State today. Let us save the records.

CHAPTER VI.

WESTERN VIRGINIA SOLDIERS IN THE ARMY ORGANIZED FOR THE SUPPRESSION OF THE WHISKEY INSURRECTION IN WESTERN PENNSYLVANIA IN 1794.

(*Source*—"Papers Relating to the Whiskey Insurrection," printed in "Pennsylvania Archives," Second Series, Vol. IV.; Documents printed in "Calendar of Virginia State Papers;" Vol. VII.)

In the year 1794, there occurred in the valley of the Monongahela river and the region contiguous thereto a series of unlawful, violent, and insurrectionary acts to which, collectively, was applied the term ''The Whiskey Insurrection,'' a term which in that application has continued in use for more than a hundred years. This was indeed, the most important movement in the early history of our Republic, for it proved to be an example showing that the Federal Government was not a rope of sand which might be broken at the will of any section of the country, whenever a State or part of a State thought a particular law might be oppressive.

At this time all that part of the State of Pennsylvania, west of the Allegheny Mountains was included in the four counties of Allegheny, Fayette, Washington, Westmoreland, and on the Western part of Bedford. The population which then numbered about 80,000, were largely Scotch-Irish, or of that descent from the Cumberland Valley and Virginia, a people whose earlier home had been beyond the sea, in a land where whiskey was the national beverage. These men in Western Pennsylvania were agriculturists—producers of grain and fruits—but there were no markets for these, and they became largely distillers of spirituous liquors. So extensive was this business that it has been said that every sixth land-owner was a distiller.

Section Eight of Article I. of the Federal Constitution which became operative in 1789, provided that one of the duties of Congress should be, ''To lay and collect Taxes, Duties, Imposts, and Excises, to pay the debts and provide for the common Defence and general Welfare of the United States.'' In compliance with this, Congress upon the recommendation of Alexander Hamilton, Secretary of the Treasury, passed ''An Act laying Duties on Distilled Spirits within the United States.'' This was approved March 3,

1791, and by its provisions the United States were divided into fourteen districts—one State in each—in each of which there was to be appointed a "Supervisor of the Revenue," under whose management all collections of the revenue were to be made. Each District was sub-divided into "Surveys of Inspection" with an Inspector in each, all under the direction of the Supervisors of the Revenue. Further, it was provided that after June 30, 1791, there should be paid on every gallon of spirits distilled in the United States from any article of the growth or produce of the United States, duties ranging from nine to twenty-five cents according to per cent below or above proof. When the provisions of this law became known, there was great dissatisfaction therewith; and the people of Western Pennsylvania agreed to not only remonstrate, but to resist the enforcement of the law. This marked the beginning of the famous Whiskey Insurrection, the crisis of which—that of armed resistance—was reached in the autumn of 1794.

Liberty poles were erected throughout all the insurrectionary districts, and on them floated banners with the significant words, "Liberty; No Excise; Death to Traitors." Any man who refused to assist in erecting a liberty pole was deemed an enemy to the common cause. David Bradford, with the rank of Major-General, was at the head of the insurrectionary army. He desired to secure the co-operation of the people of the counties—Monongalia, Ohio, Harrison and Randolph—in Northwestern Virginia. In an effort to do this he issued the following:—

ADDRESS TO THE INHABITANTS OF MONONGALIA COUNTY.

Washington, (County, Pa.) *August* 6, 1794.

Gentlemen:—I presume you have heard of the spirited opposition given to the excise law of this State. Matters have been so brought to pass here, that all are under the necessity of bringing their minds to a final conclusion. This has been the question amongst us some days: Shall we disapprove of the conduct of those engaged against Neville, the excise officer, or approve? Or in other words, shall we suffer them to fall a sacrifice to Federal Prosecution, or shall we support them? On the result of this business we have fully deliberated and have determined with head, heart, hand and voice that we will support the opposition to the excise law. The crisis is now come, submission or opposition. We are determined in the opposition. We are determined in future to act agreeably to system, to form arrangements, guided by reason, prudence, fortitude and spirited conduct. We have proposed a general meeting of the four counties of Pennsylvania, and have invited our brethren in the neighboring counties of Virginia to come forward and join us in council

and deliberation on this important crisis, and conclude upon measures interesting to the western counties of Pennsylvania and Virginia. A notification of this kind may be seen in the Pittsburg paper. Parkinson's Ferry is the place proposed, as most central, and the 14th of August the time. We solicit you (by all the ties that an union of interest can suggest) to come forward to join with us in our deliberations. The cause is common to us all; we invite you to come, even should you differ from us in opinion; we wish you to hear our reasons influencing our conduct.   Yours with esteem,
          DAVID BRADFORD.
See "Pennsylvania Archives," Second Series, Vol. IV. pp. 111, 112.

A few days later a body of men from Western Pennsylvania entered Morgantown, Monongalia county, West Virginia, where Edward Smith, was Collector of Revenue. That official fled to Winchester in the Shenandoah Valley, where he wrote Edward Carrington, Supervisor of the Revenue, at Richmond, and said:—[1]

"I am threatened from all quarters in my own county, and the Pennsylvanians came into our Town and ordered me to give up my papers, or they would come and destroy them with all of my property. In the meantime, no collection can go on, as our distillers will not pay until they see the event."

When Governor Henry Lee had information of the condition in the valley of the Monongahela, he, on August 20, 1794, issued the following:—

PROCLAMATION BY THE GOVERNOR OF VIRGINIA.

"Whereas I have received information that a banditti from the Western parts of Pennsylvania have in defiance of law and order, passed into this Commonwealth, and by threats and other evil doings compelled an officer of the United States living in Morgan Town, in the County of Monongalia, to abandon his home and seek personal safety by flight; And whereas I have reason to believe that the said banditti are a part of that deluded combination of men described in the President's proclamation of the 7th day of this present month, who, forgetful of all obligations human and divine, seem intent only on rapine and anarchy, and therefore endeavor by their emissaries and other illegal means to seduce the good people of this Commonwealth inhabiting the Country bordering on the State of Pennsylvania, to unite with them in schemes and measures tending to destroy the tranquility and order which so happily prevails, and thereby to convert the blessings we so eminently enjoy under our free and equal government into the most afflicting miseries which can possibly befall the human race.

To arrest these wicked designs; to uphold the majesty of the law; to preserve our fellow citizens from evil and our country from disgrace, I

---

1. "Calendar of Virginia State Papers," Vol. VII, pp. 265, 266.

have thought proper, by and with the advice of the council of State, to issue this, my proclamation calling on all officers, civil and military, to exercise with zeal, diligence, and firmness, every legal power vested in them respectively for the purpose of detecting and bringing to trial every offender or offenders in the premises.

And I do moreover specially require and enjoin that all persons coming into this Commonwealth from that part of our sister State, at present so unhappily distracted, be particularly watched, and if they shall be found disseminating their wicked and pernicious doctrines, or in any way exciting a spirit of disobedience to government, thereby violating the peace and dignity of this Commonwealth, that they be immediately apprehended and dealt with according to law.

Given under my hand as Governor, and under the seal of the Commonwealth, at Richmond, this twentieth day of August, in the year of our Lord one thousand seven hundred and ninety-four, and of the Commonwealth the nineteenth.   HENRY LEE.[2]

Accompanying this proclamation was the following circular letter from Governor Lee to the Delegates, Militia Commandants, Courts, and Commandants of Volunteer Militia, from the District of Monongalia, and also Brigadier-General Benjamin Biggs:—

Richmond, Virginia,
SIRS: August 20, 1794.

You will readily discover from the enclosed Proclamation how very solicitous the executive are to save their fellow citizens and Country from the horrors and disgrace which afflict and defame a sister State; and you will perceive our apprehensions that the Insurgents may, by their acts and emissaries, mislead some of our Countrymen, unless counter-exertions are made in time by the good and influential citizens.

In this situation, I not only forward to you by express the endorsed act of Government, but also address you particularly, entreating you to prove your duty to the Commonwealth, love of order, and love of Country, to avail yourself of every means in your power to counteract the latent designs of your deluded neighbors, and to bring to punishment all who openly in any manner, violate the Peace and Dignity of the Commonwealth.

Disagreeable as it is to point the bayonet against the breast of a fellow citizen, it is still more so to obey the mob, and therefore, but one opinion prevails among all orders of people in every part of the State from which I have as yet heard, viz: detestation of the Pennsylvania Insurgents; of their principles, and actions and determination to compel their submission to legal authority.

Orders have been issued for a large detachment of our militia to march under the command of General [Daniel] Morgan, at a moment's warning and the whole body of militia are ready to follow, was the same necessary.

---

2. "Calendar of Virginia State Papers," Vol. 7, pp. 265-266.

With reliance on your due exertions and confidence that my fellow citizens of your county will act the part which our common good and common happiness so strongly dictates, I remain, etc.,

HENRY LEE.3

The proclamation and circular letter of Governor Lee were borne by an express rider, who on his arrival at Morgantown, was to deliver them to Hon. Thomas Wilson. From the following letter we learn of the delivery of these documents:—

LETTER FROM COLONEL WILLIAM McCREERY, OF MONONGALIA COUNTY, IN REPLY TO THAT OF GOVERNOR LEE.

Morgan Town, Va.

SIRS: 28th of Aug. 1794.

Your express arrived here today with sundry letters addressed to the care of Mr. Thomas Wilson, who happened not to be at home; thinking it right (in this alarming time) I received the Papers & Passed a receipt for them. Mr. Wilson will be at home tomorrow & no doubt will send them instantly forward to their address.

We are all in this, Harrison & Randolph counties in Peace, & also Ohio with some exceptions; a state of neutrality is all we are able to support, and, indeed, we are in this town much threatened now for lying still by our Powerful neighbors. However I trust we will support it until the Government takes measures to bring about Peace—the Commissioners who attended at Pittsburg, by order of the President of the United States, and also by order of the Governor of Pennsylvania, but nothing has yet transpired that can be relied upon; a Committee of 12 men from the insurgents met them, and it is reported that no terms but a repeal of the Excise Law will be accepted by the People—however this is only report. I am in heast Sir.

Your Excellency's Most Obedient Servant,

WILLIAM McCREERY.4

A UNITED STATES ARMY ORGANIZED FOR THE SUPPRESSION OF THE INSURRECTION.

Meantime, the insurrection grew apace, and the National Government, and the State of Pennsylvania as well, had sent commissioners to Pittsburg, for the purpose of adjusting matters so as to secure the enforcement of the law. This resulted in failure and resort to arms became necessary on the part of the Government. President Washington issued a call for troops to be raised and

---

3. "Governor's Letter Book. No. 63, pp. 487, 488;" in Virginia State Library.
4. "Executive Papers of Virginia", August Files, 1794; in Virginia State Library.

equipped in the States of Pennsylvania, New Jersey, Maryland, and Virginia, as follows:—

	Infantry.	Cavalry.	Artillery.	Total.
Pennsylvania	4,500	500	200	5,200
New Jersey	1,500	500	100	2,100
Maryland	2.000	200	150	2,350
Virginia	3,000	300	...	3,300
	11,000	1,500	450	12,950

THE MILITARY ESTABLISHMENT OF VIRGINIA.

The military establishment of Virginia in 1794, was that provided for in the Acts of Assembly passed December 22, 1792, and December 2, 1793. This consisted of four Divisions, the third of which embraced all the regimental organizations then existing in what is now West Virginia. Of this Division Major-General Daniel Morgan, of Revolutionary fame, was the commander. This Division was composed of seven Brigades, viz: the Seventh of four Regiments; the Tenth of nine Regiments; the Thirteenth of nine Regiments; the Sixteenth of four Regiments; the Seventeenth of nine Regiments; the Eighteenth of three Regiments; and the Nineteenth of five Regiments. Of these Regiments the 4th was in Ohio county; the 11th in Harrison county; the 14th in Hardy; the 46th in Pendleton; the 55th and 67th in Berkeley; the 77th in Hampshire; the 76th and 104th in Monongalia; the 79th in Greenbrier; the 80th in Kanawha; the 103d in Ohio, but afterward in Brooke; and the 108th in Greenbrier, but afterward in Monroe. Of these the 4th, 11th, 76th, 103d, 104th, and 107th formed the Tenth Brigade, of which Brigadier-General Benjamin Biggs, of Ohio county, was the commander, and Robert McClure of the same county, was Brigade Inspector. The 79th and 80th were in the Thirteenth Brigade commanded by General John Bowyer of Botetourt county, the Brigade Inspector being Stephen Trigg of the same county. The 55th and 67th were in the Sixteenth Brigade, Brigadier-General William Darke, of Berkeley county, commanding The 108th belonged the same county, being the Brigade Inspector. The 14th, 46th, and the 77th, formed the Eighteenth Brigade, Brigadier-General Joseph Neville, of Hardy county commanding. The 108th belonged to the Nineteenth Brigade. Such was the organization of the Western Virginia troops.

On the 15th of August, 1794, Governor Lee in his capacity of Commander-in-Chief of the Military Establishment of Virginia, issued a "General Order" stating that the President of the United States had called upon the Commonwealth for three thousand Infantry, and three hundred Cavalry for immediate service. By this Order these troops were to form a Division commanded by General Daniel Morgan, and be divided into two Brigades, that from the eastern part of the State, to be under Brigadier General James Mathews of Norfolk; the other composed of western men to be under command of General William Darke. of Berkeley county. the Commandant of the Sixteenth Brigade of the 3rd Division. In this Order the 4th Regiment in Ohio county; the 11th in Harrison county; the 76th in Monongalia county; the 79th in Greenbrier county; and the 80th in Kanawha county; were exempted from furnishing any of the levies for the suppression of the Whiskey Insurrection, "because they consist of frontier inhabitants who are exposed to constant Indian warfare." Thus it is seen that with the exception of these West Virginia Regiments, General Morgan must get his Western men from the 103d Regiment of Ohio county; the 104th of Monongalia; the 107th of Randolph; of Brigadier General Biggs' 10th Brigade; the 14th of Hardy; the 46th of Pendleton, and the 77th of Hampshire, composing the 18th Brigade of General Joseph Neville: and the 55th and 67th of Berkeley county, which belonged to General William Darke's 16th Brigade. Meantime, the President had made another requisition on Virginia for an additional fifteen hundred troops which brought her total levies up to four thousand eight hundred men. Winchester in the Shenandoah valley, was made the place of rendezvous for the eastern men, while Moorefield in Hardy county, was designated as the place of rendezvous for the western men.

GENERAL ORDERS ISSUED BY MAJOR-GENERAL MORGAN.

The Brigades composing the First Division are immediately to furnish three thousand and forty-one men, officers included, properly equipped, and ready to march at a moment's warning. As no accurate returns have been made to the Adjutant-General's office, the Commander-in-Chief has ordered that each Brigade shall furnish an equal number of men: General Darke's Brigade will therefore furnish six hundred and nine men; General Zane's Brigade, six hundred and eight men; General Bigg's Brigade, six hundred and eight men; and General Bowyer's Brigade, six hundred and eight men. In the formation of the several corps the Brigades will be pleased to pay due attendance to the General Orders of the 20th of June. They are also requested to comply as early as possible with the General Orders of the 19th of June. Mr. Thomas Parker is appointed Aid-de-camp to the General, and is to be respected and obeyed as such. He is ordered to furnish the commanding officers of the Brigades with the General Orders referred to.

DANIEL MORGAN.
Major-General, Third Division.
"Saratoga" August 23, 1795.5

Of the men thus called into service by Major-General Morgan, fully twelve hundred were from Military Organizations then existing within the present limits of West Virginia. How many of these men reported at the rendezvous at Moorefield, we do not know —probably all of them. In this connection the following item, bearing date Sept. 4, 1794, and appearing on page 293, of Volume VII. of the "Calendar of Virginia State Papers," is of much interest to the student of our State History:—

"Money advanced Brigadier-General Biggs on an estimate of Expence, which may probably be increased, for provision in marching 308 men from his Brigade to Moorefield, being about 60 miles, supposed to cost 7d. each per day, and to require 4 days, going 15 miles per day, including lost time for rest... £35.19.0
4 Baggage and provision wagons finding themselves 4 days, at
15s. per day each going................................... 12:00.0
Ditto for returning empty, 25 miles per day................. 9:00.0

£56.19.0

Who were these three hundred and eight men who belonged to the Brigade commanded by Brigadier-General Biggs, and whom he marched to Moorefield? Evidently they composed the levies from the 11th and 107th Regiments in Harrison and Randolph counties. The whole number of troops which rendezvoused at Moorefield, proceeded to Cumberland, Maryland, where they joined the other Virginia troops, with whom they marched into Western Pennsylvania. Governor Henry Lee was Commander-in-Chief of the army composed of the men from the States previously mentioned, and when the order was issued for this army to return, he detailed General Morgan with twenty-five hundred men, to remain in the vicinity of Pittsburg during the winter of 1794-95. A portion of these at least were evidently the West Virginians belonging to Brigadier-General Darke's Brigade. No rolls or Rosters of them have been found, but

---
5. See The Virginia Chronicle and Advertiser, September 1, 1794.

these—some of them at least—may be deposited in the Archives of the War Department, and may hereafter be printed.

CHAPTER VII.

WEST VIRGINIANS IN THE SECOND WAR WITH ENGLAND—THE WAR OF 1812—CORRESPONDENCE CONNECTED THEREWITH.

WEST VIRGINIA COUNTIES IN THE MILITARY ESTABLISHMENT OF VIRGINIA IN THE WAR OF 1812, AS ARRANGED UNDER ACT OF ASSEMBLY, JANUARY 28, 1804.

(*Source*—Organization of the Militia of the State of Virginia. A Bulletin issued from the office of Moses Green, Adjutant-General of the Commonwealth, June 1, 1814.)

"We trusted to the moral feeling of the country x x x x Nor had the war, that of 1812, continued, would that trust have been in vain—But while the war lasted, did it furnish no evidence of the common sympathy which binds the West to the East? x x xThere was not a mountain, a river, a valley of the West that did not respond with animation, to this appeal to the patriotism of Virginia. 'At the cry of invasion and danger from the East, every man of the West from the summit of the Blue Ridge to the shores of the Ohio, capable of bearing arms, mounted his horse, strapped on his knapsack and turned his face from home—there was no distinction of the rich from the poor. Gentlemen who had occupied conspicuous places in our halls of legislation—the ploughman from fresh fallow field—officers, soldiers, and citizens—all moved with one accord. In a fortnight, 15,000 men were mustered in sight of Richmond among them the largest body of cavalry that was ever reviewed in our portion of the continent. In one morning a thousand of them were discharged as supernumeraries. On their return home they met on the mountains the eagles of the West still sweeping their flight to the East. Their course was turned to their mountains, only when danger had ceased." Speech of Charles Fenton Mercer in the Constitutional Convention of Virginia, delivered, Thursday, November 5, 1829.—Journal p. 203.

The following exhibits the names of West Virginia counties then existing; the number of the Regiment in each with number of the Brigade and Division to which each of said Regiments belonged; together with Names of Colonels and Majors, and dates of their Commissions.

COUNTIES.	DIVISION.	BRI-GADE.	REGI-MENT.	REGIMENTAL OFFICERS.	DATE OF COMMISSION.
Berkeley	3d	16th	67th	Colonel Elisha Boyd, jr.	July 22, 1807.
do	do	do	do	Major Andrew Waggoner	July 22, 1807.
do	do	do	do	Major Dougald Campbell	December 27, 1809.
Brooke	do	do	10th	103d	Colonel John Connell	March 27, 1799.
do	do	do	do	Major Garrett Snediker	January 6, 1812.
do	do	do	do	Major George Swearingen	January 6, 1812.
Cabell	do	do	13th	120th	Colonel Elisha McComas	July 5, 1813.
do	do	do	do	Major Manoah Bostick	July 6, 1809.
do	do	do	do	Major Samuel Smiley	July 5, 1813.
Greenbrier	2d	do	do	79th	Colonel Thomas Beard	April 18, 1811.
do	do	do	do	Major James W. Mathews	January 18, 1809.
do	do	do	do	Major Andrew McClung	April 18, 1811.
Hampshire	do	18th	77th	Colonel William Vanse	September 19, 1807,
do	do	do	do	Major Daniel Collins	May 11, 1802.
do	do	do	do	Major Isaac Means	June 25, 1813
do	do	do	114th	Colonel Samuel Porter	October 13, 1807.
do	do	do	do	Major John Higgins	October 13, 1807.
do	do	do	do	Major John Sargent	November 8, 1808.
Hardy	do	do	14th	Colonel Jacob VanMetre	December 6, 1809.
do	do	do	do	Major Isaac Chrisman	December 6, 1809.
do	do	do	do	Major Daniel Shobe	June 20, 1812.
Harrison	3d	20th	11th	Colonel Benjamin Wilson	July 21, 1810.
do	do	do	do	Major James Pindall	May 17, 1808.
do	do	do	do	Major Daniel Morris	December 29, 1810.
do	do	do	119th	Colonel Isaac Coplin	February 3, 1812.
do	do	do	do	Major Mathias Winters	January 26, 1810.
do	do	do	do	Major John Somerville	February 3, 1812.
Jefferson	do	do	16th	55th	Colonel Joseph Crane	June 25, 1810.
do	do	do	do	Major Van Rutherford	December 22, 1808.
do	do	do	do	Major James Hite	June 25, 1810.
Kanawha	do	do	13th	80th	Colonel David Ruffner	March 30, 1814.
do	do	do	do	Major John Stark	December 17, 1813.
do	do	do	do	Major Claudius Buster	March 30, 1814.
Mason	do	do	do	106th	Colonel John Henderson	May 20, 1814.
do	do	do	do	Major Peter Hogg	July 2, 1810.
do	do	do	do	Major John Cantrell	May 20, 1814.
Monongalia	do	do	10th	108th	Colonel James Scott	November 2, 1812.
do	do	do	do	Major John West	July 25, 1808.
do	do	do	do	Major John Laugh	September 30, 1813.
do	do	do	do	104th	Colonel James McGrew	March 23, 1812.
do	do	do	do	Major Benjamin Shaw	January 14, 1813.
do	do	do	do	Major Nathaniel Ashby	December 2, 1813.
do	do	do	76th	Colonel John Fairfax	January 1, 1814.
do	do	do	do	Major Rawley Scott	May 28, 1811.
do	do	do	do	Major Charles Byrne	January 1, 1814.
Monroe	do	do	19th	108th	Colonel Richard Shanklin	May 1, 1811.
do	do	do	do	Major Samuel Clark	March 13, 1809.
do	do	do	do	Major Conrad Peters	September 16, 1811.
Ohio	do	do	10th	4th	Colonel Archibald Woods	December 5, 1809.
do	do	do	do	Major Benjamin Jeffey	February 7, 1814.
do	do	do	do	Major Lewis Bonnett	February 7, 1814.
do	do	do	10th	123d	Colonel Moses Shepherd	February 7, 1814.
do	do	do	do	Major Jonathan Prudy	February 7, 1814.
do	do	do	do	Major John Witten	February 7, 1814.
Pendleton	2d	do	18th	46th	Colonel John Hopkins	July 21, 1806.
do	do	do	do	Major William McCoy	July 21, 1806.
do	do	do	do	Major Peter Hull	July 27, 1807.
Randolph	3d	do	20th	107th	Colonel Isaac Boothe	December 10, 1807.
do	do	do	do	Major John Crouch	August 30, 1806.
do	do	do	do	Major Hiram Goff	December 10, 1807.
Wood	do	do	do	113th	Colonel John Stokeley	June 27, 1809.
do	do	do	do	Major Thomas Tavenner	June 27, 1809.
do	do	do	do	Major Jacob Beeson	January 26, 1810.

A Declaration of War.

On the 18th of June, 1812, Congress passed an Act declaring: "That War be and the same is hereby declared to exist between the United Kingdoms of Great Britain and Ireland, and the dependencies thereof, and the United States of America and their Territories." Of this the President, James Madison, on the next day made proclamation thereof.

A Requisition on Virginia for Troops.—Letter of William Eustis, Secretary of War, to Governor Barbour.

War Department,
April 15, 1812.

I am instructed by the President of the United States to call upon the Executives of the several States to take effectual measures to organize, arm, and equip according to Law, and hold in readiness to march at a moment's warning their respective proportions of one hundred thousand Militia—officers included. * * *

This, therefore, is to require of your Excellency to take effectual means for having Twelve thousand of the Militia of Virginia (being her quota) detached and fully organized in Companies, Battalions, Regiments, Brigades, and Divisions within the shortest period that circumstances will permit, and as nearly as possible in the following proportions of Artillery, Cavalry, and Infantry, viz.: One-twentieth part of Artillery; one-twentieth part of Cavalry, and the residue Infantry. There will, however, be no objection on the part of the President of the United States to the admission of a proportion of Riflemen duly organized in distinct corps, and not exceeding one-tenth part of the whole quota of the States respectively. Each Corps should be properly armed and equipped for actual service. * * * *

I am, &c.

Four days after the receipt of the above—April 19, 1812—Governor Barbour issued "General Orders," to the Brigadier-Generals of the State Military Establishment, thus calling into service the quotas of each Brigade sufficient in number to make twelve thousand men as required from the Commonwealth by the President of the United States. The Companies, thus called into service from Virginia counties, now embraced in West Virginia, were as follows; that is to say :—

1. Captain Willson's Rifle Company attached to the 76th Regiment of Monongalia County; estimated at 50 men.
2. Captain Morgan's Rifle Company attached to the 104th Regiment of Monongalia County; estimated at 50 men.

3. Captain Pugh's Rifle Company attached to the 103d Regiment of Brooke County, estimated at 50 men.
4. Captain Simmon's Rifle Company attached to the 120th Regiment of Cabell County, estimated at 50 men.
5. Captain Van Sickle's Rifle Company attached to the 106th Regiment of Mason County, estimated at 50 men.
6. Captain Kerney's Rifle Company attached to the 55th Regiment of Jefferson County, estimated at 50 men.
7. Captain Mason's Rifle Company attached to the 67th Regiment of Berkeley County, estimated at 50 men.
8. Captain Bodkin's Rifle Company attached to the 46th Regiment of Pendleton County, estimated at 50 men.
9. Captain Heiskell's Rifle Company attached to the 77th Regiment of Hampshire County, estimated at 50 men.
10. Captain Peck's Rifle Company attached to the 11th Regiment of Harrison County, estimated at 50 men.
11. Captain James Faulkner's Artillery Company attached to the 67th Regiment of Berkeley County, estimated at 50 men.

Each of the above counties to furnish one Colonel, one Major, and a due proportion of Captains, Lieutenants, Ensigns, non-commissioned officers, musicians, etc., and allowing 60 men, (officers included) to each company.

Then the Governor added: "It would be a source of pride and exultation to Virginia were her sons, animated by that heroic spirit and love of Country the distinguishing characteristics of their character, in this important crisis, to come forward and make a tender of their services. * * * Should this event happen, and it is confidently anticipated, such tenders to be accepted; and should the number of Volunteers exceed the quota of the respective Brigades, their services may nevertheless be previously accepted, subject to the pleasure of the Executive."[2] The Western Virginians took advantage of this last proposition and there was witnessed the scene described in the extract from the speech of Charles Fenton Mercer, appearing at the head of this chapter.

THE WESTERN VIRGINIA BRIGADE WITH GENERAL HARRISON IN THE NORTHWESTERN ARMY.

Previous to the Declaration of War General William Hull with about two thousand men was ordered to proceed to Detroit. This army arrived at the head of Lake Erie, about the time the war was declared. General Hull, after concentrating his forces at Detroit

---

2. Governor's Letter Book, 1811-1812, pp. 242-249, in Virginia State Library.

crossed over the river to Sandwich and issued a Proclamation to the inhabitants of Canada. In this he said:—

"The Army under my command has invaded your country; and the standard of the Union now waves over the territory of Canada. To the peaceable, unoffending inhabitants, it brings neither danger nor difficulty. I come to find enemies, not to make them. I come to protect, not to injure you."

On the 10th of July Colonels Cass and Miller, attempted to surprise a British post, three hundred strong, distant about five miles from Malden; a slight skirmish ensued when the British retreated, leaving eleven men killed and wounded on the field; and the Americans returned to their headquarters at Sandwich. The British returned to post from which they had fled, and there was skirmishing on the 19th and 20th with trifling success on either side. Previous to leaving Detroit, large bodies of Indians tendered him their services, but he stated that he was not authorized to accept them, and that he wished them to remain silent spectators, and not engage on either side; but this was not their choice, and they at once crossed over to Malden where they were accepted and put into service of the British. Then, too, British forces arrived at Amherstburg, eighteen miles below Detroit, at which place Major-General Isaac Brock made his headquarters. An advance was made by the British and Indians in great force; and the Americans recrossed the river to Detroit on the 8th of August. Here they were besieged and attacked. On the 15th General Brock demanded the immediate surrender of Fort Detroit. To this General Hull replied by saying: "I am prepared to meet any force which you may have at your disposal." This proved to be untrue, for, on the next day he surrendered the American Army prisoners of war.[3] Thus Detroit and all Michigan Territory passed under the British dominion. Of this General Brock made immediate proclamation.

CALL FOR FIFTEEN HUNDRED TROOPS FROM WESTERN VIRGINIA.

Intelligence of the disaster at Detroit reached Washington before the end of August, and the Government at once resolved to recover Detroit, and the Michigan Territory, and thus save the Northwest to the Union. With this object in view it was resolved to create a Northwestern Army to be under the command of General William

---

3. Official Documents in "Historical Register of the United States," Vol. II. pp. 50, 51.

Henry Harrison. It was to be composed of men from Kentucky, Ohio, and Western—now West Virginia.

On the 1st day of September, 1812—sixteen days after the surrender of General Hull—William Eustis, Secretary of War, wrote Governor James Barbour, of Virginia, as follows::

War Department,
September 1, 1812.

SIR:—

I am commanded by the President to request your Excellency to call out, arm and equip fifteen hundred of the detached Militia Infantry of Virginia as soon as practicable

This force is destined to co-operate with the Northwestern army, and it is submitted to your Excellency to have the troops detached and rendezvoused at such part of the State as you may judge most convenient for their march to the western frontier of Ohio.

The recent issues of arms, equipments, and Camp equipage, render it necessary to require these troops should furnish themselves, or be supplied for their march from the Arsenals of the State.

I am, &c.

Governor Barbour hastened to comply with the request of the President and on the day on which this was received, he issued an order or proclamation providing for the formation of a Western Virginia Brigade, as follows:—

GENERAL ORDERS ISSUED BY GOVERNOR JAMES BARBOUR, SEPTEMBER 3, 1812, CALLING INTO THE FIELD 1,500 WESTERN VIRGINIA SOLDIERS TO AID IN RETRIEVING THE LOSS IN THE NORTHWEST BY THE SURRENDER OF GENERAL HULL.

Council Chamber (Richmond, Va.)
September 3, 1812.

"In obedience to the request of the President of the United States, signified to the Secretary of War, by his letter bearing date the 1st current, I have thought proper to require the following portion of the late requisition, agreeably to my orders of the 19th of April last, making in the aggregate 1500 men forthwith to take the field and repair to Point Pleasant, in the county of Mason, on the Ohio River, established hereby, as the place of General Rendezvous for the said detachment, viz:

The whole of the Infantry, of the line, Light Infantry, and Riflemen, detached from the 10th and 20th Brigades.

Also the whole of the detachment of Infantry of the Line, Light Infantry, and Riflemen,

From the 4th Regiment in Ohio county.
" " 14th Regiment in Hardy county.
" " 76th and 118th Regiments in Monongalia county.

" " 77th and 114th Regiments in Hampshire county.
" " 79th Regiment in Greenbrier county.
" " 80th Regiment in Kanawha county.
" " 103d Regiment in Brooke county.
" " 106th Regiment in Mason county.
" " 107th Regiment in Randolph county.
" " 120th Regiment in Cabell county.

And Captain James G. Laidley's company of Volunteers, of the 113th Regiment in Wood county."

BRIGADIER-GENERAL AND FIELD OFFICERS.

This detachment will be under the command of:

Brigadier-General Joel Leftwich, of Bedford county.
Colonel John Connell, of the 103d Regiment, Brooke county.
Colonel Dudley Evans, of the 76th Regiment, Monongalia county.
Major Samuel McQuire, of the 77th Regiment, Hampshire county.
Major David Scott, of the 4th Regiment, Ohio county.
Major James W. Mathews, of the 79th Regiment, Greenbrier county.
Major Jacob Beeson, of the 113th Regiment, Wood county.

The Commandants of Regiments from which companies are drawn, will provide for the transportation of the baggage, belonging to each company, either by water or land, as may best promote the public service, having regard to expedition, and the nature of the country thro' which the troops must pass. Should there be any difficulty in procuring the necessary means of conveyance, together with such camp equipage, as prescribed by the 43d section of the Militia law of the 28th of January, 1804, the Commandants will resort to the impressment, as authorized by that section.

Until the troops shall arrive at the place of rendezvous, where they will be furnished by a regular contractor, the Captains of the respective companies are to provide the necessary supplies, and draw on the paymaster, to be stationed at Point Pleasant, for the amount.

The Riflemen will take with them their rifles and accoutrements, in complete order. Should any rifle company, however, be unprovided with arms, the Commandant of the Regiment to which it is attached, is to place in its hands the best public arms belonging to the Regiment. The Infantry of the line and Light Infantry, will go unarmed to the general rendezvous, to which place one thousand and fifty stand of muskets, of the best quality, with the necessary accoutrements, will be forthwith sent, ready to be placed in their hands, on their arrival.

Tents and knapsacks will be immediately sent to Point Pleasant, (from Richmond) for the accommodation of the troops.

Brigadier-General Leftwich, will organize the detachment into Regiments and Battalions, as soon as his force shall be concentrated; and will wait the orders of the Secretary of War."

Here Governor Barbour inserted the following address:

CITIZEN SOLDIERS OF WESTERN VIRGINIA!

"Your country, after submitting to every insult and injury from Great Britain, which power, guided by injustice, could offer, or inflict,—after having essayed, in vain, every attempt to procure redress, which was calculated to influence a nation, which respected either justice or honor,—after practising a degree of forbearance which, whilst it testified her solicitude for peace, exposed her character to a humiliating imputation, appealed to Arms. In the moderation of our government will be found, the most conclusive evidence that this solemn appeal originated neither from the thirst of glory, nor the wish for conquest, but from a solicitude to maintain our honor free from pollution, and our rights from invasion. It was a measure not only dictated by necessity, but called for by the people, and is emphatically their War.

The first effort has failed of success—Gen. Hull and his army are prisoners of War!—Your implacable enemy contemptuously disregarding the dictates of honorable warfare have again called to their aid their old allies, the Indians, and have acquired thereby a temporary success. Our Western Frontier is laid bare to their inroads. Our women and children are exposed to the ruthless vengeance of the savage, who thirsting for blood, are advancing on, holding in one hand the tomahawk, that never spared,—in the other, brandishing the burning torch. To shield them from these calamities, our Brothers of the Wilderness call for our aid.—Rise, my beloved countrymen, obey this sacred summons, and rally around the unfurled banner of your country.—Confiding in the justice of your cause,—reposing upon the aid of Providence, with your arms nerved with your Country's wrongs, and with the Glory of our ancestors beaming from the fields of Saratoga, Eutaw, and York, a sacred light illuminating your path,—advance,—meet the perfidious foe, strike him home, and by a severe lustration, wipe off the stain upon the character of our country.

The present crisis is in travail with our future destines and calls for an exertion and energy proportionate to the occasion. Our enemies, foreign and internal, indulge in unhallowed auguries; they impiously foretell the destruction of our government, and the ruin of our cause. They revel, by anticipation, in our misfortune, whilst rumor, too monstrous, however, to be believed, ascribes to a desperate faction, the not to be forgiven sin of preparing to lift its paricidal hand aginst their Country.—Let it be the pride of Virginia, to exhibit an honorable contrast to this picture. Let our actions correspond with our professions. Let us encounter the privation and dangers of War, even unto death in the holy cause of our Country, looking for our reward in the pleasure arising from the consciousness of having done our duty, and the appropation of a world. For remember, that impartial history will delineate, with fidelity, the line which separates the lukewarm friend and traitor, on the one hand, and the ardent, patriotic

Citizen on the other, and succeeding ages whilst they contemn and execrate the former will pay due homage to the latter.
Given under my hand at Richmond, the day and date above.

JAMES BARBOUR.[4]

EQUIPMENT AND SUPPLIES FOR THE WESTERN VIRGINIA BRIGADE—
HOW GOVERNOR BARBOUR SECURED THEM.

Governor Barbour having issued General Orders for the rendezvous of the Western Virginia Brigade at Point Pleasant, at the mouth of the Great Kanawha river, hastened to make provision for supplying it with the necessary equipment to enable the men to render the service for which they had been called into the field. There was no public money to meet this demand. His Contingent Fund was exhausted, and he appealed to the patriotism of the citizens of Richmond. In this appeal he said:—

"The character of your country has sustained a wound in the surrender of General Hull. Our brethren of the Frontier are exposed to the Tomahawk of the savage. A prompt exertion must be made to cure the one and repel the other. FIFTEEN HUNDRED VIRGINIANS were called to unite with the Army of the West, in holy cause of their Country; for whose accommodations (within four days) 250 Tents and 1500 knapsacks are wanting. To your patriotism, and particularly to that of the Ladies I appeal, and ask for all aid you can furnish to further their completion.

Those who are willing to promote this desirable object, will signify to me, without a moment's delay, the number of hands they can furnish. Compensation will be made to those who wish it. Every room in the Capitol, not otherwise engaged, will be opened for the accommodation of those who may attend. Such as prefer continuing at home will have their portion of work sent them.

All persons conversant with the cutting and making of Tents, will confer a favor by attending and lending their aid.

JAMES BARBOUR.[5]

Accompanying this Appeal Governor Barbour added the following Statement:—

"The new detachment from Virginia will march for the West, most convenient to the points of action—from .the counties of Ohio, Monongalia, Brooke, Harrison, Randolph, Wood, Mason, Cabell, Kanawha, Greenbrier, Hampshire and Hardy, being the whole of the requisition from the Tenth and Twentieth and parts of the Thirteenth and Eighteenth Brigades—to place of rendezvous, Point Pleasant on the Ohio—under the command of Brigadier-General Leftwich."

---

[4]. Governor's Letter Book, 1812-1813, pp. 29-33, in the Virginia State Library.
[5]. See Richmond Enquirer, September 4, 1812.

The Response by the People to the Appeal of Governor Barbour.

In evidence of how the citizens of Richmond made response to the appeal of Governor Barbour, the following is quoted from the *Enquirer* of that city, of September 4, 1812:—

"Last evening the Capitol exhibited a scene of public spirit which cheered the heart—every one was crowding for work—tents and knapsacks are preparing for the defenders of their country."

Making Tents and Knapsacks in the Capitol for the Western Virginia Brigade.

The *Enquirer* of September 8th told how the work of the citizens of Richmond was progressing in the matter of making tents and knapsacks. It said:

"The citizens of Richmond vied with each other in obtaining the work. Knapsacks were cut out in one room of the Capitol, and the tents in another. Persons entered into contests with each other for the work; some snatched it out of the hands of others and many went away disappointed that they could not get more to execute. The scene will not readily be forgotten by those who witnessed it. It was an affecting offer of a volunteer service on the altar of our country. The consequence is that more work has been accomplished than is absolutely necessary; that instead of 1500 knapsacks, 1900 will be ready—and instead of 250 tents, 262 will be prepared. The wagons will probably start for the place of rendezvous—Point Pleasant on the Ohio, tomorrow. * * * Our brethren of the West are already marching in all directions to the relief of the Frontier."

Letter from Governor James Barbour to General Joel Leftwich, Telling How the Citizens of Richmond Aided in Furnishing Supplies.

Council Chamber, Richmond, Sept. 14th 1812.

Genl. Joel Leftwich, Bedford per Mr. Moody.

Sir:—

Your letter of the 8th Current was not received in time to answer it by mail, and therefore this is sent by a private friend. The appointment of Quartermaster not having been made and the Secretary of War having sent me a Commission in blank to fill up as I wished, I have acceded to your wishes, and those of Mr. Edward Watts for whom I entertain a very high respect. The appointment of Surgeon and mate was made, before the receipt of your letter. Dr. Hugh Stannard a regularly tried Physician, and of most respectable talents, and Mr. Salle his mate. There are however two Regiments, and if upon your arrival at the Point, you and the Colo: should be of opinion that an additional Surgeon & mate are wanting, and there is no Gentleman in that country of capacity willing to accept the station the Gentleman named in your letter may be assigned to one of the Regiments with such a mate as shall be deemed advisable, and this will be your authority for so doing. It was to me a subject of regret that I could not complete the knapsacks in time. I was therefore constrained to send on the wagons and the tops of the knapsacks subsequently. The Soldiers will have merely to sew them on—We had indulged a hope that by voluntary contribution we could have procured a considerable number of blankets but succeeded only in getting between thirty and forty to be given to the most necessitous. A present of 1600 or 1800 weight of good chewing Tobacco is also sent; it is due to the liberal donor to communicate his name,—Mr. Benjamin J. Harris of this place—Every canteen that could be procured in time was sent on.

With sentiments of respect

JAMES BARBOUR.6

GOVERNOR BARBOUR INFORMS THE GENERAL ASSEMBLY AS TO HOW THE EQUIPPAGE FOR THE WESTERN VIRGINIA BRIGADE WAS OBTAINED.

The Governor in his Message to the General Assembly, bearing date November 30, 1812, informs that body as to how supplies were obtained for the Western Virginia Brigade. He says:—

"As, however, this emergency—that of equipping the Western Brigade—was entirely unexpected, and considerable pecuniary means were necessary for the equipment of the detachment, we were not without embarrassment. * * * The Contingent Fund was exhausted * * * and I thought proper to appeal to the patriotism of the citizens of Richmond and so solicited their aid in the making of tents, knapsacks, etc. It is a tribute of gratitude I owe them, which I cheerfully pay, to make known to you, the representatives of the people, the promptitude with which they complied with my request. Every age, every sex, and every condition seemed animated by one sentiment. Thousands claimed a share of the pious undertaking; and in the course of a few days, the whole equipage was made and dispatched to the place of rendezvous, designated for the detachment which has since joined the Northwestern Army under the command of the brave General Harrison, soon, I trust, to redeem the wounded honor of our Country, and take just revenge on her perfidious enemies and their savage allies."

GATHERING OF THE WESTERN VIRGINIA BRIGADE AT POINT PLEASANT, AT THE MOUTH OF THE GREAT KANAWHA.

On the 4th of September, 1812, an editorial in the *Richmond Enquirer* emphasized Governor Barbour's address to the "Citizen Soldiers of Western Virginia," by saying:—

6. Governor's Letter Book, 1812, 1813, pp. 48-49., in Virginia State Library.

"Who is not aroused! The patriotism of the Country is blazing, and we shall again see the spirit of 1776 display itself—Deeds of valor and valor and disinterestedness will be achieved, which shall shine in American Annals. Fifteen hundred Virginians are required by the General Government, and ordered out by an energetic Governor. Canvass is purchased; the Governor has made an appeal to the patriotism of our ladies; and they are assisting to make tents and knapsacks for the soldiers of our Country. They will march at a day's notice—The spirit of individuals is awakened, volunteers are rousing—such as cannot leave their families, and homes, will make contributions towards those who volunteer their services, and men of the first standing will be seen stepping forth to seek the post of honor and danger. It is adversity that tries nations. Are you ready, my dear countrymen, to prove yourselves worthy of the blessings you enjoy? What say ye, Sons of Western Virginia! Will you not sympathize with the brave sons of Kentucky and Ohio!! To arms my Countrymen!:"

But addresses and appeals were not necessary. These early West Virginians—sons of noble sires and sires of noble sons—were ready. Many of them were the sons of Revolutionary soldiers, and all or nearly all had in their early years withstood the shock of barbarian warfare. Contemporary documentary evidence is the best of all evidence, and we therefore insert the following documents, or extracts therefrom, that the reader may know from official sources of the service of these West Virginians in the Northwestern Army in the War of 1812.

THE OBJECT OF THE ORGANAZATION OF THE WESTERN VIRGINIA BRIGADE.

In his message to the General Assembly of Virginia, bearing date November 30, 1812, Governor Barbour says:

"A letter from the Secretary of War, was received September 2d, communicating the request of the President of the United States, that I should cause 1,500 of the detached Militia immediately to take the field, and to rendezvous at some convenient point in this State, with a view ultimately to join the Northwestern Army. * * * My General Orders issued in pursuance of this request, were obeyed with a promptitude honorable to the citizens composing the detachment. The requisition for 1,500 Militia was made necessary in consequence of the disastrous occurrence at Detroit; which, whilst it exhibited the mortifying spectacle of an American Army surrendering without a blow, to the forces of Great Britain, laid bare our defenceless frontier, to the incursions of our enemy and their ferocious allies, whose deeds of cruelty were everywhere manifested by the indiscriminate slaughter of men, women and children. To arrest this horrible warfare it was necessary that the utmost dispatch should be used."

As early as the 1st of September, 1812—the very day on which the Secretary of War informed Governor Barbour of the call of the President for the Western troops—the citizens of Brooke county had heard of the surrender of General Hull, and were taking action acordingly. The following letters written by John Connell, Colonel of the 103d Regiment in that county; and James Marshall, a citizen of Wellsburg, in said county, contain information as to the action then being taken.

LETTER FROM COLONEL JOHN CONNELL TO JAMES BARBOUR.

(*Source*—"Calendar of Virginia State Papers," Vol. X., p. 162.)

Wellsburg, Brooke County, Va., September 1, 1812.

TO HIS EXCELLENCY, GOVERNOR JAMES BARBOUR:
Richmond, Virginia.

Your order under date of June 25 was not delivered to me until the 20th ult'o—before this time you will have received intelligence that the Traitor Hull has sold our army and our Country so far as was in his power. Our fellow citizens of the State of Ohio requested our aid. I communicated that request by express to General Biggs, of Ohio county, and on the same day on further information received by me, I repeated my application as you will observe by the enclosed copies. His answer was verbal, that he had received no orders that would ustify him in ordering out the volunteers. Your orders of June 25th were at that time in his possession (since delivered to me). I, however, continued to rouse the spirit of the Regiment, believing that our voluntary aid given in this hour of danger would be approved by your Excellency and by the General Government. A committee of respectable Gentlemen came forward and offered their aid in furnishing supplies. You will learn with pleasure that 250 of your sons are now assembling at this point, determined to avenge our Country's wrongs. We shall march tomorrow completely equipt with arms, ammunition, provisions, waggons, tents, &c., unless it shall appear that our assistance is not necessary. Our Cavalry volunteered, although without arms generally, determined to take Rifles, and act as occasion may require. Think of us as to arms, &c. The mail is waiting, I shall advise you of our movements.

I am, &c.,

LETTER FROM JAMES MARSHALL, OF BROOKE COUNTY, WESTERN VIRGINIA, TO GOVERNOR JAMES BARBOUR.

(*Source*—"Calendar of Virginia State Papers," Vol. X., p. 163.)

Brooke county, Virginia,
September 1, 1812.

On receiving authentic information that General Hull had surrendered the Fort of Detroit with all the Troops under his command to the British army under General Brock, it was believed by a number of respectable inhabitants of this county to be our duty to raise a volunteer corps for the protection of the Frontiers until the Government should provide more adequate means to repel the enemy. Colo. John Connell, an officer of some experience, tendered his services, and is this day ready to march to the Frontiers in the direction to Detroit, with about two hundred volunteers, but on receiving information that the Frontier inhabitants immediately opposite to us are sufficiently covered at present, we have thought it most advisable to suspend the march of this detachment for a few days; in the meantime, they will be held in readiness to act as circumstances may require. For the equipment of this Detachment, four other citizens of this county, viz., George Jetter, Robert Hartford, William Wartenbe, Jacob De Camp and myself, have also volunteered our services and supplied about thirty days provisions, with such quantity of arms, ammunition and tents, &c., as were in our power to procure, together with baggage wagons and pack horses for their transportation. It will perhaps be satisfactory to my colleagues to have your Excellency's approbation for this service, together with such assurance as you shall think proper to give, that we shall be reimbursed our actual expenses, which will be very trifling indeed if the service of this Detachment shall not be required. In that case the principal expense will be money advanced for the linen which is made into tents and knapsacks for the men. On the provisions, ammunition, &c., there will be no loss either to the public or to us, every article being purchased at the current cash price. Permit me to observe that the want of arms is severely felt in this County, particularly Rifles, and swords and pistols for the Cavalry. Ammunition is also much wanted. If these articles are furnished by the Government, your Excellency may rest assured the Militia of Brooke county will do their duty.

I am, &c.

Under date of September 15th, Colonel John Connell in a letter to Governor Barbour expresses his appreciation of the honor conferred upon him as Colonel of the First Regiment in the Western Virginia Brigade, and informs him that with the Brooke County troops he is ready to start to the place of rendezvous—Point Pleasant, at the mouth of the Great Kanawha. This was as follows:—

LETTER FROM COLONEL JOHN CONNELL TO GOVERNOR JAMES BARBOUR.

(*Source*—"Calendar of Virginia State Papers," Vol. X., p. 165.)

Wellsburg, Brooke county, Virginia,
September 15, 1812.

TO HIS EXCELLENCY, GOVERNOR JAMES BARBOUR,
    Richmond, Va.
    Your favors of the 3d and 4th current were duly received by your Ex-

press last night. I am truly sensible and grateful for the distinguished honor conferred on me by the appointment to so distinguish a command, and confidently hope that such services as I am capable of rendering will meet your approbation, and that of every friend to our beloved country.

I have issued orders to the several Captains of the Infantry of the line, and to Capt. Pugh of the Rifle Corps, to meet me at Charles Town, (now Wellsburg), on Tuesday the 22nd with the requisition required by your orders of the 19th of April last, and doubt not but that your sons of the North-West corner of the State will do their duty.

My staff is complete, and formed of Gentlemen fit and capable of performing service. My Quarter Master is now employing the necessary conveyance of the Baggage.

I shall proceed to Point Pleasant by water, that being the cheapest and most expeditious way of arriving there.

Capt. Wilcoxon's and Capt. Congleton's Companies of Light Infantry and Capt. William McClany's Troop of Light-horse feel damped at not having the honor to be on the first call.

The Infantry have arms. The Cavalry have none. I feel ashamed to meet those brave men when asked by them for arms.

For God's sake—for my sake—for our country's sake, arm these people as soon as possible. They are brave, active, and willing and ready to do duty. With regret I have to leave these men. God bless you and prosper our cause.

I am, &c.

On the 26th of September, 1812, Brigadier-General Leftwich arrived at Point Pleasant, at the mouth of the Great Kanawha. Here he found Captain Anthony Van Sickle's Company of Mason County Riflemen, the first at the rendezvous. The Harrison county men arrived September 30th. October 3d three hundred men embarked at the mouth of the Little Kanawha—now Parkersburg—for Point Pleasant; and the next day 200 more passed Marietta, Ohio, descending the river to the same destination.[7] The two following letters written at Point Pleasant, contain information as to the formation of the Brigade:

LETTER FROM BRIGADIER-GENERAL JOEL LEFTWICH TO GOVERNOR JAMES BARBOUR.

(Source—"Calendar of Virginia State Papers." Vol. X., p. 167.)

Point Pleasant, Virginia, October 3, 1812.

TO HIS EXCELLENCY, GOVERNOR JAMES BARBOUR.
　　Richmond, Virginia.

I have the honor to inform your Excellency that I arrived at this place on the 26th ult., at 3 o'clock P. M., finding only a Lieutenant and eighteen

---

7. Richmond Enquirer, October 13, 1812.

men, part of the quota from the county of Mason. A few days after which the troops began to come in briskly, and detachments arrive almost daily. The whole of the field officers are now present except Major McGuire, and from the morning reports of this day, including a few that are absent on furlough, there are in Camp 825 men, officers inclusive. There have been no arrivals of troops from the Counties of Hampshire, Hardy, Monongalia and Randolph. But it is understood that they are in motion, and are expected in five or six days.

Those present are generally fine looking men, in high spirits and healthy, and as far as I have yet observed, discover a disposition to pay due respect to the commands of their officers. Among the Rifle companies there is a considerable deficiency of Rifles. Those unarmed appeared on their arrival to be much opposed to the idea of receiving muskets, but the necessity of complying with the requisitions of your Excellency being explained, the opposition appears mostly to have subsided.

Information has just been received that the military stores and camp equipage are afloat on the Kanawha and will probably be here to-morrow, a circumstance that will be truly pleasing to me and gratifying to the troops who have heretofore encamped in Companies and detachments under the direction of their officers, as best suited their convenience and accommodation. From the best information I have received respecting the route we expect to march as hinted in your Excellency's special orders of the 4th ult., it is considered almost impracticable to march an army with expedition without a traveling forge, for the procuring of which I have made arrangements, but am not yet certain that my purpose will be effected. The difficulty of procuring cartridges appears to be insurmountable in consequence of the scarcity of powder. Flints are stated to be in great demand towards the place of destination.

Your Excellency will please to receive these hints relative to inconveniences as arising from a consciousness o my duty to make the representation. And be assured, Sir, that every exertion shall be made in my power to cause the troops I have the honor to command to be serviceable to our country, and an honour to the State from which they are about to be detached. I anticipate the pleasure of having the troops shortly arranged and equipped ready to execute the orders of your Excellency or the Secretary of War.

I am, &c.

LETTER FROM BRIGADIER-GENERAL JOEL LEFTWICH TO GOVERNOR JAMES BARBOUR.

(*Source*—"Calendar of Virginia State Papers," Vol. X., pp. 168, 169.)

Point Pleasant, Virginia, October 12, 1812.

TO HIS EXCELLENCY, GOVERNOR JAMES BARBOUR,
Richmond, Virginia.

I have at length the satisfaction to inform your Excellency by Express, that the troops which I have the honor to command have collected at the general rendezvous, except some small detachments which are yet expected from the 14th and 106th Regiments which have not produced but little more than half their quotas.

A partial organization has been effected for the better regulation and disciplining of the troops subject to alterations when the whole are collected, the last company of which came in last evening. The organization shall now be effected immediately, and a correct return forwarded to your Excellency. From the Regimental morning reports of this day there are in camp and on furlough, thirteen hundred and eleven men, including Officers, and 319 Blankets are wanting. It seems impracticable to procure them, without which the troops must evidently suffer greatly, as they have to act in a very cold climate and at a severe season of the year. It is confidently hoped that if possible the interposition of Government will remedy this inconvenience. We are also in want of ammunition, axes, spades and shovels, and such articles as are absolutely necessary, all of which might be readily procured *if we had funds*. The Paymaster stationed here refused to reimburse the Captains with the money they expended for provisions in conveying their companies to this place. They have been at considerable expense, and murmured on being refused the money they had expended for the public good. The Paymaster did not think himself authorized by his instructions to satisfy such claims, and it was with much difficulty I could silence their murmurings, by stating that some unintentional failure had produced this inconvenience, and the willingness of Government to discharge such claims.

I rece'd a letter from the Honorable Secretary of War directing me to march as soon as possib'e to the frontier of Ohio, and report myself to the commanding officer of the N. W. army. The same day I rece'd one from General Harrison, dated "Piqua, Sept'r 27th," in which I was informed that my destination is Wooster, in the County of Wayne, 45 miles west of Canton, and my route through New Lisbon and Canton. The Virginia detachment and that from Pennsylvania unite at Wooster and from the right wing of the army, to be commanded by the Senior Officer, and march to the rapids of Miami.

I am preparing with all possible speed to hasten on to Wooster, and expect to start in a very short time. All the troops not having arrived, I shall leave an officer at this place to conduct them after us when they arrive.

I found it indispensible to appoint a Brigade Staff *pro tem.*, and have made some arrangements to get ammunition.

The military Stores arrived the 4th inst., without much injury. The Tents are distributed and a regular encampment formed. The Infantry are furnished with arms and accoutrements, and such of the riflemen as are without Rifles will have muskets placed in their hands to-morrow.

As we shall march up the Ohio, if your Excellency should have any communication to make relative to reimbursing the Capt's or furnishing pecuniary supplies to purchase indispensible requisites, an express could intercept us at Charleston (now Wellsburg,) on the Ohio. The troops appear brave and willing to encounter any inconvenience that can be surrounded, but that of blankets is insurmountable.

I am, &c.

The Brigade crossed the Ohio river, into the State of Ohio, October 20, 1812; and thus proceeded by way of Gallipolis, Gallia County; Chillicothe, Ross County; Circleville, Pickaway County; Franklinton, on Sciota river, opposite site of Columbus, Franklin County; Delaware, Delaware County; Marion, Marion County; Upper Sandusky, Wyandott County; Finley, Hancock County; and onward across the then terrible Black Swamp[8] in what is now Wood county, to Fort Meigs, at the foot of the Maumee Rapids in the extreme north-western part of the State. The Western Virginia Troops aided in the erection and also the defense of Fort Meigs. Early in February, 1813, General Harrison left General Leftwich in command at this fort while he visited Upper and Lower Sandusky, Delaware, Franklinton, Chillicothe, and Cincinnati, to hasten forward the troops with provisions and munitions of war.[9] The term for which the Western Virginians had enlisted at length expired; four companies, were discharged April 1, 1813, and the remainder fifteen days later, when all returned to their homes. The following documents contain information relative to the history made by this Brigade in the Northwestern Army.

LETTER FROM GENERAL JOEL LEFTWICH TO GENERAL JAMES WOOD.

(*Source—Richmond Enquirer*, November 27, 1812.)

Chillicothe, Ohio.
October 31, 1812.

* * * He says: "We have been unavoidably detained at Point Pleasant longer than I expected, on account of the great difficulty of procuring wagons. But being now on the march, I hope sho·t'y to be united with the Northwestern Army and in time to render our country some service.

---

8. The approach to, and passage through, the Black Swamp is described by a correspondent with the Virginia Volunteers:—
"On that day we marched 30 miles under incessant rain; and I am afraid you will doubt my veracity when I tell you that in 8 miles of the best of the road it took us over our knees, and often to the middles. The Black Swamp (4 miles from Portage River and 4 miles in extent) would have been considered impossible by all but men determined to surmount every difficulty to accomplish the object of this march. In this Swamp you lose sight of terra firma altogether; the water was about 6 inches deep on the ice, which was very rotten, often breaking through to the depth of 4 or 5 feet. The same night we encamped on the very wet ground, but the driest that could be found, the rain still continuing. It was with difficulty we could raise fires; we had no tents; our clothes were wet, no axes, nothing to cook in, and very little to eat. A Brigade of pack-horses being near us, we procured from them some flour; killed some hogs (there being plenty of them along the road.) Our bread we baked in the ashes, and the pork we broiled on the coals—a sweeter morsel I never partook of; when we went to sleep it was on logs laid close to each other to keep our bodies from the damp ground. Good God! What a pliant being is man in adversity!!"—See Richmond Enquirer, of April 13, 1813, quoted from Petersburg Intelligencer.
9. Atwater's "History of the State of Ohio," pp. 214-215.

The Brigade is as likely militia, as any in the Union; and want nothing but some supplies of blankets and clothing to enable them to perform their duties incident to a winter campaign."

I have the honor to be with perfect respect, Sir,

Your Ob't Serv't,

JOEL LEFTWICH, B. G.

LETTER FROM COLONEL JOHN CONNELL TO GOVERNOR JAMES BARBOUR.

(Source—"Calendar of Virginia State Papers," Vol. X., pp. 169, 170.)

Camp Delaware, Ohio, November 11, 1812.

TO HIS EXCELLENCY, GOVERNOR JAMES BARBOUR,
Richmond, Virginia.

Agreeably to your orders I have repaired to Point Pleasant with the Quota of men from Brooke, where we arrived on the 2nd of October. I confess that I felt disappointed on finding that no person was authorized to pay the expenses of furnishing the troops, boats, wagons, &c., the whole of which was furnished by some Gentlemen of Brooke and myself.

The accounts of expenses will be forwarded, and I hope will be immediately discharged. For want of funds and troops were detained several days, and with all the aid of Major Turner our movements were slower than could have been wished.

General Harrison is now at this place making arrangements for our further movements. The Paymaster Gen'l of the U. States has decided that the Staff shall be taken from the line, or only receive ten dollars per month. Under the laws of Virginia, which I conceive leave the choice with the Colo' of each Regiment, I made the best selection in my power, and should the General Assembly not justify, but let the U. States absorb all the power of construing the State Laws, and of course compelling me to select from materials not competent to discharge the duties, I shall with regret retire to private life and there await the fate of my country.

I am compelled from a sense of duty to inform your Excellency that several of the officers and privates have shamefully abandoned the Standard of their Country, and disgraced the name of themselves as Virginians.

Capt. Peck of Harrison, and Lt. Larimore of Hampshire, have both resigned, I believe more from Bashfulness than ability. I hope their names will be blotted from the Records of Virginia. A number of men have deserted, but we are now daily bringing in, and some returning of their own accord, fearing that which shall be fully inflicted, the punishment of the law.

Please to accept my best respects, and present them to all my acquaintances now at Richmond in hopes of a successful campaign.

I am, &c.

LETTER FROM GOVERNOR JAMES BARBOUR TO GENERAL JOEL
LEFTWICH.

Richmond Council Chamber, Jany. 21st, 1813.

GEN'L JOEL LEFTWICH OF THE N. W. ARMY, DELAWARE, [OHIO.]
Dear General.
Your letter of the 18th Ultimo from Delaware, has just been received—I was particularly gratified, to learn that the Detachment under your command has so conducted itself as to receive the approbation of the Commander-in-Chief—The fame it may acquire in common property to every Virginian, who rejoices in the prosperity and character of his Country; all such look with sensibility to the part it may perform on the interesting theatre upon which it has been called to act. Tender to the whole Corps (officers and privates) an expression of my high regard with an assurance that I have presented to the Representatives of the People now convened in General Assembly, the tribute due to their worth, which has been paid by the Commander-in-Chief and an evidence whereof has been furnished by your letter.

It is also gratifying to me that the patriotic donation, from this place, has been received and distributed, it will be the more grateful to the troops as it was the spontaneous effusion of Brotherly love and a proof of the ardor of their devotion.

Relatively to the course you have pursued in supplying the vacancies which have occurred in your Detachment, I am sorry to advise you that insuperable difficulties occur in issuing Commissions. For example some of the nominees, upon the expiration of the Service of the Detachment would hold Commissions in Counties different from the residence, as illustrated in the case of Moses McClintick. We have therefore deemed it more eligible to suffer your appointees to hold their stations, to which they have been called, rather by your General orders than by Commission.

With very high respect
I am yours &c
JAMES BARBOUR.[10]

EXTRACT FROM A LETTER OF JOHN MALLORY, QUARTERMASTER GENERAL, TO GOVERNOR JAMES BARBOUR.

(*Source*—"Calendar of Virginia State Papers," Vol. X., pp. 182-183.)

Delaware, Ohio.
January 24, 1813.

At 4 o'clock this morning, I received a letter informing me that General Leftwich had received orders from General Harrison by express for the Virginia troops to march without the least possible delay to the Rapids of Miami of the Lakes. On the 18th, General Harrison wrote General Leftwich, that Colonels Lewis and Allen had advanced to the River Raisin with

---

[10]. Governor's Letter Book, 1812, 1813, pp. 152-153, in Virginia State Library.

about 800 men, and expected to be engaged with about the same number of British and Indians. The express that brought the last letters states that he saw a letter from General Purkins (who is at the rapids) stating that our detachment had attacked the enemy in their fortification, carried and took possession of them. 18 of the enemy were found dead in the field. The number of wounded is not ascertained. Our loss was 8 killed and wounded. But since it is thought that a cannonading has been heard in 'he direction of the River Raisin. Whilst writing I have received information by Mr. Bartlett, who is Field Commissary General, that the above statement is correct, and Lewis drove the British and Indians two miles. It is probable that British have got a reinforcement from Malden, which is only 18 miles from the River Raisin. General Harrison has sent on a reinforcement to Lewis, but they have double the distance to march that the British have. General Harrison has given me liberty to go on with the army, provided I can get some person to attend here to purchase corn for the teams that are passing with their loads. I have loaded at this place within the four last days, 700 pack horses, 60 wagons, and 100 sleds with flour and Q. M. stores. I am giving $2 per bushel for corn delivered at Upper Sandusky, and you must know from the quantity necessary to supply the army that it takes the cash by whole-sail. You may rest assured that we shall do something of consequence soon as we have a sufficiency of provisions forwarded, and all our Artillery was started the 18th from Sandusky for the rapids, and we have forwarded a sufficient supply of Ammunition. I cannot account for not receiving a letter from you. I calculate that you have made arrangements with the Bank of Virginia to settle with the Bank of Chillicothe. I am getting tolerably fond of a soldier's life, if it was not for leaving my family. * * *

I am, &c.

NOTE—The Western Virginia Brigade made a forced march of three days to re-enforce General Winchester, who was then sorely pressed at the River Raisin, but it did not reach its destination until after his disastrous defeat at that place, January 12, 1813.

LETTER FROM COLONEL JOHN CONNELL TO GOVERNOR JAMES BARBOUR.

(*Source*—"Calendar of Virginia State Papers," Vol. X., p. 228.)

Wellsburg, Brooke county, Va., May 5, 1813.

To HIS EXCELLENCY, GOVERNOR JAMES BARBOUR,
Richmond, Virginia.

You will have information before this reaches you that the Virginia Brigade have returned home without having it in their power to meet the enemies of our Country, and I hope without disgrace to their parent State.

The imprudent advance of General Winchester from the rapids completely defeated the object of the campaign, and left us so far in the rear of time that no other alterative presented itself to the Commander-in-Chief but to advance to the Rapids and there build a Fort sufficiently strong to protect the public stores; and from thence, if an opportunity offered, to attack the enemy. But the term of service for which the troops from Kentucky and Ohio—being about to expire, they would not agree to volunteer for a longer term, and were discharged, leaving the Pennsylvania and Virginia Brigades, the Petersburg, Pittsburg, and Greensburg Blues, with a few Companies of Regulars, to finish and defend the Fort. An attack from the enemy was expected, but they chose to content themselves with the advantage they had gained. From the best information I could obtain from some of those who were in the action, it was to them a dear bought victory, and to us a melancholy reflection that it deprived us of the opportunity of seeing Malden, there to die or Conquer. That, I believe, was the determination of the troops, and they appeared to have the highest confidence in the Commander-in-Chief, and in my opinion *it was by him* justly merited.

You will, no doubt, also have learned that the greater part of the Arms furnished by the State of Virginia to the Brigade were left at Delaware, upper Sandusky, &c.

This was contrary to my opinion; I urged the propriety of the men's returning the arms into the State, observing that a loan was not a gift, and that the men were bound to carry and return them, if not at a particular place, at least in the Regiment from whence they were drafted.

This, however, was contrary to the opinion of a majority of the officers then present; of course the men were suffered to deposit the arms as above stated.

Knowing what an immense loss the State will sustain, and believing that every stand of arms will be wanting to defend us against our enemies, I would advise that measures be immediately adopted to have the arms collected and secured, as they will be daily diminishing in number and value. Should your Excellency think proper to direct that the arms should be secured, and at the same time consider me a proper person to have it done, I shall willingly undertake the same for the good of my country, and confide the business to such persons only as will discharge this duty with fidelity and for a reasonable compensation.

I am, &c.

LETTER FROM GOVERNOR JAMES BARBOUR TO GENERAL JOEL LEFTWICH.

Richmond, May 22nd, 1813.

GENERAL JOEL LEFTWICH, BEDFORD.

SIR:

The period of service of the detachment under your command in the North Western Army having terminated and no further necessity on the part of this Commonwealth to furnish the various equipments into which she gave with a view to the accommodation of her troops, I request you to furnish me with a report which shall disclose the destination of the arms, tents, &c. furnished your command. Permit me to congratulate you upon your safe return, and upon the fidelity with which you have discharged the duties of your station.

I tender you assurances of
high respect

JAMES BARBOUR.[11]

EXTRACTS FROM THE JOURNAL OF PETER DAVIS,[12] WITH OBSERVATIONS THEREON.

(*Source*—Peter Davis' Journal, printed in full in Haymond's History of Harrison County, West Virginia. pp. 307, 308, 309, 319, 311.)

October 20, 1812—"Brigade crossed the Ohio river and encamped in a field on the opposite bank."[13]

October 21, 1812—Encamped at Gallipolis."[14]

October 23, 1812—"Encamped on Big Raccoon Creek, at the sign of the "White Horse."

October 25, 1812.—"The Brigade arrived at the Scioto Salt Works."

October 26, 1812—"Marched down Salt Creek fifteen miles and encamped at New Richmond within three-quarters of a mile of the Big Sciota river."

October 27, 1812—"Marched nine or ten miles; waded Big Sciota river; proceeded four miles further and encamped on the edge of the town of Chilicothe."

October 31, 1812—"Struck the tents; waded the Sciota river on a cold, blustering morning; marched fifteen miles, and encamped on the Pickaway Plains."

November 1, 1812—"Marched through the Plains; at the distance of four miles passed a small town called Jefferson; three miles further, passed through Circleville; proceeded twenty miles this day, and encamped on a large creek."

---

11. Governor's Letter Book, 1812-1813, pp. 272-273., in Virginia State Library.
12. Peter Davis, the author of this Journal, was born at Shrewsbury, New Jersey, September 16, 1783, and came with his parents to the vicinity of the town of Salem, Harrison county, West Virginia, when but six years of age. Here he grew to manhood and served with the Harrison County troops in the Western Virginia Brigade, with the Northwestern Army in 1812-13. On his return from the war he settled on Middle Island Creek, about four miles below West Union, now in Doddridge county, West Virginia, but later removed to "Westfield" in Lewis county. He was for many years a devoted minister of the Seventh Day Baptist Church. He died March 4, 1873, aged ninety years.
—V. A. L.
13. This encampment was in Gallia county, Ohio.
14. This town was then as now, the Seat of Justice of Gallia county, Ohio.

November 2, 1812—"Started and marched up the Sciota and encamped in a town called F"[15]

November 4, 1812—"Marched twelve miles."

November 5, 1812—"Marched thirteen miles and encamped near a small town called De.aware,[16] situated on Whetstone river, a fork of the Big Sciota river. Met General Harrison here and remained until the 21st of December."

December 21, 1812—"Started and arrived at Norton at three o'clock, and here we continued until the 2d day of January, 1813, for the purpose of guarding the stores which were at a fort called Fort Monroe."[17]

January 2, 1813[18]—"Started for Upper Sandusky. The day before we started it began to rain; continued all day and part of the night, and then it began to snow, and at eleven o'clock the snow was half leg deep. Went four miles and encamped. The fourth day the snow ceased falling and we started, the snow being about knee deep, and we reached the blockhouse in the Sandusky Plains; it being extremely cold. The next day we started very early and marched fifteen miles and encamped on the Plain with the Pennsylvania troops, about four miles from a town of the Wyandotte Indians, called Greentown."

"January 23—In the evening it began to rain. The snow began to melt and it being a level piece of ground, the water ran into our tents. We were baking and cooking and preparing to march to the Rapids. It was about three hours when our fires were all out and about three o'clock the water was knee deep in our tents, and we were obliged to retreat from our tents and build a fire on higher ground, where we continued until day, it being a very rough night. When daylight came we had to wade to our tents to hunt our baggage, which we found floating about the tents.

About 11 o'clock we started and it being very level we had to wade sometimes knee deep. We continued our march for eight miles and encamped on a piece of woodland but very low and muddy. That night it began to snow. In the morning we marched two miles and were stopped by a small river, it being very high. Here we continued two days, and at that time we built two canoes, but at the expiration of the two days it

---

15. Franklinton, on the west bank of the Scotia river, opposite Columbus. It was the Seat of Justice of Franklin county at this time
16. This town was then and continues to be the Seat of Justice of Delaware county. It is the seat of the Ohio Wesleyan University.
17. This fort was in Marlborough Township, in Delaware county, Ohio.
18. Under this date the Journalist groups three day's marches. The last encampment was distant thirty miles from Fort Monroe, and was the village of Upper Sandusky, now the Seat of Justice of Wyandotte county.

was so extremely cold that the river froze completely so that it bore the troops comfortably. We all crossed safely and that day we marched eighteen miles and encamped in a piece of woodland very level and rich."

January 28, 1813—"We took up the line of march at nine o'clock and marched through very low and swampy land. x x x Marched fifteen miles and came to where General Harrison was lying with about two thousand men from Ohio and Kentucky."

January 29, 1813—"The whole command marched seven miles."

February 1, 1813—"Marched eight miles and reached the Rapids of the Maumee. Marched four miles on the ice down the river and encamped on the Southeast side of the river."[19]

March 30, 1813—"This day received my discharge, and Captain John McWhorter his company and Captain L and Captains Prince and Simmons and their companies were discharged and left Fort Meigs for the purpose of returning home. When we left the Fort we had to wade, and we waded two miles and encamped on a branch of the river."

March 31, 1813—"Marched six miles and crossed Carrying river.[20] Went eight miles further and encamped on a branch of the Sandusky river."

April 1, 1813—"Marched six miles and reached the Carrying Block-House. Here we continued until the next day and our Ensign and some of our men went to the Lower Sandusky for provisions."

April 2, 1813—"This day we marched over four miles of dry land passing two miles below Sandusky." Upper Sandusky a small town on Sandusky river. x x x We traveled ten miles and encamped on the Sandusky river.

April 3, 1813—"Had a hard and rough march of about twenty-five miles and reached Fort Sandusky."

April 4, 1813—"Marched 15 miles and encamped at the Sciota Block-House."

April 5, 1813—"This day we reached Fort Monroe in the township of Marlborough, (Delaware County.)[21]

19. Here the months of February and March were spent at Fort Meigs, which the West Virginians helped to build.
20. The stream then called Carrying river, is now known as Portage river in Wood county, Ohio.
21. It was here that the Brigade halted December 21, 1812,—three months and fourteen days before. From Fort Monroe the Brigade proceeded to the Ohio river where the regiments were disbanded, and the companies returned to the several West Virginia counties whence they came.

COMPANIES FROM VIRGINIA COUNTIES NOW EMBRACED IN WEST VIRGINIA, WHICH SERVED AT NORFOLK AND OTHER PLACES ON THE ATLANTIC SEABOARD IN THE WAR OF 1812.

(*Source*—For Cavalry and Artillery Companies, see "Statement issued from the office of Moses Green, Adjutant-General of Virginia, Richmond, June 1, 1814." For other Companies, see Reference connected with each.)

Of these Companies seventeen were, at some period of the war, attached to the Third Regiment of Virginia Cavalry, of which Henry Bowyer of Botetourt county, was the Lieutenant-Colonel commanding; with Robert Grattan, of Augusta county, Major of the First Battalion; and Alexander Shields, of Rockbridge county, Major of the Second Battalion; five of the Third Regiment of Virginia Artillery of which Alexander King, of Hampshire county, was the Lieutenant-Colonel commanding, and James Faulkner, of Berkeley county, the Major commanding the First Batalion. The other Companies were of Light Infantry or Riflemen attached to various Regiments of these arms of the service.

CAVALRY COMPANIES:—

1. Captain Samuel McClure's Company from Ohio county.
2. Captain Charles W. Lewis' Company from Monroe county.
3. Captain Nimrod Saunders' Company from Wood county.
4. Captain William N. Jarrett's Company from Monongalia county.
5. Captain John Welch's Company from Greenbrier county.
6. Captain David Robertson's Company from Harrison county.
7. Captain Thomas Kincaid's Company from Pendleton county.
8. Captain Carver Willis' Company from Jefferson county.
9. Captain Rawley Martin's Company from Monongalia county.
10. Captain Peter H. Steenbergen's Company from Mason county.
11. Captain Solomen Collett's Company from Randolph county.
12. Captain Archibald B. Wilson's Company from Harrison county.
13. Captain William Brumfield's Company from Cabell county.
14. Captain John Cunningham's Company from Hardy county.
15. Captain William McClung's Company from Brooke county.
16. Captain Silas Reynold's Company from Kanawha county.
17. Captain Forbes Britain's Company from Harrison county.

ARTILLERY COMPANIES:—

1. Captain Robert Wilson's Company from Berkeley county.
2. Captain Samuel Beck's Company from Ohio county.
3. Captain James Dailey's Company from Hampshire county.
4. Captain Samuel Kennedy's Company from Monongalia county.
5. Captain George J. Davidson's Company from Harrison county.

LIGHT INFANTRY AND RIFLE COMPANIES:—22

1. Captain Joseph Johnson's Rifle Company from Harrison county.23
2. Captain ——— Buckmaster's Light Infantry Company from Berkeley county.24
3. Captain John Johnson's Company from Pendleton county.25
4. Captain William McDaniel's Company from Monroe county.26
5. Captain James Hill's Company from Monroe county.27
6. Captain John Bonnett's Company from Ohio county.28
7. Captain Moses Congleton's Company from Brooke county.29
8. Captain James Hervey's Company from Monongalia and Brooke counties.30
9. Captain William Irwin's Light Infantry Company from Ohio county.31
10. Captain Matthias McCowan's Company from Monongalia (now Preston) county.32
11. Captain Jesse Hinkle's Company from Pendleton county.33
12. Captain Joseph Grantham's Company from Jefferson county.34
13. Captain Van Rutherford's Company from Jefferson county.35
14. Captain Christain Conn's Company from Monongalia (now Preston) county.36

COMPANIES FROM VIRGINIA COUNTIES, NOW EMBRACED IN WEST VIRGINIA, WHICH SERVED IN THE WESTERN VIRGINIA BRIGADE WITH THE NORTH-WESTERN ARMY IN THE WAR OF 1812.

15. Captain John McWhorter's Company from Harrison county.37
16. Captain John H. Elson's Company from Brooke county.38
17. Captain Anthony Van Sickle's Rifle Company from Mason county.39

---

22. As yet no accurate list of Western Virginia Companies serving in the War of 1812, has been prepared, nor is it known that the necessary data therefor, is in existence. How many of these went to Norfolk and other points on the Atlantic Seaboard, we do not know; nor do we know how many were in the Western Virginia Brigade with General Harrison's Northwestern Army, or of the number whose places of service are unknown; there were several calls on Virginia for troops, as indicated by the General Orders of the Governor. Prominent among them being that of April 19, 1812; of July 18, 1812; of September 3, 1812; and of March 31, 1814. To each and every one of these calls there was a ready response on the part of the Western Virginians—and now—after the lapse of a hundred years—the exact number of companies furnished by them may never be known.—V. A. L.
23. Haymond's "History of Harrison County, West Virginia," p. 307.
24. "Calendar of Virginia State Papers," Vol. X p. ——.
25. Arrived at Norfolk, October 4, 1813. See Documents accompanying Governor's Message to the General Assembly, December 6, 1813. p. 33.
26. Arrived at Norfolk. October 4, 1813. See Documents accompanying Governor's Message to the General Assembly, December 6, 1813. p. 33.
27. Arrived at Norfolk, October 4. 1813. See Documents accompanynig Governor's Message to the General Assembly, December 6, 1813. p. 33.
28. Newton's "History of the Pan Handle," p. 377.
29. Newton's "History of the Pan Handle," p. 319.
30. Wiley's "History of Monongalia County," p. 430.
31. Newton's "History of the Pan Handle," p. 207.
32. Wiley's "History of Preston County," p. 202.
33. Morton's "History of Pendleton County, West Virginia" p. 402.
34. Printed Muster Roll preserved in State Department of Archives and History.
35. "Calendar of Virginia State Papers," Vol. X, p. 173.
36. Wiley's "History of Preston County," p. 204.
37. Haymond's "History of Harrison County, West Virginia," p. 307
38. Newton's "History of the Pan Handle," p. 319.
39. "History of the Kanawha Valley," Vol. I, p. 263.

18. Captain L————— Company from ————— county.40
19. Captain ————— Prince's Company from ————— county.41
20. Captain ————— Simmon's Company from Cabell county.42
21. Captain James G. Laidley's Rifle Company from Wood county.43
22. Captain Leonard Cupp's Company from Preston county.44
23. Captain ————— Peck's Company from Harrison county.45
24. Captain ————— Pugh's Company from Brooke county.46
25. Captain ————— Wilcoxon's Company from Brooke county.47

COMPANIES FROM VIRGINIA COUNTIES, NOW EMBRACED IN WEST VIRGINIA, WHICH SERVED IN THE WAR OF 1812, BUT WHOSE PLACE OF SERVICE HAS NOT BEEN ASCERTAINED.

26. Captain John Wilson's Company from Kanawha county.48
27. Captain Jesse Ice's Company from Monongalia (now Preston) county.49
28. Captain James Morgan's Company from Monongalia county.50
29. Captain Samuel Wilson's Company from Monongalia county.51

ROSTERS OF EIGHTEEN OF THE COMPANIES FROM VIRGINIA COUNTIES, NOW EMBRACED IN WEST VIRGINIA, WHICH SERVED IN THE WAR OF 1812.

The following Rosters, eighteen in number, are in the State Department of Archives and History, either in manuscript or printed copies. "A Resolution adopted by the General Assembly of Virginia, March 31, 1851, directed the Governor to cause to be obtained authentic copies of all Muster Rolls of the Virginia Militia who served in the War of 1812, and in the War with Mexico; and that he caused five hundred copies to be printed." This volume was printed the next year, but strangely enough, it contained but two of the Rosters of the organizations from Virginia counties now included in West Virginia; and there is no mention whatever, of the service of Western Virginians in the Western Virginia Brigade, in the Northwestern Army—nor indeed of their service at Norfolk or elsewhere on the Atlantic coast. But the Secretary

40. Mentioned in Peter Davis' Journal.
41. Mentioned in Peter Davis' Journal.
42. Mentioned in Peter Davis' Journal.
43. "Calendar of Virginia State Papers," Vol. X, p. 147.
44. Wiley's "History of Preston County," p. 292.
45. "Calendar of Virginia State Papers," Vol. X, p. 170.
46. "Calendar of Virginia State Papers," Vol. X, p. 165.
47. "Calendar of Virginia State Papers," Vol. X, p. 165.
48. "Pay Rolls, Virginia Militia,. War of 1812." p. 80.
49. "Wiley's History of Monongalia County," p. 499.
50. Original Muster Roll in possession of the State Department of Achives and History.
51. Wiley's "History of Monongalia County," p. 490.

of War in announcing to the Governor, the requisition for troops, added: "Your Excellency will please to direct that correct Muster Rolls and Inspection Returns be made of the several Corps and that copies thereof be transmitted to this Department as early as possible." How many of these Muster Rolls, of the Western Virginians, the War of 1812, are preserved in the Archives of the War Department, can not be known until printed.

MUSTER ROLL OF CAPTAIN WILLIAM N. JARRETT'S CAVALRY COMPANY FROM MONONGALIA COUNTY, IN THE THIRD REGIMENT OF VIRGINIA, IN SERVICE IN 1813.

(*Source*—"Muster Rolls of the Virginia Militia in the War of 1812." p. 480.)

OFFICERS.

William N. Jarrett.. Captain
Robert Hawthorn...Lieutenant
Ralph Berkhire.....Lieutenant
Marmaduke Evans..Cornet

PRIVATES.

Daniel Balzet	Cornelius Barkshire	Francis Billingly
Benjamin Dowey	Henry Darby	James Doran
John Davis	John Evans	Mathew Gay
Archibald Hamilton	Reason Holland	Brice Holland
John Jolliff	Fielding Kizer	William B. Linsey
Nehemiah Power	Henry Runner	James Runner
George Reed	Thomas S. Swearingen	Jonathan Salyards
Frederick Swisher	Alpheus P. Wilson	Augustus Werninger

MUSTER ROLL OF CAPTAIN JOHN CUNNINGHAM'S CAVALRY COMPANY, FROM HARDY COUNTY, IN THE THIRD REGIMENT OF VIRGINIA CAVALRY. IN SERVICE IN 1814.

(*Source*—"Virginia Pay Rolls," p. 255; also "Virginia Muster Rolls" p. 257.)

OFFICERS.

John Cunningham.........................Captain.

John G. Harness....1st Lieutenant	Jacob Neff ....1st Corporal
Valentine Simmons. 2d Lieutenant	Thomas Wheeler....2d Corporal
William Gourlay....1st Sergeant	Joseph Williams....3d Corporal
Ambrose Updegraff. 2d Sergeant	Jacob Barger.......Trumpeter
Adam Bishop.......3d Sergeant	Mathew Toler.......Cornet
James Gray........ 4th Sergeant	

PRIVATES.

John Bailey	John Bishop	Oliver Bliss
Jesse Cunningham	Joseph Evans	Thomas Evans
Obediah Edwards	Joseph Fry	Henry Fry
Moses Hutten	Gideon Hutten	Isaac Hutten
Job Hutten	Solomon Harness	George Harness
Adam Harness	Henson Lewis	Abram Lorance
Isaac Lorance	Henson Marshall	John Marshall
James Miles	John Miles	Strother McNeil
John Meloy	Joseph Neville	John O. Brannon
Miles Parsons	James Russell	Jacob Rumer
William Snodgrass	John Stump	Elijah Veach
William Wilson	Jacob Wilson	John Wilson
Jacob Yoakum	John Yoakum	Michael Fisher
David Miles	Charles Machir	Abram Shobe

MUSTER ROLL OF CAPTAIN SAMUEL KENNEDY'S ARTILLERY COMPANY, FROM THAT PART OF MONONGALIA COUNTY NOW INCLUDED IN PRESTON COUNTY, IN THE THIRD REGIMENT OF VIRGINIA ARTILLERY. IN SERVICE IN 1813.

(*Source*—Wiley's "History of Preston County," pp. 293-294.)

OFFICERS.

Samuel Kennedy,...Captain,	Noah Ridgway,.....Sergeant,
Michael Shively,....Lieutenant,	Philip Shively,.....Corporal,
Robert Courtney,...Lieutenant,	James Hamilton,...Corporal,
John Shively,......Sergeant,	Levi Jones,........Corporal,
George Bell,........Sergeant,	Abraham Huffman,.Corporal,
Josiah Little,.......Sergeant,	Fielding Ramsey,..Drummer,

PRIVATES.

John Amos,	Amariah Augustine,	William Ayers,
John Butler,	Benjamin Butler,	William Burris,
Harvey Burnes,	John Brumasin,	Mathew Campbell,
John Clayton,	Aananias Davis,	John Davis,
William Davis,	Eli Fanner,	Thomas Glisson,
Robert Guthrie,	Edmund Guthrie,	Jacob Gilmore,
Jesse Hanway,	John Haught,	Jacob Haughtman,
Isaac Hunce,	David Jackson,	Samuel Jewell,
John King,	Gabriel Leap,	William Lollis,
Job Lee,	Samuel Lazzell,	John Laidly,
William Lemmor,	George Laugh,	David Mathiney,
David Michael,	John Myers,	James Mooreland,
James Montgomery,	Robert Meins,	John Martin,

Henry Pride,
Morgan Scott,
Ephraim Sayers,
Jesse Tucker,
Caleb Tribbett,
William Woods,
John Young,

Jacob Hodeheaver,
Thomas Scott,
John Samuels,
Joel Tatler,
Henry Wolfe,
John Watts;

Jacob Ringer,
George Steel,
Philip Short,
William Tennant,
Daniel Wolfe,
John Wheeler,

ROSTER OF CAPTAIN ANTHONY VAN SICKLE'S COMPANY OF MASON COUNTY RIFLEMEN.

(*Source*—"History of Great Kanawha Valley, Vol. I., pp. 263, 264.

OFFICERS.

Anthony Van Sickle..................Captain.

Nicholas Yeager,....Lieutenant,   Benjamin Lewis,... Drummer,
James Ball,.........Ensign,   Abraham Roush,... Fifer.
Jesse Bennett,...................Surgeon.

PRIVATES.

George Riffle,
George Clendenin,
Leonard Cooper,
John Yeager,
Charles Taylor,
Henry Nease,
Harry Van Meter,
Lewis Roush,
Arthur Edwards,
John McIntire,
Michael Rickard,
Samuel McCulloch,
Samuel Bumgardner,
Robert Bryan,
Nathaniel Kimberling,
Paul Chamberlain,
William Sterrett,
Jacob Rottenhery.

Joseph Rader,
Thomas Lewis, Sr.[52]
John Johnson,
Isaac Taylor,
Isaac Johnson,
Resin Van Meter,
Henry Van Sickle.
George Eckard,
James Stephenson,
Jacob Peck,
Robert Johnson,
James McLure,
David Bumgardner,
John Craig,
William Tucker,
Robert Pruit,
George Sebrill,
—— Mallory,

John Eckard,
Jacob Rickard,
Cornelius Miller,
William Roach,
Abraham Brinker,
Charles Collins,
Samuel Somerville,
Emmanuel Nease,
Jacob Aleshire,
William Cooper,
Sheldon Gibbs,
John Van Meter,
James Hall,
William See,
John Jackson,[52]
Lieutenant Brown,
John Jackson,
—— Russell.

[52]. John Jackson and Thomas Lewis died of injuries received while working on the defenses of Fort Meigs.

MUSTER ROLL OF CAPTAIN WILLIAM IRWIN'S "WHEELING LIGHT INFANTRY." IN SERVICE IN 1812.

(*Source*—Newton's "History of the Pan-Handle, West Virginia," p. 207.)

OFFICERS.

William Irwin,............................Captain.
John Kecheson,......Lieutenant, George Dulty, ...Ensign.

PRIVATES.

John Adams,	Jacob Adams,	Thomas Adams,
William Eskew,	Thomas W. Eskew,	Archibald Armstrong,
John Brown,	William Bell,	Thomas Baird, Jr.,
Absolam Bushhan,	Soloman Bushhan,	John Bushhan,
Jacob Bently,	Thomas Campbell.	Thomas Crespin,
John Carrol,	—— Campbell,	William Caldwell.
William Crawford,	Robert Prittyman,	Josiah Parlit,
John Rodeheffer,	Morris Rosling,	Joseph Smith,
Robert Stewart,	William Stichler,	Robert Snodgrass,
William Stevenson,	David Thornburg,	Daniel Irwin,
John McDonald,	Robert Arbutton,	Henry Dement,
John Doun,	Michael Dulty,	Arnold Evans,
John Fulton,	John Fawcett,	William Grous,
Thomas Johnson,	Peter Loffer,	John Lowery,
Hugh Lachey,	David Moore,	Zedicl Masters,
John D. Miller,	Alexander McConal,	Joseph McKnight,
Zeb. Mix,	James Minnis,	William Montgomery,
Samuel McClain,	Moses Thompson,	John Tegarden,
Thomas Tourner,	George Tibergen,	George Venon,
John Canon,	Aaron Varney,	William Williamson.
Robert Williamson,	William Williams,	John Williams,
Soleman Wardle,	Abram Westbrook,	Thomas Williams,
Hiram Anderson,	Alexander White,	

MUSTER ROLL OF CAPTAIN MOSES CONGLETON'S COMPANY FROM BROOKE COUNTY, LIGHT INFANTRY, VIRGINIA, IN SERVICE IN 1812.

(*Source*—Newton's "History of the Pan Handle, West Virginia," p. 319.)

OFFICERS.

Moses Congleton..........................Captain.
John Miller............Lieutenant Edward Nicholas...Corporal
William Williams...Ensign David Smiley.......Corporal
John Myers.........Sergeant John Dougherty.....Corporal
Philip P. Doddridge.Sergeant Henry Linton ......Corporal
Daniel Tarr........Sergeant William Plantenberg Fifer
Isaac Jones........Sergeant James Snider.......Drummer

PRIVATES.

Oliver Ashenhurst	Harvey Bonten	Nenier Boyles
D. Walton Blair	Hugh Bane	John Brown
John Bonner	Samuel Burke	Thomas Connell
Benjamin Crouch	Elijah Cornelius	James Craft
John Crowley	Jona Cooper	Robert M. Dawson
Thomas Edgington	Ezekiel Fuller	Isaac Goudy
William Griffith	Elias Johnston	William Johnston
James Kidwell	Alexander Lather	Andrew Lyons
Arnold Lee	Alexander McConnell	William McMillen
Levi Muncy	John Moren	John Mobley
Jacob Mendal	Samuel Pennington	Perry Petticord
William Patton	Mathew Richardson	Joseph Ray
William Ridgley	Joseph Smith	William Strain
John Tarr	Hanson Wheeler	John Holmes
Charles Wells	John Worstell	James Long
John Long	James Early	Sylvester Fowler,
John Gorley	Nicholas Gosuch	Thomas Gosuch

MUSTER ROLL OF CAPTAIN JOSEPH GRANTHAM'S COMPANY OF LIGHT INFANTRY OF JEFFERSON COUNTY. CALLED INTO SERVICE UNDER GENERAL ORDERS OF MARCH 31, 1814.

(*Source*—Roster supplied to the State Department of Archives and History, by Hon. Braxton Davenport Gibson, of Charles Town, Jefferson County, West Virginia.)

OFFICERS.

Joseph Grantham...Captain   Richard Williams...Second Lieut.
Braxton Davenport.First Lieutenant   Thomas Briscoe....First Ensign
George Fayman..................Second Ensign.

PRIVATES.

Joseph Alexander	George Arvin	James Barr
Elias Brown	Uriah Bradshaw	William Brawner
John Brown	George Bruce	Thomas Burnett
Cornelius Beasley	Joseph McCormick	George L. McCormick
Eden Carven	Abram Cole	James McClure
William Carr	Mathew Columber	William Cage
John McCloy	David Dillow	Samuel Duke
James Duke	John Dodenhaver	Thomas Duke
David Farman	Joseph Feagans	Jacob Grove
Robert Games	John Grove	Raleigh T. Hedges
Thomas Hall	John Hawkins	Jacob Hummer
John Johnson	Rudolph Jacobs	Benjamin Johnston

William James	William LaRue	Ashel Lucas
John McFallin	James Merchant	Jesse Mercer
William Mercer	William Mappins	Jesse Marmaduke
James Milburn	John McKnight	James Novis
Christian Newman	James Oldfield	Robert O'Neill
George Price	William Parmer	Elisha Park
William Quingley	John Tellers	Benjamin Tansberry
Daniel Sufferans	William Southerns	George Snyder
Philip Sagle	Timothy Shirly	Thomas Toul
Andrew Toul	Jonathan Van Metre	John L. Vanzant
Philip Wilhelms	John Watson	John C. Young
Thomas Fitzgerald	John Taylor	Jacob Trope
William Callahan	John Mustin	Daniel Drew
Lewis Ervin	Benjamin Games	Samuel Lancaster
Cary Thompson	Levi Tarr	Elias Waggoner
John Avis	Samuel Atwell	Ephraim Beller
John Cornicle	Solomon Van Metre	Thomas Jordan
John Howell	Philip Haines	Daniel Staley
Nathan O'Ferrel	Samuel Poland	John Colbreth
James Edmondson	Thomas McClanahan	James Heskitt
William Beasley	Richard Johnson	Thomas O'Neill

I certify that this Muster Roll exhibits a true statement of a Company of Infantry, under my command, and that the remarks set opposite the men's names are accurate and correct.

Signed BRAXTON DAVENPORT,
1st. Lieut. Commanding.

We certify that this Muster Roll exhibits a true statement of Captain Grantham's Company of Infantry and that the remarks set opposite the men's names are accurate and just.

Signed VAN BENNETT, Mustering Officer.
J. WOOD, Surgeon.

MUSTER ROLL OF CAPTAIN JAMES HERVEY'S COMPANY FROM MONONGALIA AND BROOKE COUNTIES. IN SERVICE AT NORFOLK, IN 1814.

(*Source*—Wiley's "History of Monongalia County," pp. 490-491.)

OFFICERS.

James Hervey,..... Captain,	Peter Tennant,..... Sergeant,
John Carothers,.....Lieutenant,	Lewis Turner,...... Corporal,
Joseph Pickenpaugh Ensign,	George Ashby,...... Corporal,
George McCrea,.... Sergeant,	Carden Burgess,....Corporal,
Thomas S. Haymon Sergeant,	Lewis Smith,.......Corporal,
Samuel Brand,......Sergeant,	Isaac Cox,......... Corporal,
John Street,........Sergeant,	Morgan S. Morgan,..Corporal.

PRIVATES.

George Amos,
Nelson Bolen,
Jacob Brookover,
David Bates,
Thomas Bland,
Jacob Brumagen,
Joseph Barrett,
John Bennett,
George Buchannon,
James Buchannon,
William Brown,
Walter Brownlee,
Edward Bozeman,
James Collen,
Turner Compton,
Michael Conner,
Morris Canada,
Isaac Cohen,
Thomas Clayton,
Jesse Cheshire,
Henry Dusenberry,
Elisha Dawson,
William Demoss,
James Everly,
Edward Evans,
John Fisher,
Peter Fox,
Richard Fawcett,
Richard Fields,
Elisha Ford,
Jacob Flanagan,
Jacob Goff,
Joseph Haught,

Harry Howard,
Patrick Haney,
Jacob Hickman,
John Harris,
William Hardesty,
Silas Hedges,
Ephraim Johnson,
Thomas Jones,
Zachariah Jones,
George Keller,
John Lemasters,
Philip Lewellen,
John Lipscomb,
Andrew Luzader,
George Low,
Edward Mathews,
Peter Myers,
William Murphy,
Uriah McDavitt,
William McCants,
James McGee,
David Mathews,
William McMillen,
John Mathews,
Aaron McDaniels,
Evan Morgan,
James Moorehead,
Caleb Merriman,
Abe McAtee,
Richard Nuzum,
Robert Perfect,
Samuel Pixly,
William Pratt,

James Price,
Joel Rhodes,
Aaron Riggs,
Benjamin Reed,
Cyrus Riggs,
Steve Ridenour.
John Roberts,
Edward Sanders,
William Stewart,
Patrick Shean,
James Stoneking,
David Swindler,
Jacob Swisher,
William Shaw,
Samuel Sheppard,
Jacob Stone,
Philip Shewman,
George Smith,
William Strait,
George B. Smith,
John Townley,
Garrett Thomas,
Aaron Titchner,
Abe Tennant,
Joseph Tennant,
Joseph Trickett,
Alexander Winders,
Joseph Williams,
John Wiley,
William Wyatt,
James I. West,
David West,
John Wood,

Many of the men from the mountain region of West Virginia, died at Norfolk, during the War of 1812, and were buried in the sands at that place. A movement was put on foot in 1836, to suitably mark their burial places. The following is in evidence of this:—

"THE BURIAL PLACE OF THE MOUNTAINEERS.—It is with the liveliest satisfaction we inform our readers, that the Common Council of Norfolk, at their meeting yesterday afternoon contracted for building a brick wall around the burial place of the brave and patriotic yeomanry of the upper country, who marched to the defense of our town during the late war, and who fell victims to the terrible plague which ravaged the country in the memorable winter of 1814-15. Too long has this duty been delayed, while every citizen of Norfolk has felt it as a reproach, that no public tribute of respect and gratitude had been paid to the memory of their gallant defenders, but for twenty years their graves had been left uninclosed, and without any mark to distinguish them from the sod of the field. It is contemplated to have their remains disinterred and deposited in one common grave, to mark the spot by a monument to their memory, inscribed with their names as far as they can be ascertained.53

MUSTER ROLL OF CAPTAIN JOHN BONNETT'S COMPANY FROM OHIO COUNTY. IN SERVICE AT NORFOLK IN 1814.

(Source—Newton's "History of the Pan-Handle, West Virginia," p. 377.)

OFFICERS.

John Bonnett,......Captain,
James Ewing,......1st Lieutenant,
Peregrine Wells,....2d Lieutenant,
Jacob Keller,.......Ensign,
Daniel Wells,.......Ensign,
John Boner, ...Sergeant,
Vaehel Harding,....Sergeant,

Jonah Porter,.......Sergeant,
Jonathan Thomas,..Sergeant,
James Vanscyal,....Sergeant,
Daniel Toviel,........Corporal,
Thomas Adams,.... Corporal,
Jacob Crow, ... Corporal,
William Bills,.......Corporal,

Cornelius Ogden,........................Corporal.

PRIVATES.

Augustus D. Alton,
Aaron Ankrum,
John Baker,
Daniel Bludgett,
John Bogard,
James Buchanan,
John Carroll,
Joseph Cox,
Justice Chanot,
Daniel Darling,
Levi Darnell,
John Evans,
Bruce Enoch,
Levi Greeg,
George Goodrich,
John G. Hicks,
James Jefferson,
John Kyger,
James Knox,
Aaron Lewis,
Jacob McVay,
David Medly,

Uriah Morgan,
David McCarty,
William Murphy,
Alexander Martin,
John Owens,
Bethnel Rush,
Henry Riggle,
John Stone,
William Smith,
William Taylor,
Nicholas Vandwender,
Daniel Ward,
John Whitkanach.
James Aikine,
John Betts,
William Bell,
John Bond,
Isaac Blake,
Isaac Brown,
Daniel Carland,
John Carmichael,

John Cline,
William Dougherty,
Chage Doty,
George Evans,
James Francis,
Neal Gwin,
Moses Grindstaff,
Jonathan Howell,
Abraham Jones,
Andrew Kyger,
David Lyon,
Samuel Martin,
Asa Martin,
William McClelland,
Horace McCardle,
Thomas More,
Nicholas Morland,
Elijah Mart'n,
David Patterson,
James Robison,
Henry Ryan,

---

53. Quoted from the Norfolk Herald by the Richmond Whig and Public Advertiser, issue of Friday, May 13, 1836.

Joseph Stone,	Thomas Clegg,	Morgan Morris,
John Smith,	Daniel Day,	James McCrerey,
Isaac Underwood,	James Denison,	Ferdinand More,
William Watson,	Archibald Neal,	Andrew Marvis,
Samuel Westbrook,	Robert Edging,	William Orr,
John Wayman,	William Fletcher,	Jacob Price,
James Burns,	James Gray,	Levi Roberts,
William Ankrum,	John Glaspy,	Pardon Starks,
Spencer Biddle,	Richard Hanlan,	John Sims,
Francis Burris,	Samuel Hover,	James Taylor,
Benjamin Baker,	Thomas Kiggins,	John Vansyoc,
Barney Belford,	Daniel Lyon,	James Weekly,
John Bulliman,	John Maly,	Jacob White,
David Craig,	William Melong,	Robert Barclay.

MUSTER ROLL OF CAPTAIN MATTHIAS McCOWAN'S COMPANY, FROM MONONGALIA, NOW PRESTON COUNTY, IN SERVICE AT NORFOLK IN 1814.

(*Source*—Wiley's "History of Preston County," pp. 292-293.)

OFFICERS.

Matthias McCowan,....Captain,	Robert Johnson,...Sergeant,
Thomas Montgomery,..Lieutenant,	Eli Bently,........Corporal,
Hiram Hansford,......Lieutenant.	Rice Miller,.......Corporal,
James King,..........Ensign,	Jesse Cain,.......Corporal,
John Stephenson,.....Ensign,	Henry Harris, ...Corporal,
John Hull,...........Sergeant,	John D. Maupin,..Corporal,
Amariah McGrigg,.....Sergeant,	William Bohan,...Corporal,
Levi Ross,...........Sergeant,	George Corbin,....Drummer,
Cunningham McColgan,Sergeant,	James Hayman, ...Fifer.

PRIVATES.

Altz Adams,	Eli Anderson,	Isaac Asher,
Ezekiel Aldeman,	Samuel Billups,	Meredith Bird,
Samuel Beach,	Stephen Bice,	Arnold Bohand,
Isaac Callison,	William Chilcot,	David Chilcot,
Robert Curry,	John J. Carto	William Curny,
John Duke,	James Day,	John Deatz,
John Dewit,	Henry Dewit,	Adam Deatz,
William Edwards,	John Foster,	James Frame,
Philip Fout,	James Given,	William Gribble,
John Goff,	John Gilmore,	James Goodman,
John Greathouse,	John Hicks,	Abel Huddleson,
Elliot Hawkins,	Achilles Hicks,	Abner Howell,
John D. Hobright,	John Hubbert,	William Hendrick,

Peter Hannick,
John Hill,
Abraham Hays,
Charles Harrison,
Thomas Jopling,
Benjamin Jeffers,
Peter Kingory,
Elisha Legg,
Moses Moss,
Jacob Newal,
Westly Payne,
Jonathan Pearson,
Benjamin Parsinger,
William Hatfield,
Noah Robinson,
Jordon Smith,
Anderson Stephenson,
Benjamin Wells,
James Walker,
James Williams,
Samuel Wise,
Joseph Wright,

Jiles Hally,
Jilson Hannick,
Thomas Heb,
John Jenkins,
Edward Irwin,
William Jones,
William King,
Benjamin Lawson,
George McNeely,
John Newal,
John Parson,
William Pearson,
Christopher Ringsburg,
Aaron Rice,
Alexander Ragsdale,
Solomon Sevier,
Thomas Thomas,
John Williams,
George Witsell,
William Winos,
Francis Wilson,
Joseph Windon,

Isaac Hugh,
William Roach,
John Harris,
Henry Johnson,
Joshua Lawson,
Elisha Jones,
John Kilburn,
David McColgin,
Robert McCoy,
Richard Oly,
Jacob Parsinger,
William C. Philips,
William Rich,
William Roberts,
William A. Saint,
Frederick Snider,
Nothan Vanzant,
Thomas Wyat,
John Wallace,
John Weaver,
Andrew Wilson,
James Wheeler.

MUSTER ROLL OF CAPTAIN JESSE ICE'S COMPANY. IN SERVICE IN 1813.

(*Source*—Wiley's "History of Monongalia County," p. 489.)

OFFICERS.

Jesse Ice,..................................Captain,
Moses Cox,..........Lieutenant,   Peter Haught,......Sergeant,
Peter Bates,........Ensign,   David Helmick,.....Corporal,
James Kelley,.......Sergeant,   Joseph Neely,......Corporal,
Nathan Hall,.......Sergeant,   Abner Hall,........Corporal,
Abram Cox,.........Sergeant,   George Lough,......Corporal,

PRIVATES.

Samuel Aulton,
John Brown,
Benjamin Baldwin,
Jesse Coombs,
Aaron Foster,
Peter Haught,
James Henderson,
David Jenkins,

Henry Ashton,
George Baird,
John Brookover,
Thomas Clayton,
Alexander Hart,
William Hayhust,
Nicholas Haught,
Henry Jansen,

Stephen Archer,
James Brand,
Jacob Brookover,
Jacob Claus,
Benjamin Hayhust,
John Harker,
James Holbert,
John Jones,

John Knox,	John King,	James Lough,
Virgil Lancaster,	Philip Moore,	Nimrod Lancaster,
John Morgan,	Rawley Morgan,	Henry Martin,
John Martin,	John McMasters,	Charles Martin,
John McCallister,	Richard Postlewaite,	Daniel Rich,
Philip Rutherford,	Philip Sherman,	William Stewart,
Jacob Tennant,	William Underwood,	Joseph Varner,
Daniel Varner,	John Walton,	Azariah Wilson.

MUSTER ROLL OF CAPTAIN JAMES MORGAN'S COMPANY, MONONGALIA COUNTY. IN SERVICE IN 1813.

(*Source*—Wiley's "History of Monongalia County," p. 489.)

OFFICERS.

James Morgan, ...Captain,

Isaac Cooper,......Lieutenant,	Hopkins Rose,......Sergeant,
Silas Stevens,.......Ensign,	John Cobun,........Corporal,
Henry Watson,..... Sergeant,	Thomas Leach,.....Corporal,
Thomas McGee,......Sergeant,	Simeon Stevens, ...Fifer,
Joseph Lewis,......Sergeant,	Thomas Rose,......Drummer.

PRIVATES.

George Grim,	John Powers,	George Gay,
Turner Quick,	Joseph Bunner,	William Huggins,
Nathaniel Reed,	James Cobun,	J. Jones,
Joseph Rader,	John Chipps,	Luke Jane,
John Rix,	John Cobun,	Hezekiah Joseph,
Job Springer,	Abraham Devault,	John Keller,
John Squires,	Amos A. Deal,	Thomas Lewellen,
Thomas Stafford,	Thomas Franklin,	Amos Powell,
Thomas Stewart,	William Ford,	William Powers,
Alex. Wilson,		

MUSTER ROLL OF CAPTAIN SAMUEL WILSON'S COMPANY, FROM MONONGALIA COUNTY, IN SERVICE IN 1813.

(*Source*—Wiley's "History of Monongalia County," p. 490.)

OFFICERS.

Samuel Wilson,.....Captain,	Joseph Guseman,...Corporal,
Godfrey Guseman,..Lieutenant,	Isaac Guseman,....Corporal,
Robert Stewart,....Sergeant,	William Allender,...Corporal,
Thomas Dunn,..... Sergeant,	George Reese,......Corporal,
John Howell,.......Sergeant,	Francis Pierpont,...Ensign,
John Foster,.......Sergeant,	John Sullivan,.....Drummer.

PRIVATES.

James Adair,	Asael Gifford,	Geo.ge Morris,
Joseph Austin,	William Hall,	Larkin Pierpont,
John Atkison,	James Herrington,	Zackwell Pierpont,
William Baldwin,	William Hartley,	John Pride,
John Baker,	Henry Henthorn,	John Robinson,
Reuben Baker,	William Huston,	Thomas Robinson,
William Boyd,	George Hopkinson,	William Robe,
Archibald Boyd,	Joseph D. Hill,	James Reed,
Benjamin Bartlett,	Abram Hess,	George Randolph,
George Cropp,	Levi Jenkins,	Philip Smell,
James Donaldson,	Joseph Jones,	William Stafford,
Isaac Davis,	John Jenkins,	Peter Smell,
Isaac Dean,	John Kern,	Clayton Swindler,
John Dean,	Asa Lewellen,	Hezekiah Wells,
William Davis,	Robert Lemon,	John Watts,
William Darnell,	William May,	Clark Williams,
John Foster, Jr.,	Job Magill,	Augustine Wells,
Isaac Forman,	Eli Moore,	William Wison,
Philip D. Gordon,	Henry May,	William Watson,
John Guseman,	James Marty,	John Magill.

MUSTER ROLL OF CAPTAIN JOHN H. ELSON'S COMPANY, FIRST VIRGINIA REGIMENT, IN SERVICE IN 1812.

(*Source*—Newton's "History of the Pan-Handle, West Virginia," p. 319.)

OFFICERS.

John H. Elson,..........................Captain,
Thomas McCreary,.. Lieutenant, James Gap......... 4th Sergeant,
William Creale,..... Ensign, George Templeton,. 1st Corporal,
Joshua Everitt,.....1st. Sergeant, Andrew McCamman 2d Corporal,
Jacob Foulty,...... 2d. Sergeant, David Irwin,........ 3d Corporal,
William Atkinson,.. 3d. Sergeant, Josiah McGuire,.... 4th Corporal.

PRIVATES.

John Ashanhast,	James Atkinson,	John Brownlee,
James Burns,	Newman Billings,	John Brady,
William Chambers,	William Conighan,	Isaac Conighan,
Walter Cain,	James Campbell,	Francis Duke,
Aaron Elliot,	Enoch Fowler,	John Freeman,
William Francis,	Ezekial Hoitt,	Thomas Hopkins,
Peter Homlet,	Samuel Hedges,	Silas Hedges,
George Hedges,	Francis Hindman,	Jacob Hanes,
James Lee,	Thomas Lee,	William Leeper,

George McCormick,	David Morris,	Robert McGuire,
Henry Merlatt,	John Munsey,	Joshua Mummy,
Valentine Mendle,	George McCally,	Thomas Nicholls,
Michael Parsons,	Samuel Roberts,	William Roberts,
Thomas Ray,	John Redding,	John Stewart,
Jacob Stevens,	Ebenezer Strain,	David Smiley,
John V. Swearingen,	William Tarr,	Venosdoll Cornelius,
John Walker,	Thomas Williamson,	Isaac Workman,
Samuel Williamson,	Henson Wheeler,	Samuel Wheeler.
Nathaniel Wells,		

MUSTER ROLL OF CAPTAIN JOHN WILSON'S COMPANY, FROM KANAWHA COUNTY. IN SERVICE IN 1812.

(*Source*—"Pay Rolls, Virginia Militia, War of 1812." p. 80.)

OFFICERS.

John Wilson.......Captain	James Sisson......4th Sergeant
Robert Wilson......Lieutenant	Chisholm Ellis......1st Corporal
William C. Wilson. Ensign	Henry Cartmille...2d Corporal
Thomas Mathews...1st Sergeant	Hiram Cobbs......3d Corporal
Isham Bagby.......2d Sergeant	John Donnally.....4th Corporal
Dabney Jones......3d Sergeant	John Fisher.......Fifer.

PRIVATES.

Isham Bailey	Moses Brown	Thomas Cobbs
Thomas Casdorp	Jacob Casdorp	Alexander Cartwright
John Campbell	Solomon Casdorp	John Cooper
Leonard Cooper	Joseph Dawson	Gabriel Dawson
James Fowler	William Fowler	Asa Fowler
Joshua Fowler	Leonard Fisher	John Guthrie
Thomas Hensley	James Hensley	Thomas Lowe
John Medley	Thomas Milam	Moses Milam
Malcolm McCown	James Newport	Thomas Parish
Nimrod Paul	Archibald Price	Edmund Price
Samuel Priestley	Joel Rucker	John Ray
Andrew Slaughter	John Smith	Joseph Still
Elisha Smith	Luke Shiverdecker	Alexander Taylor
George Weldy	Langston Ward.	
Henry McLaughlin	Simeon Milam	John McCown

MUSTER ROLL OF CAPTAIN LEONARD CUPP'S COMPANY, FROM WHAT IS NOW PRESTON COUNTY, IN SERVICE IN 1812.

(*Source*—Wiley's "History of Preston County," p. 292.)

OFFICERS.

Leonard Cupp,.....Captain,
Jacob Paul.........Lieutenant,
Robert Gibson,.....Ensign,
William Brandon,..Sergeant,
Henry Synes,.......Sergeant,

George Smith,.........Sergeant,
Peter Reihart,........Sergeant,
John Wolff,...........Corporal,
Jacob Wolff, Jr.,.....Corporal,

John Synes,..............................Corporal.

PRIVATES.

John Bryte,
Jacob Cale,
Joseph Earley,
Michael Hartman,
Usuel Johnson,
Edward Larew,
Abraham Penrose,
Henry Syner,
Christian Teets,
William Waller,
Samuel Wolff,
James Miller,

Levi Bryte,
John Cupp,
William Edenfield,
Jonathan Jenkins,
John Kimmery,
Henry Miller,
George Kinger,
Samuel Smith,
Michael Teets,
Samuel Waller,
Henry Woods,
Eli Deberry,

William Boyce,
Peter Earley,
John Feather,
Evan Jenkins,
James Kelley,
Jacob Martin,
W. Syner,
Adam Teets,
Jacob Teets,
Joseph Waller,
Solomon Wilhem.

MUSTER ROLL OF LIEUTENANT CHRISTIAN CONN'S COMPANY, FROM MONONGALIA, NOW PRESTON COUNTY. IN SERVICE IN 1815.

(*Source*—Wiley's "History of Preston County," pp. 294-295.)

OFFICERS.

Christian Conn,......................Lieutenant,

Burget Minor,.....Ensign,
Robert McGuire,...Ensign,
Richard Conner,...Sergeant,

James Gibson,......Sergeant,
Peter Mason,.......Corporal,
Samuel Crane,......Musician.

PRIVATES.

Isaac Armstrong,	George Benson,	Simon B.andon,
John Conner,	Jacob Frankhouser,	Thomas Gibson,
Levi Gibson,	George Hartman,	William Limmin,
Thomas McCollum,	Nathaniel Metheny,	Stephen Osburn,
John Starling,	David Smith,	Daniel Smith,
John Sevrance,	Philip Sterling,	Stephen Zichimal,
William Tervie,	Charles Walls,	Moses Woods,
Jacob Cress,	Solomon Herndon,	John King,
James Paugh,	Jonathan Johnson,	John Stinebuck,
John Ashby,	William Mitchell	James Metheny,
Jacob Metheny,	James Benson.	

DIRECT TAX ASSESSED BY THE UNITED STATES GOVERNMENT IN 1813, AND AMOUNT THEREOF PAID BY VIRGINIA COUNTIES NOW EMBRACED IN WEST VIRGINIA.

The collection of a Direct Tax by the General Government is only resorted to in cases of great emergency. The Second Section of Article I. of the Federal Constitution declares that "direct taxes shall be apportioned among the several States, which may be included within this Union according to numbers;" while the Ninth Section of the same Article provides that "no capitation or other direct tax shall be laid unless in proportion to the census or enumeration herein before directed to be taken." The first time that Congress availed itself of these constitutional provisions, was to aid in the prosecution of the Second War with England—that of 1812. The American Armies had sustained many reverses, and the national treasury was depleted. To raise funds, Congress availed itself of this last resort—that of a direct tax—and, August 2, 1813, passed an Act entitled *"An Act to lay and collect a Direct Tax within the United States."* It was as follows:—

"Be it enacted by the Senate and House of Representatives of the United States of America in Congress Assembled: That a direct tax of three millions of dollars shall be and is hereby laid upon the United States and apportioned to the States respectively," x x x

Further, the Act apportioned this sum, first among the several States, and secondly, among the several counties comprised in each of the respective States. The part assigned to Virginia was $369,018.44. Of the counties now in West Virginia, sixteen then had an existence. These with the Congressional Assessment upon each, were as follows:—

Monroe	$ 1,030.50	Ohio	$ 1,907.50
Greenbrier	1,650.44	Brooke	1,195.50
Kanawha	2,167.50	Pendleton	1,428.50
Cabell	1,546.50	Hardy	2,126.50
Mason	1,130.50	Hampshire	3,795.50
Randolph	5,465.50	Berkeley	6,147.22
Harrison	2,672.50	Jefferson	6,876.28
Wood	1,338.50		
Monongalia	2,992.50	Total	$43,469.94

Thus it is seen that the present counties of West Virginia, nearly eighty years ago, paid the sum of $43,469.94, as a direct tax to the General Government, to aid in the prosecution of the Second War with Great Britain.

CHAPTER VII.

WEST VIRGINIA SOLDIERS IN THE WAR WITH MEXICO.

When the Mexican Minister, as the representative of his government officially notified Congress that in the event of the passage of the bill providing for the admission of Texas into the Union, war would follow, his declaration attracted but little attention. But when General Santa Anna equipped an army and began his march from the city of Mexico toward the Rio Grande, at the same time announcing to the excited populace of the capital of the Montezumas, that before his return he would water his horse in the Potomac river, the Americans realized the truth of the declaration made by the minister before leaving Washington. Hostilities began April 25th, 1846, and by an Act of Congress passed May 13, 1847, it was declared that, "by an Act of the Republic of Mexico, a state of war exists between that Government and the United States." There is nothing more contagious than military enthusiasm, and though philanthropists depict the blessings of peace and dilate on the horrors of war, let the drum beat and the bugle sound and the field and workshop will be deserted and the young and brave follow in their wake in quest of glory and adventure. Such was the existing condition in the United States, at the time of the declaration of war against Mexico. The President, James K. Polk, issued a call for troops and a requisition was made on Virginia. This was as follows:—

LETTER FROM WILLIAM L. MARCY, SECRETARY OF WAR, TO WILLIAM SMITH, GOVERNOR OF VIRGINIA.

War Department,
November 16, 1846.

SIR:—

x x x The President now directs me to notify your Excellency that one Infantry regiment of volunters from your State is required for immediate service, and to be continued therein during the war with Mexico, unless sooner discharged. The regiment will consist of—

Field and Staff:—1 Colonel, 1 Lieutenant Colonel, 1 Major, 1 Adjutant, (a Lieutenant of one of the Companies, but not in addition.)

Non-commissioned Staff:—1 Sergeant Major, 1 Quartermaster Sergeant, 2 Principal Musicians, and 10 Companies, each of which to consist of one Captain, 1 First Lieutenant, 2 Second Lieutenants, 4 Sergeants, 4 Corporals, 2 Musicians, and 80 Privates.

Should the number of Privates, on being mustered, not fall below sixty-four effective men in a Company it will be received.

Guyandotte is designated as a place of rendezvous for the several companies as fast as they shall be organized, and where they may be further organized into a regiment, if not already done under a previous call. The regiment will be inspected and mustered into service by an officer or officers of the United States Army, who will, in every case, be instructed to receive no man who is in years apparently over 45 or under 18, or who is not of physical strength and vigor. x x x

W. L. MARCY,
Secretary of War.

To his Excellency William Smith, Governor of Virginia.[1]

On the 18th of November—that on which Governor Smith received the above communication—he issued a proclamation calling for ten companies of volunteers to constitute a regiment to serve according to the terms of the requisition of the President. These companies when organized and their officers commissioned, were to rendezvous at Guyandotte in Cabell county, now in West Virginia, there to be mustered into the service of the United.[2] On the same day William H. Richardson, Adjutant-General of Virginia, issued "General Orders" declaring that the Infantry Regiment of Volunteers required by the Governor's Proclamation, should consist of the officers and privates as designated in the President's Requisition.[3]

Nowhere else did the call for volunteers meet with a readier response than in the Virginia counties now included in West Virginia. In the issue of the *Martinsburg Gazette*, of November 26th, there appeared a call for a meeting of citizens of Berkeley county, on Friday evening, the 27th ensuing to respond to the proclamation of Governor Smith. The result of this meeting was that Captain Ephrain G. Alburtis, editor of the *Berkeley County Republican*, and Captain of the "Independent Blues" tendered to the Governor the services of himself and company and these were promptly accepted. The roster of this company was as follows:—

1. Richmond Enquirer, Wednesday, November 18, 1846.
2. Richmond Enquirer, November 19, 1846.
3. Richmond Enquirer, November 20, 1846.

MUSTER ROLL OF CAPTAIN EPHRAIM G. ALBURTIS' COMPANY, FROM BERKELEY COUNTY, IN THE FIRST REGIMENT OF VIRGINIA VOLUNTEERS, COMMANDED BY COLONEL JOHN F. HAMTRAMCK CALLED INTO THE SERVICE OF THE UNITED STATES BY THE SECRETARY OF WAR UNDER THE ACT OF CONGRESS APPROVED MAY 13, 1846, FROM THE TWENTY-FIRST DAY OF JANUARY, 1847, (DATE OF THIS MUSTER) DURING THE WAR WITH MEXICO UNLESS SOONER DISCHARGED.

(*Source*.—The original Manuscript Roster supplied to the State Department of Archives and History, by Hon. Gray Silver, of Martinsburg, West Virginia.)

NAMES PRESENT AND ABSENT. (Privates in Alphabetical Order.)	RANK.	AGE.	JOINED FOR DUTY AND ENROLLED.		
			WHEN.	WHERE.	BY WHOM ENROLLED.
Ephraim G. Alburtis	Captain		21 Nov., 1846	Martinsburg	Captain Alburtis.
Otho H. Harrison	1st Lieut		21 Nov., 1846	Martinsburg	do
David W. Gray	2d Lieut		27 Nov., 1846	Berkeley	do
George W. Chambers, Jr.	2d Lieut		20 Dec., 1846	do	do
Edward W. Maxwell	1st Sergt	28	21 Nov., 1846	do	do
John C. Reed	Sergeant	30	27 Nov., 1846	Morgan	do
Robert Pollock	do	28	6 Jan., 1847	Berkeley	do
John Jamison	do	22	27 Nov., 1846	do	do
Daniel Poisal	Corporal	27	21 Nov., 1846	do	do
William H. Page	do	23	26 Dec., 1846	do	do
Thornton Coontz	do	26	29 Nov., 1846	do	do
William Sherrard	do	26	27 Nov., 1846	do	do
John W. Keef	Drummer	18	21 Nov., 1846	do	do
Benjamin W. Blondell	Fifer	18	30 Dec., 1846	do	do
Bennett, Anderson	Private	30	6 Jan., 1847	Berkeley	Lieutenant Harrison.
Beales, John A	do	22	21 Nov., 1846	do	Captain Alburtis.
Blessing, John H	do	18	27 Dec., 1846	do	do
Brown, John	do	35	6 Jan., 1847	do	do
Brown, Peter A	do	22	11 Jan., 1847	Alexandria	do
Brown, William J	do	18	6 Jan., 1847	Berkeley	Lieutenant Harrison.
Blakeney, George W	do	19	21 Nov., 1846	Martinsburg	Captain Alburtis.
Crowl, Jacob	do	30	19 Dec., 1846	do	do
Cain, William C	do	31	1 Jan., 1847	do	do
Creamer, John Q	do	22	21 Nov., 1846	do	do
Done, William D	do	19	6 Jan., 1847	do	Lieutenant Harrison.
Duffey, Andrew	do	26	30 Nov., 1846	do	Captain Alburtis.
Dobb, Carlisle	do	23	6 Jan., 1847	do	do
Dunn, William W	do		21 Jan., 1847		
Evans, James	do	31	9 Dec., 1846	do	do
Erwin, Charles	do	21	6 Jan., 1847	do	Lieutenant Harrison.
Freer, Henry S	do		21 Jan., 1847		
Gordon, Aaron K	do	35	21 Nov., 1846	do	Captain Alburtis.
Gainor, Robert	do	18	30 Nov., 1846	do	do
Grove, Lewis H	do	30	26 Dec., 1846	do	do
Griffin, Andrew M	do	43	4 Jan., 1847	Richmond	Lieutenant Harrison.
Gallaher, John S., Jr	do	32	6 Jan., 1847	Berkeley	Captain Alburtis.
Hagan Arthur	do	18	6 Jan., 1847	do	Lieutenant Harrison.
Heilfeinstein, Jacob H	do	25	24 Nov., 1846	do	Captain Alburtis.
Heller, Josiah	do	42	16 Dec., 1846	do	do
Heck, David	do	18	19 Dec., 1846	do	do
Hodges, George	do	22	6 Jan., 1847	do	Lieutenant Harrison.
Hood, John W	do	22	1 Dec., 1846	do	Captain Alburtis.
Hunter, John H	do	18	26 Dec., 1846	do	do
Harwood, James D	do	21	16 Dec., 1846	Richmond	do
Hooven, William	do	33	6 Jan., 1847	Berkeley	Lieutenant Harrison.
Hooser, Francis W. M	do		21 Jan., 1847		
Jones, John	do	18	6 Jan., 1847	Berkeley	Captain Alburtis.
Johnston, Joseph	do	25	6 Jan., 1847	do	do
Kisinger, Otho	do	36	17 Dec., 1846	do	do
Klein, Charles H	do	21	6 Jan., 1847	do	do
Kimley, William	do	22	6 Jan., 1847	do	do
Loftin, Charles	do		6 Jan., 1847	do	Lieutenant Harrison.
Lewis, James	do	24	22 Nov., 1846	do	Captain Alburtis.
McCommack, William	do	19	6 Jan., 1847	do	Lieutenant Harrison

MUSTER ROLL OF CAPTAIN EPHRAIM G. ALBURTIS' COMPANY, FROM BERKELEY COUNTY.—*Continued.*

NAMES PRESENT AND ABSENT. (Privates in Alphabetical Order.)	RANK.	AGE.	JOINED FOR DUTY AND ENROLLED.		
			WHEN.	WHERE.	BY WHOM ENROLLED.
Mansford, Robert	Private	31	28 Dec., 1846	Berkeley	Captain Alburtis.
Miller, John M	do	21	15 Dec., 1846	do	do
Mason, Thompson	do	29	21 Dec., 1846	do	do
McMinn, Joseph	do	22	15 Dec., 1846	do	do
Moore, Richard G	do	21	6 Jan., 1847	do	Lieutenant Harrison.
Mimey, John	do	24	6 Jan., 1847	do	Captain Alburtis.
Magee, Bernard D	do	18	6 Jan., 1847	do	Lieutenant Harrison.
Maguire, Patrick	do	19	6 Jan., 1847	do	do
McCorkle, Alexander C.	do		21 Jan., 1847		
Nople, William	do	28	6 Jan., 1847	Berkeley	Lieutenant Harrison.
Ott, John H	do	26	21 Nov., 1846	do	Captain Alburtis.
Prather, Socrates	do	22	4 Dec., 1846	Hampshire	do
Peare, James	do	29	14 Dec., 1846	Berkeley	do
Pentony, James	do	21	14 Dec., 1846	Morgan	do
Peare, John	do	29	12 Dec., 1846	Berkeley	do
Rinor, Jacob	do	18	23 Dec., 1846	do	do
Robbins, George T.	do	20	6 Jan., 1847	do	Lieutenant Harrison.
Reese, Jeremiah R	do	22	27 Nov., 1846	do	Captain Alburtis.
Reamy, John T	do	20	1 Jan., 1847	Richmond	do
Shoemaker, William L	do	34	6 Jan., 1847	Berkeley	Lieutenant Harrison.
Stewart, John P	do	36	23 Nov., 1846	do	Captain Alourtis.
Shank, Jacob	do	30	27 Nov., 1846	Morgan	do
Seigler, William	do	19	27 Dec., 1846	Berkeley	do
Stephens, Richard H	do	26	29 Dec., 1846	do	do
Sorber, William	do	21	6 Jan., 1847	do	do
Vanhorn, John C	do	20	6 Jan., 1847	do	Lieutenant Harrison.
Vanmetre, Abram G	do	19	26 Nov., 1846	do	Captain Alburtis.
Vaden, Paskil	do	35	13 Jan., 1847	Richmond	do
Vanlier, John	do	22	6 Jan., 1847	Berkeley	Lieutenant Harrison.
Weast, George L	do	19	18 Dec., 1846	do	Captain Alburtis.
Wilhelm, Henry	do	20	26 Dec., 1846	do	do
Williams, John R	do	21	6 Jan., 1847	do	do
Winter, Richard	do	26	6 Jan., 1847	do	do
Whiteman, Charles	do	18	6 Jan., 1847	do	Lieutenant Harrison.

I certify, on honor, That this Muster Roll exhibits the true state of Captain Epraim G. Alburtis' Company of the first Regiment Virginia Volunteers for the period herein mentioned; that each man answers to his own proper name in person; and that the remarks set opposite the name of each officer and soldier are accurate and just.

E. G. ALBURTIS,
Commanding the Company.

I certify, on honor, That each non-Commissioned Officer, musician, and private of this company, has furnished himself six months clothing or will in due time so furnish himself under my supervision agreeably to the intention of the law in authorizing an advance to be made on account of clothing.

E. G. ALBURTIS,
Commanding the Company.

I certify, on honor, That I have carefully examined the men whose names are borne on this Roll, and have accepted them, into the service of the United States during the war with Mexico, from this 21st day of January 1847.

LARKIN SMITH,
Capt. 8th Inf'y,
Mustering Officer.

The Governor's call for volunteers met with a response as enthusiastic in Jefferson county as it did in Berkeley; and while Captain Alburtis, was drilling the "Independent Blues" of Martinsburg. Captain John William Rowan was organizing the "Jefferson County Volunteers" at Charles Town and Shepherdstown. The roster of this Company was as follows:—

MUSTER ROLLS OF CAPTAIN JOHN WILLIAM ROWAN'S COMPANY, IN THE FIRST REGIMENT OF VIRGINIA VOLUNTEERS. COMMANDED BY COLONEL JOHN F. HAMTRAMCK, CALLED INTO THE SERVICE OF THE UNITED STATES BY THE SECRETARY OF WAR, UNDER THE ACT OF CONGRESS APPROVED MAY 13, 1846. FROM THE 27TH DAY OF JANUARY 1847. (DATE OF THIS MUSTER,) FOR THE TERM OF DURING THE WAR WITH MEXICO, UNLESS SOONER DISCHARGED.

(*Source*—Muster Rolls. Virginia Militia, War of 1812; pp. 73, 74.)

NAMES.	RANK.	WHEN ENROLLED.
J. W. Rowan	Captain	Dec. 1, 1846
John Avis	1st Lieut.	Dec. 1, 1846
Lawrence B. Washington	2d. do	Dec. 6, 1846
William McCormick	2d. do	Dec. 12, 1846
George Wm. Fairfax	1st Sergeant	Dec. 10, 1846
John W. Gallaher	2d do	Dec. 1, 1846
Lewis D. Ball	3d do	Dec. 9, 1846
John M. English	4th do	Dec. 20, 1846
James W. Duke	Corporal	Dec. 1, 1846
James R. Copeland	do	Dec. 1, 1846
Joseph Jones	do	Dec. 12, 1846
Wm. C. McClure	do	Jan. 4, 1847
Thomas H. Douglass	Drummer	Jan. 2, 1847
John Cunningham	Fifer	Jan. 1, 1847
William A. Baker	Private	Dec. 24, 1846
William F. Bragg	do	Dec. 29, 1846
Benjamin H. Bradford	do	Jan. 5, 1847
John P. Brock	do	Jan. 26, 1847
William Bryant	do	Jan. 5, 1847
James H. Boxer	do	Dec. 9, 1846
James B. Ball	do	Dec. 9, 1846
Peter Boughn	do	Dec. 24, 1846
William Birkit	do	Dec. 24, 1846
Vance W. Bush	do	Jan. 20, 1847
Emanuel Beam	do	Jan. 1, 1847
Cornelius P. Barr	do	Dec. 20, 1846
James W. Bateman	do	Jan. 20, 1847
Cornelius Carlin	do	Dec. 17, 1846
Fayette Cole	do	Jan. 26, 1847
Andrew J. Copenhafer	do	Dec. 9, 1846
Henry L. Cabell	do	Dec. 9, 1846
Henry Davy	do	Dec. 27, 1846
Joseph L. Everett	do	Dec. 11, 1846
Joseph Evans	do	Dec. 11, 1846
Samuel Ellis	do	Dec. 20, 1846
Charles French	do	Jan. 20, 1847
William C. Gover	do	Jan. 1, 1847
Carter Gibson	do	Jan. 24, 1847
John Grandberry	do	Dec. 26, 1846
David B. Glasscock	do	Jan. 21, 1847
Henry Gallenar	do	Jan. 21, 1847
Joseph L. Hampton	do	Dec. 29, 1846
John A. B. Harding	do	Dec. 4, 1846
Dennis Herrington	do	Dec. 17, 1846
Joseph Henning	do	Dec. 29, 1846

MUSTER ROLL OF CAPTAIN JOHN WILLIAM ROWAN'S COMPANY.
Continued.

NAMES.	RANK.	WHEN ENROLLED.
Stephen D. Hurst	Private	Dec. 7, 1846
John M. Heflin	do	Jan. 20, 1847
Morriss B. Howell	do	Dec. 17, 1846
John F. Hogan	do	Dec. 20, 1846
Richard W. Heafer	do	Dec. 13, 1846
James M. Harry	do	Dec. 20, 1846
John V. Howell	do	Dec. 14, 1846
William Hillard	do	Dec. 29, 1846
William Kirk	do	Dec. 11, 1846
William Kendall	do	Dec. 20, 1846
George W. Kile	do	Jan. 2, 1847
Beverley W. Lancaster	do	Dec. 6, 1846
James W. McKinney	do	Dec. 25, 1846
Pilate McKay	do	Dec. 11, 1846
Thomas McCroig	do	Jan. 20, 1847
Peter Miller	do	Dec. 24, 1846
Joseph Meyer	do	Jan. 20, 1847
Elijah L. Mindenall	do	Dec. 20, 1846
George W. Mack	do	Dec. 26, 1846
John F. Poland	do	Jan. 20, 1847
Thomas R. Satterfield	do	Dec. 20, 1846
James F. Shryock	do	Dec. 20, 1846
William P. Shipman	do	Dec. 28, 1846
James C. Seabright	do	Dec. 28, 1846
John William Sheets	do	Dec. 1, 1846
Barnardt Shelling	do	Dec. 25, 1846
James Thompson	do	Dec. 26, 1846
Charles M. Thompson	do	Dec. 20, 1846
Henry G. Vonreason	do	Jan. 20, 1847
John B. Whiting	do	Dec. 9, 1846
Charles Waddell	do	Dec. 23, 1846
Treadwell S. Wall	do	Dec. 23, 1846
David H. Watson	do	Jan. 20, 1847
Andrew J. Wood	do	Dec. 29, 1846

ORGANIZATION OF THE REGIMENT.

On the 10th day of December, 1846, Governor Smith writing the Secretary of War, said: "Give me the privilege of mustering both battalions at Richmond, and I will promptly furnish as fine a Regiment as the world can produce." With the request, the President and Secretary of War complied, and the place of rendezvous was thus changed from Guyandotte, on the Ohio, to Richmond on the James. The reasons assigned for this change were that the greater number of companies were organized east of the Blue Ridge; and that because of the bad roads and deep snows in the Alleghenies at that season of the year rendered the march to Guyandotte almost impossible. Speedily the various company organizations including those from Berkeley and Jefferson counties, gathered at Richmond where they were mustered into service by Captain Larkin Smith of the Eighth Regiment, United States Infantry. On the 22d of December the Governor and Council of State appointed John F.

Hamtramck. of Shepherdstown, Jefferson county, now in West Virginia, Colonel of the Regiment, and he, arrived at Richmond on the 30th ensuing, at which time there was a great military and civic demonstration.[4] On the 3d day of January, 1847, the first battalion of five companies, left Richmond for Old Point Comfort. The same day three other companies arrived at Richmond and two others were on the march to that city. On the 26th of that month, four companies sailed in the "Mayflower" from Old Point for Mexico; fresh water and supplies were taken on board at Havanna, Cuba, February 7th, and then the voyage was continued to Point Isabel, at the mouth of the Rio Grande. February 24th, Colonel Hamtramck having completed arrangements for the sailing of the remaining companies; and having received a beautiful sword, presented by the General Assembly of the Commonwealth. left Richmond overland for New Orleans. Early in March, the Regiment, complete in its organization was at Point Isabel, whence it proceeded by steamboats up the Rio Grande and San Juan rivers to Comargo, from which place it proceeded to Monterey.

A letter written at Monterey, by Dr. E. K. Chamberlin, Surgeon of the First Regiment Ohio Volunteers, under date of April 23, 1847, says:—

"The Virginia Regiment under Colonel Hamtramck escorting a train of one hundred and eighty wagons from Comargo, arrived here yesterday. They have been sixteen days on the way, having been detained by heavy rains. They were obliged to build several bridges over streams that three weeks ago had not a drop of water in them. The Regiment is one of the largest and finest appearing ones I have seen in the field. The officers are generally military men of experienc and appear to be gentlemen of high honor and bearing. The "Old Dominion" may well feel proud of the force she has sent into the field."[5] From Monterey, the march was continued by way of Santillo to Buena Vista. No braver Regiment did battle on the plains of Mexico than this.

VOLUNTEERING IN WESTERN VIRGINIA WEST OF THE ALLEGHENY MOUNTAINS FOR THE WAR WITH MEXICO.

There was no company organization in Greenbrier county for the War with Mexico, but a number of men from this county hastened away to Staunton and enlisted in the Augusta County Company, formed at that place, and commanded by Captain Kenton Harper. The Roster of this Company is printed in the "Muster Rolls of the

---

4. R'chmond Enquirer, December 31, 1846.
5. Wheeling Argus, May 23, 1847.

Virginia Militia," pp. 69, 70. A local historian familiar with the family names in Greenbrier, would, doubtless, readily detect and classify those from that county, who served in Captain Harper's Company. This will, doubtless, be done by some interested person in the near future.

MONONGALIA COUNTY MEN IN THE WAR WITH MEXICO.

(*Source—Wheeling Argus*, June 15, 1847; also Wiley's "History of Monongalia County," p. 496.)

Lieutenant George W. Clutter, early in 1847, enlisted a detachment of thirty-two men in Monongalia county, for service in the War with Mexico. They were known as the "Mountain Boys of Monongalia," and all left Morgantown, May 21, 1847, and proceeded to Fortress Monroe, Virginia, where they were attached to Company B of the Thirteenth United States Infantry, of which John Tyler was captain. He resigned and Lieutenant Clutter was promoted to the captaincy. The Company sailed June 9, 1847, in the brig "Tuckahoe" from Old Point Comfort, to Point Isabel at the mouth of the Rio Grande, whence the Regiment marched to join the forces of General Taylor. The names of these Monongalia county men were as follows:—

Levi L. Bryte	John W. Hayes	Elliss Mitchell
William Black	Richard Hall	John McFadden (dis.)
Jesse J. Carraco	Oakley Hopkins	William Miller
William Christy (died)	Aaron Hamilton (died)	Amos Martin (died)
Henry Dean	N. N. Hoffman	Lewis Powelson
William Dean	Alexander Jenkins	William Pixler (Pa.)
Wilson Dean	John Keefover	Felix Scott
George Exline	——— John Koontz	Jeff Scott
Jacob Farr (Pa)	William Miller	Benjamin Scott (died)
Oliver Guthrie	Levi Hayes	Davis Toothman
George Hayes		

A RESPONSE TO THE CALL OF THE GOVERNOR FROM HARRISON COUNTY.

The *Harrison Republican* in its issue of June 26, 1846, states that the Eleventh Regiment of the Virginia Military establishment (that of Harrison county), was paraded at Clarksburg, under Colonel Augustine J. Smith, and that forty or fifty "fell in for Mexico."[6]

---
6. Haymond's "History of Harrison County," p. 312.

TENDER OF A COMPANY FROM KANAWHA COUNTY.

December 26, 1846, Governor Smith wrote the Secretary of War, saying: "Messrs. Kemper and Fry, two gallant young gentlemen from Kanawha, have just called on me to know if they can raise a company in that county for service in the War with Mexico." Their request was of course denied for the Regiment was already full.

READY FOR THE WAR IN OHIO COUNTY.

(*Source*—The *Wheeling Times*, and the *Wheeling Argus*.)

The *Wheeling Times*, in its issue of November 25, 1846, contained a call for a meeting of the people of Ohio county on that evening, for the purpose of organizing a company for service in the War with Mexico. The ranks of the company were filled, and on the 11th of February, 1847, a meeting was held for the purpose of organization. Colonel Benjamin F. Kelly presided, and John J. Watson acted as Secretary; Daniel S. Lee was elected Captain; George W. Clutter, First Lieutenant; and John Jay Watson, Second Lieutenant. An editorial in the *Argus*, of February 23d ensuing, recommends that the ladies of Wheeling present the Company with a flag, before its departure. But now there was disappointment; information was received from the Governor of Virginia to the effect that the Regiment called for by the president was full, and no additional troops could be received. It was now that Lieutenant Clutter, previously mentioned, proceeded to Monongalia where he enlisted the detachment which became part of Company B. of the Thirteenth United States Infantry.

As early as December 10, 1846, Governor Smith had information that a company was being organized in Cabell county, Western Virginia, for service in the War with Mexico.

A PATRIOTIC DEMONSTRATION IN CABELL COUNTY.

The *Richmond Enquirer* in its issue of January 16th, 1848, has the following under the caption, "Volunteer Movements in Western Virginia."

"A letter from Cabell C. H., of the 6th of January, alludes to the formation of a volunteer company for Mexico. The Regiment was called together on the 4th instant, when fifty-three stepped forward and enrolled themselves as ready to march and fight in their country's cause.

They were to start on the 7th for Wayne C. H., where the Regiment was to meet on the 9th, hoping to make up the requisite number. Though this company will be formed too late to be accepted by the State, it shows that there are some gallant spirits in Cabell county. The citizens of the Courthouse have subscribed $200 for their benefit, and Charles Conner (so public-spirited a gentleman deserves to be named with praise) has made a donation of $100. Again, we say, well done old Cabell! She has set a patriotic example for her neighbors, which will not be lost upon them, should the country hereafter call upon Virginia for more of her sons to fight in a good cause."

CAPTAIN ELISHA W. McCOMAS' COMPANY C. OF THE ELEVENTH UNITED STATES INFANTRY.

The Virginia Regiment being full and already gone to Mexico, Elisha W. McComas and Joseph Samuels secured Commissions as Captain and First Lieutenant, and at Wheeling, and in Cabell and other counties bordering on the Ohio, raised a company which was attached as Company C. of the Eleventh United States Infantry. The Rendezvous was Guyandotte, in Cabell county, from which the Company proceeded to Newport barracks, where it was mustered into service. "Yesterday," said the *New Orleans Delta,* in its issue of August 5, 1847, "Captain Elisha W. McComas and Lieutenant Joseph Samuels, with seventy-five privates of Company C. of the Eleventh United States Infantry of the Regular Army, arrived on the steamer "Pontiac" from Newport barracks.'"[7]

WEST VIRGINIA ORGANIZATIONS WHICH SAW SERVICE IN MEXICO.

Four West Virginia Organizations were accepted—two by Virginia and two by the United States—and saw service on the battlefields of Mexico. These were as follows:—

Captain Ephraim G. Alburtis' Berkeley County Company, in First Regiment Virginia Volunteers.

Captain John William Rowan's Jefferson County Company, in First Regiment Virginia Volunteers.

Captain Elisha W. McComas' Company C. of Eleventh Regiment, United States Infantry.

Captain George W. Clutter's Detachment of Monongalia "Mountain Boys" attached to Company B of the Thirteenth Regiment, United States Infantry.

---

7. Delta quoted by Wheeling Argus of August 16, 1847.

WEST VIRGINIA ORGANIZATIONS WHICH TENDERED THEIR SERVICES
TO THE STATE OF VIRGINIA BUT WERE NOT RECEIVED.

Ten Companies of West Virginians were enlisted, organized and tendered their services to the Governor of the Commonwealth for the War with Mexico, but were not received for the reason that the National Government called upon Virginia for only one Regiment and this, as we have seen was speedily filled by men from the eastern part of the State. These ten West Virginia Companies were as follows:—

Kemper & Fry's Kanawha Riflemen of Kanawha county.
Captain Daniel S. Lee's Volunteers of Ohio county.
Captain Elisha W. McComas' Volunteers of Cabell county.
Captain ——— Kramer's Monongalia Blues of Monongalia county.
Captain ——— Fowler's Cheat River Invincibles of Preston county.
Captain ——— Ellison's Cavalry Company of Preston county.
Captain Byron J. Bassel's Volunteers of Harrison county.
Captain Hiram W. Winters' Bridgeport Rifles of Harrison county.
Captain Cyrus Vance's Harrison Guards from Harrison county.
Captain Cruger W. Smith's Clarksburg Rifles of Harrison county.

It is thus seen that, had they been permitted, these West Virginia Volunteers would have completely filled the ranks of the First Virginia Regiment; or had a second Regiment been called for, were ready to organize it with a full complement of a thousand men.

SERVICE OF INDIVIDUAL SOLDIERS.

Among the West Virginians who served in the War with Mexico, were Lieutenant Forbes Britain, Seventh United States Infantry, of Harrison county; and Lieutenant Thomas J. Jackson, First United States Artillery, the latter born in Harrison county and reared in Lewis. He was the famous "Stonewall" Jackson, of the Confederate States Army. Others who served from Harrison county, were George Duff, Hiram Applebay, Judson Holden, and George Exline, all in Company C. of the Eleventh United States Infantry. Edgar Haymond and his brother Alfred from Braxton county, also enlisted, the former dying in Mexico, the latter soon after his return. Levi L. Bryte, of Grant District, and Alexander Jenkins of Reno District, both in Preston county, and others whose names have not been ascertained, served in this war. Isaac Lewis and ——— Knopp of Mason county, were members of Company

C. of the Eleventh Regiment United States Army. The Roster of this Company may be preserved in the War Department; if we had it it would be found to contain many familiar names of men in the West Virginia counties bordering on the Ohio river, especially those of Ohio and Cabell.

Where are the Rosters of these Company Organizations? Lost or preserved, which? Some are doubtless lost; others may yet be found in the possession of individuals; in county record offices; in the Archives of Virginia; or in the possession of the War Department of the National Government. Doubtless search will be made for them in the future.

CHAPTER VIII.

WEST VIRGINIA SOLDIERS WHO WENT TO HARPER'S FERRY IN 1859, AT THE TIME OF JOHN BROWN'S INSURRECTION AT THAT PLACE.

The intelligence that went out from Harper's Ferry on the morning of the 17th of October, 1859, sent a thrill throughout Virginia and astonished the whole nation. It was the prelude to the greatest civil war of all time, and the world has learned the story of the forcible seizure of the National Arsenal at that place; the capture, imprisonment, the killing of the people, and the almost immediate suppression and extermination of the insurgents. The madness of the attempt, the boldness—amounting to heroism on the part of the handful of men who were concerned in the movement, and especially the romantic history and personal character of the chief actor—all have given to the place and the event an interest and importance which will keep both ever prominent in American, yea in world history. No sooner was it known that an insurrection had taken place than Virginia military organizations were ordered out, and those in Jefferson and Berkeley Counties, both now in West Virginia, were the first to arrive on the scene. These were as follows:—

1. "The Jefferson Guards" of Charles Town, Jefferson county; Captain John H. Rowan, who had commanded a Jefferson County Company in the War with Mexico twelve years before. This Company was the first to arrive at Harper's Ferry on October 17, 1859, the morning after the Insurgents took possession of the Armory and Arsenal buildings. Type written copy of roster supplied by C. Frank Gallaher, of Charles Town, West Virginia.

2. "The Hamptramck Guards" formerly the Shepherdstown Light Infantry. It took its name from its Captain, John F. Hamptramck, who with the rank of Colonel, commanded the First Virginia Regiment in Mexico. This Company was on the scene at Harper's Ferry early on the day following the occupancy of the town by the Insurgents. Printed roster supplied from *Shepherdstown Register* of March 24, 1910. Typewritten roster supplied by C. Frank Gallaher of Charlestown, West Virginia.

3. Berkeley County Company; organized at Bunker Hill, Berkeley County, in 1859, and the night after the Insurrection at Harper's Ferry, it was stationed at Bedington, in said county, awaiting orders

to proceed to the scene of action. Manuscript roster supplied by Hon. Gray Silver of Martinsburg, West Virginia; also copy printed in *Evening Journal* at Martinsburg, April 10, 1910, supplied by Hon. Thomas C. Miller, of Shepherdstown, West Virginia.

4. "The Berkeley County Rifles;" Captain E. G. Alburtis, left Martinsburg early in the morning after the Insurrection, and arrived on the scene of action, shortly after noon. Typewritten roster supplied by Hon. Gray Silver, of Martinsburg, West Virginia.

5. "The Berkeley Rangers," of Berkeley County; an Infantry Company of Gerrardstown, in that county; commanded by Captain James W. Gray, hastened away to Harper's Ferry, on the first alarm. Typewritten roster supplied by Hon. Gray Silver of Martinsburg, West Virginia.

From the date of the Insurrection, October 16th, 1859, to the final execution of the last of the insurgents, fully 1700 Virginia troops were on duty, at different times, at Harper's Ferry and Charlestown; but the companies mentioned above—all West Virginia companies—were the first to arrive upon the scene.

CHAPTER IX.

WEST VIRGINIA SOLDIERS IN THE FEDERAL ARMY DURING THE WAR BETWEEN THE STATES.

THE REGIMENTAL AND OTHER ORGANIZATIONS.

INTRODUCTORY.

The world knows the story of American Civil War. Forty-five years have come and gone since the surviving soldiery of West Virginia, engaged therein, returned to their homes; and in all these years no rosters of Regiments, or other organizations have been printed by the State. The object in the preparation of "CHAPTER IX," of this Report, is to preserve data relating to West Virginia Soldiers in this war, and, at the same time, make it readily accessible to all who may care to examine it.

For the material necessary to the compilation of this, we are indebted to the care and labor of Colonel James S. Wheat,[1] and Colonel Henry J. Samuels[2], the Adjutant Generals during the period of the Restored Government; (June 20, 1861, to June 20, 1863) and to Brigadier-General Francis P. Pierpont,[3] the first Adjutant General of West Virginia.

Neither Colonel Wheat nor Colonel Samuels ever made any official report to Governor Pierpont; but each collected and preserved papers and records which were, by an Act of the General Assem-

---

1. James S. Wheat was born in the District of Columbia and came to Wheeling in 1831. Soon after he was admitted to the bar and speedily rose to distinction in his chosen profession, and as an orator as well. He was appointed Adjutant General by Governor Pierpont, on the 27th of June, 1861, and served until the 30th of September ensuing. Later, he was Attorney General under the Restored Government, and was a member of the State Constitutional Convention in 1872.—V. A. L.

2. Henry J. Samuels was appointed Adjutant General September 30th, 1861, by Governor Pierpont, and continued in office until June 20th, 1863. He was born in Barboursville, Cabell county, West Virginia, July 12, 1825. He received a liberal education, studied law, and became a distinguished jurist. For several years he was associated in the practice of law with Hon. James H. Ferguson. At the close of the war he returned to Barboursville, where for several years, a judge of the judicial circuit in which he resided, and was a member of the House of Delegates in 1891. He died, June 27, 1898, at Barboursville, and is buried near that place. On the 10th day of October, 1848, Judge Samuels wedded Rebecca Bartram, a native of Pennsylvania, but at that time a resident of Lawrence county, Ohio.—V. A. L.

3. Francis Perry Pierpont, the first Adjutant General of West Virginia, was born at Fairmont, now in Marion county, West Virginia on the 23rd day of February, 1840, his parents being Zackquill Morgan Pierpont and Martha (Vandevoort) Pierpont. When but two years of age, he was taken by them to Harris-

bly, under the Restored Government, transferred to the new State of West Virginia. It was this undigested and unclassified mass of material that came to the hands of Adjutant General Pierpont on June 20, 1863—that on which West Virginia became a State.

FIRST REPORT OF THE ADJUTANT GENERAL PIERPONT[4]— THAT FOR 1863.

General Pierpont at once set about arranging, in systematic order, the data in his office, which was to be the basis of his first Annual Report. Speaking of this Report he said:—

"I should have liked very much to have given [therein] a complete list, or complete rolls of all the troops mustered into the United States' service from this State, but owing to the great neglect of mustering officers to return to this office copies of the muster-in rolls, and of the recruiting officers to return their enlistment papers, especially of the first regiments organized. *the records of the office are very incomplete and inaccurate, and to give what the records of the office show, only would, I fear, be productive of more harm than good.* Indeed so incomplete are the records, that my report of the number of troops furnished by the State is taken from a statement from the Adjutant General's office of the United States, which I think is a very correct estimate."

Thus it appears that, because of the "incomplete and inaccurate" character of the records of the Adjutant General's office, which came into the hands of General Pierpont, he chose rather to

---

ville, Ritchie county. Here he attended the old time subscription school of his day; and then, having completed the course of study of the Fairmont Academy, he engaged in the study of law and was admitted to the bar when quite young. At the beginning of the war between the States, he assisted in recruiting the Twelfth Regiment West Virginia Infantry; and became Second-Lieutenant in Company F.; August 7, 1862, he was commissioned First-Lieutenant and Adjutant of the Regiment: and nineteen davs later was raised to the rank of Major, an office which he resigned June 16, 1863, to accept the appointment of Adjutant-General of the new State, tendered him by Governor Arthur I. Boreman. He assumed the duties of this position, June 20th ensuing, and continued therein until September 10, 1866, when he resigned and hastened away to Cambridge, Massachusetts, where he attended the Law School of Harvard University. Having graduated, he returned to Ritchie county, where he engaged in the practice of his profession; and was at once elected Prosecuting Attorney. But now his health failed, and in November, 1868, he accepted an invitation from his friend, Jacob Hornbrook, to accompany him and family to Florida. On the steamer "Grosback" all arrived at New Orleans January 1, 1869. Here General Pierpont was so ill that he was unable to proceed further. Of this he notified his relatives and his father and brother, William, hastened to him, scarcely did they see him alive for he died January 7th ensuing. The body was brought home and buried by the Masonic Fraternity in the village cemetery at Harrisville, in Ritchie county. A beautiful marble shaft ten feet in height marks the spot.—V. A. L.

4. So scarce are the three Reports of Adjutant General Pierpont, that I have never seen but two copies of that of 1863; four copies of that for 1864; and three copies of that of 1865. Two copies of the first, one of the second, and three copies of the third are in the Library of the State Department of Archives and History. It is from these Reports that the following data relative to West Virginia soldiers, in the Federal services during the Civil War, have been compiled.—V. A. L.

use data from the Report of the Adjutant General of the United States. His Report—that for 1863—covers thirty-four pages, six of which are devoted to introductory and explanatory matter, while the others contain rosters of the Field, Staff and Line Officers of sixteen Regiments of Infantry; four Regiments of Cavalry; one of Light Artillery; two Companies of Independent Exempt Infantry of the city of Wheeling; and a "Recapitulation," showing the total enlistments in West Virginia Regiments, at the close of the year 1863, to be 20,027, of which 689 were from Ohio; and deducting these, 19,338 were to be credited to West Virginia. This Report was printed as a Public Document, in the Journal of the House of Delegates, Session of 1864. Printed in the same volume is the Report of George W. Brown, the Quartermaster General of West Virginia, for the same period as that covered by that of the Adjutant General.

SECOND REPORT OF THE ADJUTANT GENERAL PIERPONT—
THAT FOR 1864.

The energy and labor of Adjutant General Pierpont is shown in the preparation of this Second Report—that for the year 1864. It is an octavo volume containing 740 pages. Explanatory matter occupies thirteen pages. Following this are Rosters of the Field, Staff and Line Officers of eleven Regiments of Volunteer Infantry; two Regiments of Veteran Infantry; seven Regiments of Cavalry; and two of Artillery. Then appear Rosters of Companies in thirteen Regiments of Infantry; two Companies of Independent Exempt Infantry of Wheeling; seven Regiments of Cavalry, three of these being Mounted Infantry; and one of Artillery.

THIRD REPORT OF ADJUTANT GENERAL PIERPONT—THAT FOR 1865
—DATED JANUARY 8, 1866.

Adjutant General Pierpont's Third Official Report—that for 1865—is an octavo volume of 444 printed pages. The war had ended when he prepared it. It is a most interesting document; one of inestimable value to the military history of the State. Nineteen pages of introductory matter describe conditions, as then existing, and the return and discharge of the Regiments. This is followed by Rosters of Field, Staff and Line Officers, of fourteen Regiments of Volunteer Infantry; two Regiments of Veteran Infantry; two Companies of Independent Exempt Infantry of Wheeling; seven Regiments of Cavalry, three of these being Mounted Infantry; and one Regiment of Light Artillery. Then comes a Roster of Colored Soldiers, credited to the State, who served in the Forty-fifth Regiment United States Colored Infantry; Lists of men who were prisoners of war at the time their Regiments were mustered out of service; names of men who died in prison, at Andersonville and Camp Lawton, Georgia, and at Belle Isle and Danville, Virginia; and Lists of Companies of State Guards, organized in different counties of the State, for the protection of such counties; and last of all, the complete roster of the Sixth Regiment of Veteran Cavalry, with casualties therein. Historical data of this Regiment appears on pp. 16-17 of this Report.

The following tabulated form shows references in Adjutant General Pierpont's three Annual Reports, to all the military organizations of the State, which were engaged in the Federal army during the Civil War:

REGIMENTS.	REF. TO ADJ. GENERAL'S REPORT FOR 1863. PAGES.	REF. TO ADJ. GENERAL'S REPORT FOR 1864.		REF. TO ADJ. GENERAL'S REPORT FOR 1865.	
		PAGES		PAGES	
VOLUNTEER INFANTRY.					
First Regiment (3 months)	7.	14, 15.	45- 73.	27.	405.
" (3 years)	8.	37, 38.	597-623.	28.	99-108.
Second 5	9.	38, 39.	626-654.	82-85.	331-339.
Third 6	10.	15, 16.	76-103.	85-90.	423-444.
Fourth	11.	16, 17.	106-133.	30-32.	108-117.
Fifth		17-19.	135-189.	33-35.	117-126.
Sixth	12, 13.	40-41.	191-226.	36-39.	126-141.
Seventh	14, 15.	40-42.	656-693.	39-43.	141-166.
Eighth 7	16.	20.	229-255.	90-93.	346-360.
Ninth	17.	21, 22.	259-285.	43-45.	166-175.
Tenth	18.	22, 23.	288-312.	46-48.	176-185.
Eleventh	19.	23, 24.	318-343.	48-51.	185-193.
Twelfth	20.	24, 25.	346-371.	51-54.	193-201.
Thirteenth	21.	25, 26.	373-398.	54-56.	201-208.
Fourteenth	22.	27, 28.	400-424.	57-59.	209-218.
Fifteenth	23.			59-62.	219-224.
Sixteenth	24.			62-63.	225-245.
Seventeenth 1 year			426-439.	63-65.	245-258.
VETERAN INFANTRY.					
First Regiment 8		29.	439-464.	65-67.	259-264.
Second Regiment 9		30.		67-68.	264-285.
VOLUNTEER CAVALRY.					
First Regiment	25, 26.	31, 32.	471-503.	69-73.	287-303.
Second Regiment	27, 28.	32, 34.	505-537.	74-77.	303-312.
Third Regiment	30, 31.	34, 35.	541-567.	78-80.	312-329.
Fourth Regiment (6 months)		36, 37.	570-606.	80-82.	329-331.
Fifth Regiment (Late 2d Inf.)		37, 38.	607-623.	82-85.	331-339.
Sixth Regiment (Late 3d Inf.)		38, 39.	626-654.	85-90.	339-346.
Seventh Regiment 7 (Late 8th Inf.)		40-42.	656-693.	90-93.	346-360.
Sixth Regiment Veteran Cavalry 10 (Late 5th & 6th Vol. Cavalry.)					
ARTILLERY VOLUNTEERS.					
First Regiment Light Artillery.	— 32.	41.	697-730.	94-95.	360-369.
INDEPENDENT COMPANIES.					
Wheeling Exempt Companies 11.			465-470.	—	391-392.
State Guards 12.				69.	286-287.

5. The Second Regiment of Infantry was changed to the Fifth West Virginia Cavalry Regiment, by an order of the Secretary of War, issued January 26, 1864.
6. The Third Regiment of Infantry was changed to the Sixth West Virginia Cavalry Regiment Veteran Volunteers by an order of the Secretary of War, issued January 26, 1864.
7. The Eighth Regiment of Infantry was changed to the Seventh West Virginia Cavalry Regiment, by an order of the Secretary of War, issued January 27, 1864.
8. The First Regiment of Veteran Infantry was formed by the consolidation of re-enlisted men of the Fifth and Ninth Volunteer Regiments, by an order of the Secretary of War, dated November 9, 1864.
9. The Second Regiment of Veteran Infantry was formed by the consolidation of the re-enlisted men of the First and Fourth Volunteer Regiments, by an order of the Secretary of War, dated December 10, 1864.
10. The Sixth Regiment Veteran Cavalry was formed by consolidation of the re-enlisted men of the 5th and 6th Volunteer Cavalries.
11. The organization known as "Independent Exempt Infantry," consisted of two companies stationed at Wheeling, as guards of the city during the War. Members thereof were exempt from other military service.
12. These were Companies—forty-four in number—organized in different counties of the State for service in their respective counties. The men composing them were sworn into the service of the State for one year, were paid and supplied by the State with arms and equipments.

TOTAL NUMBER OF ENLISTMENTS IN THE FEDERAL ARMY FROM WEST VIRGINIA FROM 1861 TO 1865.

How many West Virginians served in the Federal Army during the War between the States? A correct answer to this question has never been made; in all probability never will be. Immediately after the adoption of the Ordinance of Secession, April 17, 1861, the enlistment of troops for the National Army began at Wheeling, and speedily extended throughout the counties giving allegiance to the Restored Government. On the day on which West Virginia was admitted into the Union, June 20, 1863, fully 12,000 men within the bounds of the new State had volunteered their services, in the war for the Union. By the report of the Adjutant General, Francis P. Pierpont, for the year 1863, it is shown that the enlistments in the State up to December 31st, of that year, numbered 20,027, of which number 689 had come from Ohio. Deducting this number, it appears that at the close of the year 1863 West Virginia had furnished 19,338 men to the Federal Army. Enlistments continued to increase so that, as shown by the Report of the Adjutant General, they numbered 26,540 the 31st of December, 1864. The following statements for the whole period of the war exhibit the requisitions of the President on West Virginia for troops, and also the numbers furnished under each call—that is, "West Virginia in Account with the United States":

REQUISITIONS—THE STATE, DR.

1861 To quota of calls made that year.......................... 8,497
1862 To quota of call on July 2, that year..................... 4,650

1862	To quota of calls for 300,000 nine months men, reduced to three years standing.....................................	1,162
1864	To quota under call of February 1st that year for 500,000 men	5,127
1864	To quota under call of March 14th that year for 200,000 men	2,051
1864	To quota under call of July 19th that year for 500,000 men	5,928
1864	To quota under call of December 19th that year for 300,000 men	4,431
	Total requisitions on State........................	31,846
1861	By enlistments under calls of that year....................	12,688
1862	By enlistments under calls of July 2, that year...........	3,888
1863	By enlistments from May 26th to December 31st, that year	3,281
1864	By enlistments from January 1st to January 31st, that year	131
1864	By enlistments and re-enlistments from February 1st to August 1st, that year.................................	4,712
1864	By enlistments from August 1st to December 31st, that year	1,956
1865	By enlistments from August 1st to August 31st, that year..	2,509
	Total enlistments to August 31st, 1865..............	29,163

The foregoing statements show a deficiency on the part of the State of 2,683 troops; but this must have been made up, for by a statement of the Provost Marshall of the United States, made September 2, 1865, it was shown that on April 30, 1865, the State of West Virginia had furnished, of all arms and for different terms of service, 31,884 men, for service in the United States Army.

These figures, however, include all re-enlistments of which there were quite a large number. Of these there were two regiments of Veteran Infantry, and one of Cavalry. They were composed of three years men who re-enlisted for the war. In addition to the men composing these regiments, numbers of others re-enlisted, so that it is believed that the actual number of troops from West Virginia in the United States service during the war was about 28,000.

BOUNTIES PAID BY COUNTIES IN WEST VIRGINIA, TO VOLUNTEERS.

As the several calls by the President of the United States were made for men, the new State of West Virginia put forth every effort to supply its quota; and this was done by voluntary enlistments. To encourage these, large bounties were paid in many counties of the State. At the close of the War Governor Boreman requested General Pierpont, his Adjutant-General, to make inquiry regarding these county bounties, as to what counties paid them, and the amount paid by each. In compliance with this request, General Pierpont addressed letters to the Boards of Supervisors of the several counties in the State, requesting from them an official statement of the amount of money expended in each for the payment of Local Bounties to soldiers. In his report for 1865, dated "Wheeling, West Virginia, January 8, 1866," General Pierpont, when speaking of these letters, said: "As yet I have not received reports from all the counties, but sufficient to know that over one and a half million dollars have been paid for that purpose. A statement of the amount paid by each county is hereto annexed:—

The following is an extract from official statement received from the several counties in this State, showing the amount of money levied and paid by such counties as local bounties for volunteers mustered into the United States service, and money appropriated for the relief of soldiers' families in such counties.[13]

COUNTY.	TOTAL AMOUNT LEVIED AND PAID.	REMARKS.
Barbour	$ 46,684.91	Local bounties for volunteers.
Brooke	85,155.14	Local bounties for volunteers.
Doddridge	71,355.00	Local bounties for volunteers.
Gilmer	3,698.71	Local bounties for volunteers.
Jackson	14,000.00	Local bounties for volunteers.
Kanawha	9,400.00	Local bounties for volunteers.
Lewis	28,575.20	Local bounties for volunteers. $1,400 of this amount for relief of soldiers' families.
Monongalia	154,425.00	Local bounties for volunteers.
Marion	103,075.00	Local bounties for volunteers.
Pleasants	37,900.00	Local bounties for volunteers.
Ritchie	30,270.00	Local bounties for volunteers.
Tyler	16,330.00	Local bounties for volunteers.
Wirt	27,975.00	Local bounties for volunteers.
Mason	40,110.00	Local bounties for volunteers.
Harrison	258,438.04	Local bounties for volunteers.
Ohio	334,959.00	Local bounties for volunteers.
Preston	135,700.00	Local bounties for volunteers.
Upshur	55,843.00	Local bounties for volnnteers.
Wetzel	65,478.42	Local bounties for volunteers. $500 of this amount for soldiers' families.
Hancock	60,830.00	Local bounties for volunteers.
Marshall	181,325.65	Local bounties for volunteers. $1,500 of this amount for soldiers' families.
Putnam	12,630.00	Local bounties for volunteers.
Wood	187,791.00	Local bounties for volunteers. $8,000 of this amount for soldiers' families.
Cabell	3,600.00	Local bounties for volunteers.
Total	$1,965,549.07	

13. "There are," said Adjutant General Pierpont, "several counties from which no statements have been received, and the total amount levied and paid is probably over two millions of dollars"

INFANTRY VOLUNTEERS.

FIRST REGIMENT INFANTRY VOLUNTEERS.—*Three months service.*

This Regiment was organized at Wheeling in May, 1861, from volunteer companies from Hancock, Brooke, Ohio, and Marshall counties at "Camp Carlisle" on Wheeling Island. It participated in the battle at Philippi, Barbour county, June 3, 1861. It was mustered out of service at Wheeling, August 28, 1861.

FIRST REGIMENT INFANTRY VOLUNTEERS—*Three years service.*

This Regiment was organized in the northern Pan Handle in the autumn of 1861; served three years, and its non-veterans were mustered out of service at Wheeling, November 26, 1864, by Lieutenant Henry C. Peck of the Fourteenth United States Infantry. The veterans, or re-enlisted men of this Regiment, were, by an order of the Secretary of War dated December 10, 1864, consolidated with the veteran volunteers of Fourth Volunteer Infantry, to form the Second Veteran Infantry Regiment.

SECOND REGIMENT INFANTRY VOLUNTEERS—*Three years service.*

This Regiment was organized at Beverly in Randolph county, in August, 1861, and consisted of companies from Wood, Taylor and other counties. By an order of the Secretary of War, bearing date May 18, 1863, Company G was transferred to the First Regiment of Light Artillery. By another order of the Secretary of War, issued January 26, 1864, this Regiment was changed to "Mounted Infantry," but is known thereafter as the Fifth Regiment Volunteer Cavalry; but it was never armed or equipped as such. The non-veterans were mustered out of service in August, 1863, and the re-enlisted, two hundred in number, were, in the ensuing November, consolidated with veterans of the Sixth Mounted Infantry (then known as the Sixth Regiment Volunteer Cavalry) to form the Sixth Veteran Cavalry.

THIRD REGIMENT INFANTRY VOLUNTEERS—*Three years service.*

This Regiment was organized at Clarksburg, in Harrison County, in July 1861. January 26, 1864, the Regiment was changed to

"Mounted Infantry," but known henceforth as the Sixth Regiment Volunteer Cavalry. The non-veterans of the Regiment were mustered out of service at Beverly, in August 1864. while the re-enlisted men were reorganized into six companies which were consolidated with the re-enlisted men of the Fifth Regiment Cavalry—the "Mounted Infantry" of the Second Regiment—and thus formed the Sixth Regiment Veteran Cavalry, which should have been designated in the Military Establishment as the First Regiment Veteran Cavalry.

FOURTH REGIMENT INFANTRY VOLUNTEERS—*Three years service.*

This Regiment was organized at Point Pleasant, in Mason County, in the months of June, July, August and September, 1861. The non-veterans were mustered out of service upon the expiration of their term in the summer of 1864; and the re-enlisted men were, by an order of the Secretary of War, dated December 10, 1864, consolidated with the re-enlisted men of the First Regiment Volunteer Infantry, to form the Second Regiment Veteran Infantry.

FIFTH REGIMENT INFANTRY VOLUNTEERS—*Three years service.*

This Regiment was organized at Ceredo, in Wayne County, in the months of July and August, 1861, and was mustered into the service of the United States on the 18th of October ensuing. The non-veterans were mustered out on the expiration of their terms, in the summer of 1864; and the re-enlisted men were, by an order of the Secretary of War, dated November 9, 1864, consolidated with the re-enlisted men of the Ninth Regiment Infantry, to form the First Regiment Veteran Infantry.

SIXTH REGIMENT INFANTRY VOLUNTEERS—*Three years service.*

This Regiment was organized in August 1861, and was by special authority, recruited to fifteen companies. The non-veterans were mustered out as their terms of service expired; while the re-enlisted men, together with a large number of recruits, preserved the regimental organization until June 10, 1865, when it was mustered out of service at Wheeling.

SEVENTH REGIMENT INFANTRY VOLUNTEERS—*Three years service.*

This Regiment was organized at Wheeling and Grafton, during the months of July, August, September, and October, 1861. No other Regiment from the state saw harder service than this. The non-veterans were mustered out of service as their terms expired, but the re-enlisted men, together with the recruits which came to it continued the Regiment in the field until it was mustered out of service at Munson's Hill, Virginia, July 1, 1865.

EIGHTH REGIMENT INFANTRY VOLUNTEERS—*Three years service.*

This Regiment was organized in the Great Kanawha Valley in the autumn of 1861. On the 13th of June, 1863, it was, by an order of the War Department, mounted and henceforth drilled as "Mounted Infantry." By a second order of the Secretary of War, dated January 27, 1864, the "Eighth Mounted Infantry" was changed to the Seventh Regiment Cavalry. Now, the non-veterans were discharged, but nearly 400 members of the Regiment re-enlisted as veterans, and together with about 250 recruits, preserved the regimental organization until mustered out of the service in 1865.

NINTH REGIMENT INFANTRY VOLUNTEERS—*Three years service.*

This Regiment was organized at Guyandotte, in Cabell County, February 28, 1862, of companies from the counties of Cabell, Wood, Jackson, Mason and Roane. The men in this regiment represented twenty-four counties. In 1864, the non-veterans were discharged as their terms of service expired; but 357 members of the Regiment re-enlisted, and with the veterans of the Fifth Regiment Infantry were, by an order of the Secretary of War, dated November 9, 1864, consolidated and formed the First Veteran Infantry Regiment.

TENTH REGIMENT INFANTRY VOLUNTEERS—*Three years service.*

The organization of this Regiment was begun in March, 1862. It was mustered out of service at Richmond, Virginia, August 9, 1865.

ELEVENTH REGIMENT INFANTRY VOLUNTEERS—*Three years service.*

The organization of this Regiment was begun as early as December, 1861; but this was not completed until September, 1862. It was mustered out of service at Richmond, Virginia, June 17, 1865.

TWELFTH REGIMENT INFANTRY VOLUNTEERS—*Three years service.*

This Regiment was organized at "Camp Wiley" on Wheeling Island, on the 30th of November, 1862, and was composed of companies recruited in the counties of Hancock, Brooke, Ohio, Marshall, Marion, Taylor and Harrison. It was mustered out of service at Richmond, Virginia, June 16, 1865.

THIRTEENTH REGIMENT INFANTRY VOLUNTEERS—*Three years service.*

This Regiment was organized with eight companies at Point Pleasant, Mason County, October 10, 1862. It was mustered out of service at Wheeling. June 22, 1865.

FOURTEENTH REGIMENT INFANTRY VOLUNTEERS—*Three .years service.*

This Regiment was organized at "Camp Wiley" on Wheeling Island in the months of August and September, 1862, the organization dating from the 16th of September, that being the date of muster-in of the last company. It was mustered out at Cumberland, Maryland, June 27, 1865.

FIFTEENTH REGIMENT INFANTRY VOLUNTEERS—*Three years service.*

This Regiment was organized with nine companies, at Wheeling, and was ordered to the field October 16, 1862. The tenth Company was organized in February, 1864. The Regiment was mustered out of service at Richmond, Virginia, June 14, 1865.

SIXTEENTH REGIMENT INFANTRY VOLUNTEERS—

This Regiment has a unique history. It was organized at the old town of Alexandria on the Potomac River, nine miles below

Washington City, and was the only regiment in the Federal service from that part of Virginia east of the Blue Ridge. It was largely composed of men from the counties of Alexandria, Fairfax, Fauquier and Prince William, with quite a number from the vicinity of Norfolk. The history of this Regiment is very incomplete. Adjutant General Pierpont has scarcely any historical data relating to it, and this is true of the rosters in the office of the Adjutant General, as well. He refers to the Muster-In and Muster-Out rolls, giving a roster of the officers in the latter and of the privates in the former, but does not mention the date of either.

SEVENTEENTH REGIMENT INFANTRY VOLUNTEERS—*One year's service.*

This Regiment was organized at Wheeling in August and September, 1864, under the call of the President, dated July 14th that year, for one, two or three years men. Nearly all the men in it were enlisted for one year. It was mustered out of service at Wheeling, June 30th, 1865.

VETERAN INFANTRY VOLUNTEERS.

FIRST REGIMENT VETERAN INFANTRY—*Term of service—during the War.*

This Regiment, formed by the consolidation of enlisted men of the Fifth and Ninth Infantry Volunteers, was organized under "Special Orders No. 391" of the War Department bearing date November 9, 1864. It was mustered out of service at Cumberland, Md., July 21, 1865.

SECOND REGIMENT VETERAN INFANTRY—*Term of service—during the War.*

This Regiment was formed by the consolidation of the re-enlisted men of the First and Fourth Regiments Infantry Volunteers, in compliance with an Order of the Secretary of War, dated December 10, 1863. It was mustered out of service at Clarksburg, Harrison county, July 16, 1865.

CAVALRY VOLUNTEERS.

FIRST REGIMENT CAVALRY VOLUNTEERS—*Three years service.*

This Regiment was organized in the summer of 1861. The non-veterans were mustered out as the terms expired in the summer of 1864; but the re-enlisted men together with 223 recruits which thereafter joined therein, preserved a regimental organization until July 8, 1865, when it was mustered out of service at Wheeling.

SECOND REGIMENT CAVALRY VOLUNTEERS—*Three years service.*

This Regiment was recruited during the summer of 1861, and was mustered into the service of the United States with ten full companies November 8th, that year. It was mustered out of service at Wheeling, June 30, 1865.

THIRD REGIMENT CAVALRY VOLUNTEERS—*Three years service.*

This Regiment was not organized until early in the summer of 1864, but it was composed of companies, therein brought together but which had been privately recruited and attached to other commands. Company "A" was mustered at Wheeling, December 23, 1861; Company "C" was organized at Brandonville, Preston county, October 1, 1861; and the two constituted a battalion; Companies "B" and "D" were mustered at Wheeling, October 21, 1862; Company "H" was organized at Parkersburg, in Wood county, November 2, 1862; Company "I" was mustered into service at Bridgeport, in Harrison county, May 16, 1863; Company "M" was mustered at Buckhannon, April 4, 1864; and Company "G" was recruited and mustered into service at Point Pleasant, in Mason county. The re-enlisted men of the Regiment, together with 115 recruits, kept the Regiment in the field until June 30, 1865, when it was mustered out of service.

FOURTH REGIMENT CAVALRY VOLUNTEERS—

This Regiment was enlisted in the autumn of 1863, for six months service, and was composed of companies organized in the northern part of the State. In these companies were men from Doddridge, Tyler, Wetzel, Marshall, Ohio, Marion, Monongalia, Harrison, Wood and other counties. It was mustered out of service March 15, 1864. But little historical data has been preserved regarding the services of this Regiment. Adjutant General Pierpont's Report for 1865 contains a roster of the officers from the date of organization to that of Muster Out; and rosters of all the companies, compiled from the Muster In rolls; but no historical data whatever regarding the operations and movements.

FIFTH REGIMENT CAVALRY VOLUNTEERS—*Three years service.*

(See Second Regiment Infantry Volunteers.) This Regiment as stated, was organized in July, 1861, as the Second Regiment Infantry Volunteers, and served as such until January 26, 1864, when, by an Order of the Secretary of War, it was mounted and designated as the Fifth Regiment Cavalry. However, it was never armed or equipped as Cavalry, but continued to serve as "Mounted Infantry." As stated, its re-enlisted men were on December 1, 1864, consolidated with the re-enlisted men of the Sixth Regiment Cavalry Volunteers, (Mounted Infantry) to form the Sixth Veteran Cavalry, while the non-veterans were mustered out as their terms of enlistment expired.

SIXTH REGIMENT CAVALRY VOLUNTEERS—*Three years service.*

(See Third Regiment Infantry Volunteers.) This Regiment was, as before stated, organized at Clarksburg, in Harrison county, in July, 1861, as the Third Regiment Infantry Volunteers; and served as such until January 26, 1864, when, by an order of the Secretary of War, it was mounted and its designation changed to that of Sixth Regiment Cavalry; but it continued to serve as mounted infantry. It was never armed or equipped as cavalry. Its non-veterans were mustered out, September 7, 1864, and its re-enlisted men were consolidated with the re-enlisted men of the Fifth Regiment Veteran Cavalry.

SEVENTH REGIMENT CAVALRY VOLUNTEERS—*Three years service.*

(See Eighth Regiment Infantry Volunteers.) This Regiment, was as stated, organized in the Great Kanawha Valley, in the Autumn of 1861, as the Eighth Regiment Infantry Volunteers; and it continued to serve as such, up until June 13, 1863 when it was ordered to Bridgeport, in Harrison county, where it was mounted and drilled as "Mounted Infantry." As such it was known until January 27, 1864, when by an Order from the War Department, its designation was changed to that of the Seventh Regiment Cavalry. Its non-veterans were mustered out of service in 1864, as their terms expired; but its re-enlisted men—nearly 400 in number—together with an addition of 250 recruits sent to them, continued the regimental organization until it was mustered out of service at Charleston, West Virginia, August 1, 1865.

VETERAN CAVALRY VOLUNTEERS.

SIXTH REGIMENT VETERAN CAVALRY VOLUNTEERS—*Term of service —during the war.*

This Regiment, which should have been known as the *First* Regiment Veteran Cavalry, was formed by the Consolidation of the re-enlisted men—two hundred in number—of the Fifth Regiment Cavalry (or originally the Second Regiment Infantry) and the re-enlisted men—making six companies— of the Sixth Regiment Cavalry (originally the Third Regiment Infantry) by order of the Secretary of War.[14]

ARTILLERY VOLUNTEERS.

FIRST REGIMENT LIGHT ARTILLERY VOLUNTEERS—*Three years service.*

This was the only artillery regiment in the service of the United States from West Virginia. It consisted of eight batteries, as follows: Battery "A", was the first battery organized under the Restored Government. Its non-veterans were mustered out of

14. No other West Virginia Regiment has a more interesting history than this, it being the only West Virginia Regiment retained in service after the close of the war. Its organization took place at North Branch Bridge, West Virginia, September 7, 1864; whence the Regiment moved to New Creek—now Keyser, West Virginia. It spent the months of January and February, 1865, at Camp Remount, Pleasant Valley, Maryland; and in March it was ordered to Washington City, where it was engaged in doing Provost duty until the 16th of June, when it received orders to proceed to Louisville, Kentucky; from there it was ordered to Fort Leavenworth, Kansas, and thence across the Plains into the Territories of Colorado and Dakota. Its headquarters in the winter of 1865-66, was Fort Laramie, in the last named Territory; more than a thousand miles west of Fort Leavenworth. The Regiment was several times engaged with the Indians and was highly complimented for its gallantry. On the 22d of May 1866, it was mustered out of service at Fort Leavenworth, Kansas; and arrived at Wheeling, on the 25th, where, on the 29th, the men received their final pay and discharge; and then proceeded to their West Virginia homes.'

service August 8, 1864; its re-enlisted men being added to Battery "F". Battery "B", was mustered out October 23, 1864; its re-enlisted men being added to Battery "E". Batteries "C" and "D", continued in service without change to the close of the war. Battery "E", was recruited at Buckhannon, Upshur County, in August, 1862, and was mustered into service at Wheeling a few days later. Battery "F" was organized in 1861 as Company "C" of the Sixth Regiment Volunteer Infantry; by order of the Secretary of War it was transferred to the Artillery Regiment. It was mustered out of service September 14, 1864; its re-enlisted men, with those previously transferred to it from Battery "A" now reorganized a veteran battery designated Battery "A". Battery "G" was organized in 1861 as Company "G" of the Second Regiment Infantry Volunteers, but it was transferred to the Artillery Regiment. It was mustered out of service August 8, 1864. Battery "H" remained in service, unchanged, to the close of the war. The Regiment was mustered out at Wheeling as follows: Battery "A" (being Batteries "A" and "F" consolidated) July 21, 1865; Battery "C", June 28, 1865; Battery "D", June 27, 1865; Battery "E" (being Batteries "B" and "E" consolidated) June 28, 1865; and Battery "H", July, 1865.

WHEELING INDEPENDENT EXEMPT INFANTRY.

This was a body of Infantry consisting of two organizations known as Company "A" and Company "B", neither of which had any Regimental connection. They were composed of men enlisted in the Northern Pan-Handle, who were stationed at Wheeling throughout the war as city guards, or rather Capitol Guards, for Wheeling was not only the seat of the Restored Government, but the capitol of West Virginia after the admission of the State into the Union. These companies were on duty during the continuance of the war, and were not required to perform other military service.

LOSS OF LIFE AMONG WEST VIRGINIA SOLDIERS IN THE FEDERAL ARMY DURING THE CIVIL WAR.

More than three thousand West Virginia soldiers in the Federal Army lost their lives in the Civil War. The following tabulated statements exhibit the loss from the several causes therein shown, as ascertained by actual count from the Reports of Francis P. Pierpont, the Adjutant General of West Virginia in the years of the War. It should be observed that the Sixteenth Regiment Infantry was scarcely organized at the close of the struggle; and that the Fifth, Sixth and Seventh Regiments of Cavalry were changed from Infantry in 1864; hence the loss of life in these Regiments while serving as Infantry, appears in connection with the Second, Third and Eighth Infantry.

LIST OF WEST VIRGINIA STAFF OFFICERS WHO WERE KILLED, OR DIED OF WOUNDS OR DISEASE IN SERVICE IN THE FEDERAL ARMY.

Major-General Jesse Lee Reno, commanding the Ninth Army Corps, was killed in action at South Mountain, Maryland, September 14, 1862.
Colonel Joseph Thoburn, of the First Infantry, was killed in action at Cedar Creek, Virginia, October 19, 1864.
Major John Thomas Hall, of the Fourth Infantry, was killed in action at Beech Creek, West Virginia, August 6, 1862.
Major A. M. Goodspeed, of the Fourth Infantry, was killed in action at Vicksburg, Mississippi.
Major Ralph Ormstead, of the Fifth Infantry, was killed in action September 15, 1863.
Sergeant-Major John T. Sutton, of the Ninth Infantry, was killed in action at Halltown, Jefferson county, West Virginia, August 26, 1864.
Colonel Daniel Frost, of the Eleventh Infantry, was killed in action at Snicker's Ferry, Virginia, July 19, 1864.
Lieutenant-Colonel James Robert Hall, of the Thirteenth Infantry, was killed in action at Cedar Creek, Virginia, October 19, 1864.
Lieutenant-Colonel Thomas Morris, of the Fifteenth Infantry, was killed in action at Snicker's Ferry, Virginia, July 18, 1864.
First Lieutenant and Adjutant Sidney W. Knowles, of the First Cavalry, was killed in action at Gettysburg, Pennsylvania, July 3, 1863.
Major S. B. Conger, of the Second Cavalry, was killed in action.
Major Seymour B. Conger, of the Third Cavalry, was killed in action at Moorefield, Hardy county, West Virginia, August 7, 1864.

LOSSES BY DEATH IN THE COMPANIES OF THE REGIMENTAL ORGANIZATIONS.

	Killed in Battle	Accidentally Killed	Died of Wounds or Disease	Total Deaths
First Regiment Infantry; (Three months service)		1	2	3
First Regiment Infantry; (Three years service) (Re-enlisted men of this Regiment, served in Second Veteran Infantry).	37	4	62	103
Second Regiment Infantry; (afterward Mounted Infantry; then designated as the Fifth Cavalry)	51	8	57	116
Third Regiment Infantry; (afterward Mounted Infantry; then designated as the Sixth Cavalry)	42	5	83	130
Fourth Regiment Infantry; (Re-enlisted men of this Regiment served in Second Veteran Infantry)	40	5	138	183
Fifth Regiment Infantry; (Re-enlisted men of this Regiment served in First Veteran Infantry)	40	1	65	106
Sixth Regiment Infantry; (no change in organization)	6	15	117	138
Seventh Regiment Infantry; (no change in organization)	98	4	159	257
Eighth Regiment Infantry; (afterward Mounted Infantry; then designated as Seventh Cavalry)	18	2	164	186
Ninth Regiment Infantry; (Re-enlisted men of this Regiment served in First Veteran Infantry)	69	3	108	179
Tenth Regiment Infantry; (no change in organization)	59	3	125	187
Eleventh Regiment Infantry; (no change in organization)	27	0	106	142
Twelfth Regiment Infantry; (no change in organization)	46	2	116	164
Thirteenth Regiment Infantry; (no change in organization)	32	1	103	136
Fourteenth Regiment Infantry; (no change in organization)	48	3	162	213
Fifteenth Regiment Infantry; (no change in organization)	39	2	79	120
Sixteenth Regiment Infantry; (no change in organization)				
Seventeenth Regiment Infantry; (no change in organization)				
First Regiment Veteran Infantry; (composed of re-enlisted men of the Fifth and Ninth Infantry)	12		20	20
Second Regiment Veteran Infantry; (composed of re-enlisted men of the First and Fourth Infantry)				
First Regiment Cavalry; (no change in organization)		10	38	60
Second Regiment Cavalry; (no change in organization)		3	11	14
Third Regiment Cavalry; (no change in organization)	43	8	121	172
Fourth Regiment Cavalry; (six months service, no change in organization)	44	9	94	147
Fifth Regiment Cavalry; (formerly the Second Infantry)	31	3	115	149
Sixth Regiment Cavalry; (formerly the Third Infantry)	2	1	19	22
Seventh Regiment Cavalry; (formerly the Eighth Infantry)				
Sixth Regiment Veteran Cavalry; (composed of re-enlisted men of the Fifth and Sixth Cavalry, which had been respectively, the Second and Third Infantry)	7	4	95	106
First Regiment West Virginia Light Artillery; (eight batteries)	16	5	116	137
West Virginia Exempt Infantry; (Wheeling City Guards) two companies			12	12
General and Staff Officers	13		9	22
	820	108	2,296	3,224

Sergeant-Major Edward A. Thomas, of the Second Cavalry, was killed in action near Winchester, Virginia, July 24, 1864.

Reverend Gordon Battelle, Chaplain of the First Infantry, died of typhoid fever in Washington, D. C., August 7, 1862.

Surgeon George C. Gans, of the Tenth Infantry, died of disease at Harrisonburg, Virginia, October 4, 1864.

Surgeon Jonathan R. Blair, of the Tenth Infantry, died; cause, place and date unknown.

Commissary-Sergeant Rees Cooper, of the Eleventh Infantry, died of disease, September 1, 1864.

Surgeon John W. Moss, (of Wood county), of the Fourteenth Infantry, died of disease at Petersburg, Hardy county, (now Grant county), West Virginia, January 2, 1864.

Quartermaster-Sergeant John Starr, of the Fifteenth Infantry, died of consumption, October 19, 1864.

Major Josiah Steel, of the First Cavalry, died May 28, 1863, of wounds received in action.

Hospital Steward John R. James, of the Second Cavalry, died in hospital at Gauley Bridge, Fayette county, West Virginia, September 4, 1862.

Major Patrick McNally, of the Fifth Cavalry, died of wounds received in action at Rocky Gap, Greenbrier County., West Virginia, June 26, 1862.

COMPANIES OF STATE GUARDS ORGANIZED IN DIFFERENT COUNTIES OF THE STATE FOR THE PROTECTION OF SUCH COUNTIES AGAINST INVASION.15

COUNTIES FOR WHICH ORGANIZED.	DATE OF ORGANIZATION.	DATE OF FINAL DISCHARGE.	DATE OF CAPTAIN'S COMMISSION.	NAMES OF CAPTAINS.	REMARKS.
Barbour	Sept. 17, 1863	May 30, 1865	Sept. 17, 1863	George M. Yeager	Dismissed December 21, 1863.
"	Aug. ..., 1863		Dec. 21, 1863	M. T. Haller	This company was organized by Geo. M. Yeager. Haller was killed in action.
Braxton	Jan. 30, 1864	Mar. 10, 1865	Apr. 28, 1865	Moore McNeel	
"			Jan. 30, 1864	M. Rollyson	
"			Aug. 2, 1864	Gustavus F. Taylor	Discharged August 5, 1864.
Calhoun	Oct. 3, 1863	June 16, 1864	Oct. 3, 1863	William Ellison	
Clay	Apr. 16, 1863	May 30, 1864	Apr. 16, 1863	Benj. L. Stephenson	
Doddridge	Dec. 9, 1863	June 20, 1865	Nov. 4, 1863	H. S. Sayre	
Gilmer	May 9, 1864	May 30, 1865	May 9, 1864	William T. Wiant	
Greenbrier	Dec. 13, 1864	July 1, 1865	Dec. 13, 1864	Andrew W. Mann	
Lewis	Sept. 9, 1863	Nov. 9, 1864	Sept. 9, 1863	J. C. Wilkinson	
Jackson	Aug. 14, 1863	May 30, 1865	Aug. 14, 1863	George L. Kennedy	
"	Aug. 14, 1863	Aug. 20, 1864	Aug. 14, 1863	John Johnson	
Wood	Oct. 30, 1863	May 30, 1865	Aug. 15, 1863	William Logsdon	
Roane	Oct. 30, 1863	June 16, 1864	Oct. 30, 1863	Alex. Donaldson	
"	Oct. 30, 1863	May 30, 1865	Oct. 30, 1863	Henry Chapman	
Wirt	Feb. 18, 1864	May 20, 1864	Feb. 18, 1864	William Gandee	
"	Sept. 2, 1864	June 20, 1864	Sept. 18, 1864	H. S. Burns	
Pendleton	Apr. 8, 1863	May 20, 1865	Sept. 9, 1863	William F. Peil	Killed in action.
"		May 31, 1865	Apr. 30, 1863	E. C. Harper	Company formerly commanded by Capt. Harper, who was killed by guerrillas.
"			Apr. 30, 1864	John Boggs	Discharged expiration term of service.
Upshur	June 26, 1863	Apr. 15, 1865	June 26, 1863	Isaac Alt	
"			June 24, 1864	M. Mallow	
Putnam	Sept. 4, 1863	June 9, 1863	Sept. 4, 1863	J. L. Kesling	
"	Apr. 7, 1864	May 30, 1865	Apr. 7, 1864	John Ball	Discharged March 7, 1864.
Wayne	Dec. 9, 1863	May 9, 1864	Dec. 9, 1864	William R. Spaulding	
Preston	Mar. 1, 1864	Apr. 5, 1864	Mar. 1, 1864	M. M. Pierce	
Tucker	Jan. 20, 1864	May 30, 1865	Jan. 20, 1864	N. J. Lambert	Resigned January 20, 1865.
"			Mar. 3, 1865	James H. Lambert	
Nicholas	May 3, 1864	June 30, 1865	May 3, 1864	James R. Ramsey	
Hardy	Dec. 7, 1863	Mar. 10, 1865	Dec. 9, 1863	John S. Bond	
"	June 24, 1864	Apr. 15, 1865	June 24, 1864	John Yocum	
Wayne	Sept. 5, 1864	Mar. 10, 1864	Sept. 5, 1864	J. Rohrbough	
"	Mar. 22, 1864	May 9, 1864	Mar. 22, 1864	William Bartram	
"	Mar. 22, 1864	May 9, 1864	Mar. 22, 1864	Ira G. Copley	
"	May 7, 1864	Sept. 26, 1864	May 7, 1864	Benj. R. Haley	

Raleigh	Jan. 23, 1864	June 20, 1865	Jan. 23, 1864	William Turner
Wyoming	Jan. 23, 1864	Feb. 10, 1865	Jan. 23, 1864	Sanders Mullins
Kanawha	Jan. 28, 1864	Sept. 26, 1864	Jan. 28, 1864	Robert Brooks
Nicholas	Apr. 28, 1864	Dec. 13, 1864	Apr. 28, 1864	Isaac Brown
Marion	June 20, 1863	Dec. 10, 1864	June 20, 1863	N. Alltop
Ritchie	May 7, 1864	Apr. 30, 1865	May 7, 1864	Josiah M. Woods
Randolph	Apr. 12, 1864	Apr. 15, 1865	Apr. 12, 1864	Sampson Snyder
Pocahontas	Apr. 29, 1864	Apr. 4, 1865	Apr. 29, 1864	I. W. Allen — Discharged September 30, 1864.
			Apr. 29, 1864	Samuel Young
Cabell	Apr. 25, 1865	May 30, 1865	Apr. 25, 1865	J. H. Ferguson
Monroe	Apr. 6, 1865	June 20, 1865	Apr. 6, 1865	Benj. F. Ballard
	Apr. 1, 1865	June 20, 1865	Apr. 1, 1865	L. D. Garton
Mason	June 20, 1863	May 30, 1865	June 20, 1863	A. I. Waterson
Wirt	Sept. 2, 1863	Feb. 29, 1864	Sept. 2, 1863	C. W. Vaught
Pocahontas, Randolph & Webster	May 1, 1865	June 10, 1865	May 1, 1865	Isaac W. Allen

15 These organizations were known as "State Guards," organized for the protection of their respective counties. They were paid by the State. Many of them were in service for nearly two years; and some of them for a longer period.

COLORED SOLDIERS IN THE UNITED STATES SERVICE ACCREDITED TO WEST VIRGINIA.

In the years of the Civil War, two hundred and twelve colored men were enlisted in West Virginia for service in the Federal Army, there being no organization of colored troops from the State, these enlisted men were assigned to the Forty-fifth Regiment United States Colored Troops, in which they were mustered to the credit of the State of West Virginia.

CHAPTER XI.
WEST VIRGINIA SOLDIERS IN THE CONFEDERATE STATES ARMY.

The Military History of the State of West Virginia has never been written; and no other American State experienced the conditions that existed within its boundaries during the Civil War. In many of the counties there was presented the remarkable scene of men enlisting, and companies forming, at the same time, some for the Federal service and others for the Confederate service. The inhabitants of the counties of Central Northwestern Virginia, those bordering on western Marylaand and Pennsylvania, those in the Northern Panhandle, and thence stretching along the Ohio River to the mouth of Big Sandy River, were largely in favor of the maintenance of the Union; and it was in these that far the largest number of soldiers for the Federal Army were enlisted. In the counties of the upper New River region, in the Greenbrier Valley, the Valley of the South Branch of the Potomac, and in the lower Shenandoah Valley—now in the Eastern Panhandle—the majority of the people favored secession; and it was from these that far the greater number of West Virginians entered the Confederate service. This will be the more readily seen when it is stated that Mason County, on the Ohio, sent more than one thousand men to the Federal Army, and one company (61 men) to the Confederate Army; while Hampshire County, in the Valley of the South Branch of the Potomac, sent more than a thousand men to the Confederate Army, and but one company (73 men) to the Federal Army—largely from that part now embraced in Mineral

County. The Northern Panhandle sent thousands of men into the Federal Army, while from the Eastern Panhandle many hundreds entered the Confederate service.

In the preceeding chapter the regimental organization of the different arms of the service of the West Virginia soldiers in the Federal Army has been given. It is impossible to secure such accuracy of statement from data in hand, or ever to be obtained, relative to the Confederate Military organizations from this State. There were a part of a Company, a Company, or Companies from the counties of Barbour, Berkeley, Boone, Cabell, Calhoun, Clay, Fayette, Gilmer, Greenbrier, Hampshire, Hardy, Harrison, Jackson, Kanawha, Lewis, Marion, Mason, Mercer, Monongalia, Monroe, Morgan, Nicholas, Ohio, Pendleton, Pocahontas, Putnam, Raleigh, Randolph, Roane, Upshur, Wayne, and Wyoming.

WHAT NUMBER OF WEST VIRGINIANS WAS IN THE CONFEDERATE ARMY?

How many West Virginians served in the Confederate Army? No one now knows the exact number, nor will it ever be definitely known; but it may be approximated. There were twelve companies of West Virginians in the famous Stonewall Brigade; viz: four from Jefferson County; two from Berkeley County; two from Greenbrier County; one each from Hampshire, Hardy, Monroe and Ohio counties. The entire Twenty-second Regiment Virginia Infantry was composed of West Virginia Companies; nine companies of the Thirty-first Regiment Virginia Light Infantry were from West Virginia; as were six companies in the Thirty-sixth Regiment Virginia Infantry; while the remaining companies enumerated above were widely distributed for service in various other regimental organizations. It has been stated that more men from Mercer entered the Confederate Service than there were voters in that County. Judge James H. Miller in his "History of Summers County" gives a list of the names of two hundred men who were in the Confederate Army from the territory now embraced in Summers County; while H. T. Calhoun prepared for Morton's."History of Pendleton County," a list of names of more than seven hundred men from that county who served in the Confederate Army. In the spring and summer of 1865 Gen. John H. Ohley, with the Fifth

West Viginia Cavalry, stationed at Charleston, was in command of the Kanawha Military District, which included twenty counties, stretching from Jackson to Mercer, and from Pocahontas to Wayne; and at the close of his service here, August 1st, 1865, he reported to the Adjutant General of West Virginia that the officers of his command had parolled more than five thousand Confederates returning to counties within the said Kanawha Miiitary District.

At the close of the war there was no Adjutant General's Office or War Department in which to deposit the rosters of these companies; but this Department is now in possession of original muster rolls, pay rolls, typewritten manuscript or printed rosters of a large number of the above mentioned companies; and it is believed that a conservative estimate of the number of West Virginians in the Confederate service would approximate seven thousand.

THE BLUE AND THE GREY OF WEST VIRGINIA.

At the close of the last chapter it was stated that the total number of enlistments of West Virginians in the Federal Army should be, in round numbers, placed at twenty-eight thousand. If, now, the total number of West Virginians in the Confederate service be placed at seven thousand, we should have a total of thirty-five thousand West Virginians rendering service in the two armies. The population of the State at that time was 360,000, 9 2-3 per cent. of which, was, therefore, enlisted men—evidently the highest per centage, according to population, of enlisted men of all the states of the Union.

It was likewise shown that of the whole number of West Virginians enlisted in the Federal Army, three thousand, two hundred and twenty-four lost their lives in battle or died from wounds, disease or accidental causes—11 3-7 per cent. of the total enlistments. And now, if we assume that the loss of life in the seven thousand West Virginians in the Confederate service was equal to this, as doubtless it was, we shall have as the total number of West Virginians who lost their lives in the Civil War, four thousand and twenty-four. Enormous loss! And all the greater when it is remembered that the average age of these four thousand men was twenty-one years.

CHAPTER XII.

WEST VIRGINIA SOLDIERS IN THE SPANISH-AMERICAN WAR.

The declaration of war by Congress was made against Spain, April 23, 1898; and immediately thereafter President McKinley called upon Governor George W. Atkinson for a regiment of Infantry, to be formed, so far as possible of drilled men of the National Guard. In compliance with this the Governor, on May 2nd ensuing, ordered the Brigade of our State, Brigadier General B. D. Spillman commanding, to mobilize at Kanawha City, on the south side of the Great Kanawha, about a mile above where the steel bridge spans that river, at Charleston, the capital of the State. There was a ready response to the order of the Commander-in-Chief, and in a few days the eighteen companies composing the two regiments of the Brigade were at the place of rendezvous, and had spread their tents at "Camp Lee."

THE FIRST REGIMENT WEST VIRGINIA INFANTRY.

Of the companies composing the two Regiments, six were designated to return to their homes. The First Regiment of West Virginia. Volunteer Infantry was then formed of all the men of the remaining twelve companies physically fit, and willing to enlist; and its ranks were afterward filled to the required number from the names obtained by enlistment in different parts of the State. The Regimental organization was as follows: B. D. Spillman, Colonel; Clarence L. Smith, Lieutenant Colonel; W. H. Banks, Major; Philip A. Shafer, Major; H. Byron Baguley, Surgeon; Cassius C. Hogg, Ass't Surgeon; Charles T. Nesbitt, Ass't Surgeon; Rev. S. K. Arbuthnot, Chaplain. On May 20th the Governor caused a commission to issue to W. H. Lyons as a Major in this Regiment. On that day the Regiment left "Camp Lee" for Chickamauga, Tennessee, where it arrived in the dusk of evening the next day; and bivouacked on the great battle field. On the 18th it entered "Camp George A. Thomas." After some months spent here the Regiment moved to "Camp Poland" at Knoxville, East Tennessee. From here it proceeded to "Camp Conrad," at Columbus, Georgia, where it was mustered out of service February 7, 1899.

THE SECOND REGIMENT WEST VIRGINIA INFANTRY.

On May 25, 1898, the President of the United States requested Governor Atkinson to send forward a Second Regiment of Infantry. The Governor hastened to issue a call, and the companies hastily formed in various parts of the State, rendezvoused at "Camp Atkinson" on the north bank of the Great Kanawha, about half a mile below the mouth of Elk River, say about five squares above where the Kelly Axe Factory now stands. Here the Regiment was organized, the regimental officers being as follows, viz: D. T. E. Casteel, Colonel; O'Brien Moore, Lieutenant Colonel; Howard Atkinson, Major; Charles D. Elliott, Major; William F Henshaw, Surgeon; Zadoc T. Kalbaugh, Assistant Surgeon; William F. Bailey, Assistant Surgeon; Rev. Albert S. Kelly, Chaplain. The companies were mustered into service by Captain J. M. Burns of the 17th U. S. Infantry; the first on June 25th, and the last on the 9th of July. The Regiment left "Camp Atkinson" and moved to Middletown, Pennsylvania, where it entered "Camp Meade." Here some months were spent, after which it removed to "Camp Wethcrill at Greenville, South Carolina, where it was mustered out of service, March, 1899.

COMPANIES OF WEST VIRGINIA SOLDIERS IN OTHER REGIMENTAL ORGANIZATIONS.

In addition to the two Regiments mentioned above, four companies of West Virginians went to the field and served in other regimental organizations. They are as follows:—

Company "E," Fourth Regiment United States Volunteer Infantry, Captain W. H. Monroe; mustered into service at Parkersburg with sixty-four men.

Company "G", Fourth Regiment United States Volunteer Infantry, Captain Albert A. Franzheim, mustered into service at Wheeling, with eighty-two men.

Company "L", Eighth Regiment United States Colored Volunteer Infantry, Captain E. E. Hood, mustered into service at Charleston, with eighty men.

Company "M," Eighth Regiment United States Colored Volunteer Infantry, Captain William T. Bishop, mustered into service at Parkersburg with forty-eight men, a sufficient number of men being enlisted and sent forward to raise the aggregate of this Company to the required number.

Thus it is seen that the total number of troops supplied by the State for service in the Spanish-Amreican War was as follows:—

First Regiment West Virginia Volunteer Infantry	1,385
Second Regiment West Virginia Volunteer Infantry	1,322
Companies "E" and "G", Fourth United States Volunteer Infantry	152
Companies "L" and "M", Eighth United States Volunteer Infantry	145
A total of	3,004

West Virginia responded promptly to the calls made by the President, and the patriotism of her citizens is shown not only by the number of volunteers sent to the field, but by the fact that at the time the Adjutant General of the State received requests from two thousand additional men for service; and he expressed the opinion that had the President called for ten thousand men from the State, that number would have gone promptly to the field.

www.ingramcontent.com/pod-product-compliance
Lightning Source LLC
Chambersburg PA
CBHW051057230426
43667CB00013B/2329